First Edition

International Opportunity Recognition

and

Export Satisfaction in

SMEs

This book is the result of four years research on SMEs in Malaysia and has written

based on the author's doctoral thesis in UTM University in Malaysia.

Dedicated to my beloved mother and father

ISBN: 978-1939123275

Supreme Century, by asanashr

International Opportunity Recognition and Export Satisfaction in SMEs

Dr. Sahar Ahmadian
*Business Administration
Department, UTM University,
Kuala Lumpur, Malaysia*

Prof. Dr Abu Bakar Abdul Hamid
*Business Administration Department, UTM
University, Kuala Lumpur, Malaysia*

.

TABLE OF CONTENTS

LIST OF TABALES

LIST OF FIGURES

FIGURE NO.   **TITLE**   **PAGE**

LIST OF ABBREVIATIONS

SME	-	Small and Medium sized Enterprise
IOR	-	International Opportunity Recognition
NBV	-	Network Based View
IE	-	International Entrepreneurship
MC	-	Marketing capability
EA	-	Experience Assets
RA	-	Relation Assets
ES	-	Export Satisfaction
EI	-	Export Intermediary
GDP	-	Gross Domestic Product
EIN	-	Export Intermediary Networking

LIST OF APPENDICES

CHAPTER 1

INTRODUCTION

1.1   Research Background

Small and medium enterprises (SMEs) are important in regional, national and international levels due to their increasing number, the employment and job creation, and growth opportunities, making them worthy of further research (Moen, 2000; OECD, 2000). Firm growth is a multidimensional phenomenon and there is substantial heterogeneity in a variety of variables that may affect firm growth (Delmar *et al.*, 2003). Going into international markets especially exporting to abroad as the simplest form considers as one of the important factors for SMEs growth.

In the last decades, there is keen interested research on the internationalization in small firms. International business literature mostly focuses on large firms, and theories believe that firm could be internationalizing gradually after a period of domestic experience and growth. Despite of the stage theory in internationalization business literature, scholars in the field of entrepreneurship point to the inconsistency between the stage theory and the empirical reality of a growing number of entrepreneurially oriented firms, which tends to adopt a global focus from their conception.

In the response of small firms that are global born from their establishment, International Entrepreneurship (IE), as a new field of inquiry, appears to have drawn both from International Business (traditionally focused on larger firms) and from Entrepreneurship (focused on small firms). Therefore, IE became a new field of study which was merger of international business and entrepreneurship studies.

McDougall and Oviatt defined IE as *"the discovery, enactment, evaluation, and exploitation of opportunities across national borders to create future goods and services"* (McDougall and Oviatt, 2003; p. 7).Consequently, the heart of IE studies is the way of thinking and making decisions about recognizing and utilizing the opportunities (Shane and Venkataraman, 2000).

IE research and opportunity recognition is the attraction of universal consideration (Zahra *et al.,* 2005). This has prompted the editors of several journals to call for more research investigating how entrepreneurs distinguish or discover new opportunities for international exchange (Dimitratosa and Jones, 2005; Stylesand Seymour, 2006). Regarding to this call for more research, some studies focused on this topic such as (Park, 2005; DeTienne, 2008; Ellis, 2011).

One of the interesting topics in IE research is international opportunity recognition (IOR) by small and medium size firms in international markets because of their importance in the whole economy and the role of internationalization on SMEs performance. The root of opportunity recognition is originally in the classic entrepreneurship study (Park, 2005) and it considered on how firm and people are able to recognize opportunities for entering into global markets at the beginning of their internationalization (Park, 2005; Chandra, 2008).

The primacy of opportunity identification in the entrepreneurial process is now well-established (Aldrich and Zimmer, 1986; Corbett, 2007; Eckhardt and Shane, 2003; Kirzner, 1979; Ozgen and Baron, 2007; Schumpeter, 1934; Shane, 2000; Venkatarama, 1997). However, the questions of "how opportunities in foreign markets can be identified" and the "techniques used by entrepreneurs for recognize opportunity" remains under explored in the IE literature (Singh 2000; Young *et al.,* 2003) and is still mainly immature (Hills *et al.,* 1999; Shane, 2000; Collarelli-O'Connor and Rice, 2001).

Availability of firm resources has the significant role in international opportunity recognition and internationalization. Previous studies on "how entrepreneur recognize opportunities in international markets" is focused on individual and firm characteristics while SMEs are suffering from their individual and firm characteristics. Now, SMEs understood that without resources are not able to recognize opportunities. Therefore, they should pursue innovation task to compensate their resources scarcities for their internationalization.

In other hand, studies shift from the focus on individual and firm's characteristic toward a focus on relationships with multi-polar networks and now internationalization is a function of multi-polar networks involving special relationships. Now, studies show that entrepreneur's participation in social and business network is the answer of "why and how people are able to recognize and exploit the opportunities" (e.g. Aldrich and Zimmer, 1986; Arenius and DeClercq, 2005; Chen and Chen, 1998; Coviello and Munro, 1997; Johanson and Mattsson, 1988; Komulainen *et al.*, 2006; Loane and Bell, 2006; Meyer and Skak, 2002; Mort and Weerawardena, 2006; Oviatt and McDougall, 2005; Rutashobya and Jaensson, 2004; Sharma and Blomstermo, 2003; Singh, 2000). Despite of the importance of networks for SMEs to internationalization in the recent decades, less attention has provided to entrepreneurial recognition and exploitation of those opportunities.

1.2   Problem Statement

As discussed in the previous section, small and medium enterprises (SMEs) are important in terms of their contributions at the regional, national and international levels. The presence of SMEs would contribute to the economy as their contributions, would translate into an increase in the number of employment, job creation, gross domestic production (GDP) and growth opportunities in most of the developed and developing countries, thus studying SMEs is worthy of further research (Moen, 2000; Rullani, 2000). As SME's growth will affect the above-mentioned factors and one the contributors to its success is 'Internationalization'. It is a major dimension of growth, as this would lead to a strong growth potential for the SMEs (Peng and Delios, 2006).

Internationalization is crucial because if SMEs engage in international markets, they will experience further improvement in their performance (Baldwin and Gu, 2003) This exposure and participation in the international scene would bring about an economy of a larger scale as well as promote innovation and productivity growth among the enterprises (Harris and Li, 2005; Hughes, 2004). The transition from a national to international level for SMEs has been made possible due to the removal of barriers.

This can seen as there is an increasing number of entrepreneurs who are entering the international markets because of the removing the barriers of trading, advances in manufacturing transportation, advances in process manufacturing, and information technology (Knight, 2000; OECD, 1998; Bell, 1995; Steenkamp, 2001).

In order to be part of internationalization, exporting is the most common entry mode used by SMEs as this is a vital for almost any sector which wants to be part of an ever growing global economy (Bowyer, 2002). Thus, gaining access to export markets considered as crucial role for SMEs development, growth and productivity (Bowyer, 2002).In the context of this study, Malaysia is one of the countries, which strongly support the internationalization of SMEs.

Malaysia a middle-income country and a rapidly developing economy in Asia with 80% of its manufacturers are small firms that have approximately 20% exporting activities from its total output (Mahajar and Hashim, 2001). To facilitate the entry of SMEs into international markets, there are many ministries and agencies available to assist continuously SMEs to export their products (Hashim, 2000). In a survey supported by OECD (2008), that Malaysia was one of the countries that contributed to the survey, it was reported that there are government support programs for SMEs in most of the countries around the world. Most of these programs consider export as an important element of SME internationalization. The survey found that 71.6% of the programs focused totally on supporting export activities and 21.6% included exporting with other international engagements as their focus. However, 6.9% supported programs that did not have any support for export as their main focus. The survey has proven that many of the programs for SMEs organized by the governments focused on exporting. Therefore, most of the government support programs focused on exporting.

Despite government assistance on exporting and access to international market as well as providing support in ICTs, evidence shows that the share of SMEs in the international market is often noticeably lower than their share in gross domestic product (GDP). For example, Malaysian GDP was worth about 750 Billion Malaysian Ringgit of the world economy in 2010 while its national exports were worth 64 Billion Malaysian Ringgit (Bank Negara Malaysia report, 2011). This shows that there is a big difference between SMEs contribution to GDP and national export. In relation to these figures, SMEs contribution in terms of export revenue is low in comparison to their contribution to GDP. Thus, SME manufacturers have numerous opportunities to enlarge their existing share of the country's total exports and they should not miss this selling opportunity. Due to this situation, there is a need for further research on the issue of how SMEs should be more involved in exporting and internationalization (European Central Bank, 2011).

Besides that, there is a need to study further the assistance provided by domestic, foreign partners or from public sector organizations on how these sources can increase the leverage or supplement the SMEs modest sources (Susman, 2007).If these barriers or problems in the pursuit of internationalization were identified, SMEs would be able to excel and penetrate the global market. Knows the barriers that SMEs face for internationalization could be essential to assist them to remove that, make themselves stronger, and have a confidence to move to international markets.

In another report by OECD (2008) concerning barriers, SMEs face four main barriers in the exporting activities that are access, finance, business environment, and firm capabilities. The level of importance of the government support programs are accordingly: Access (53%), Finance (47%), Capabilities (35.9%) and Business Environment (9.4%) (See picture 1.2).

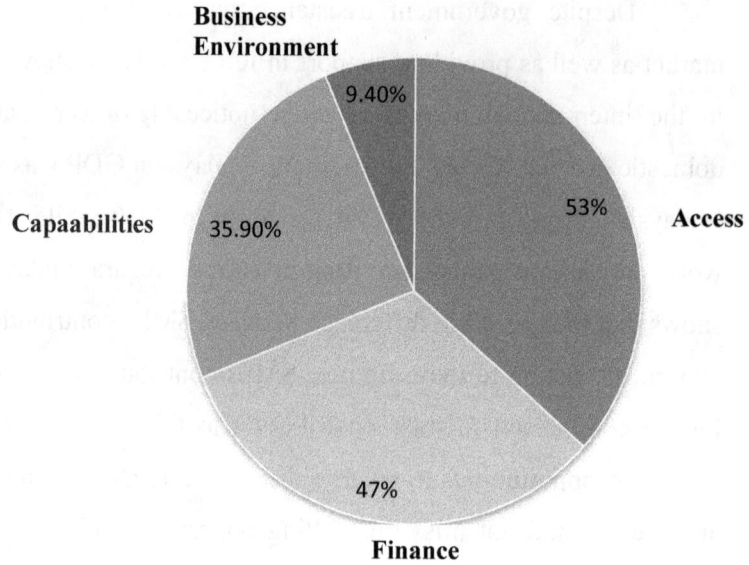

Figure 1.1   The level of government support programs on SMEs faced barriers
Source: (OECD, 2008)

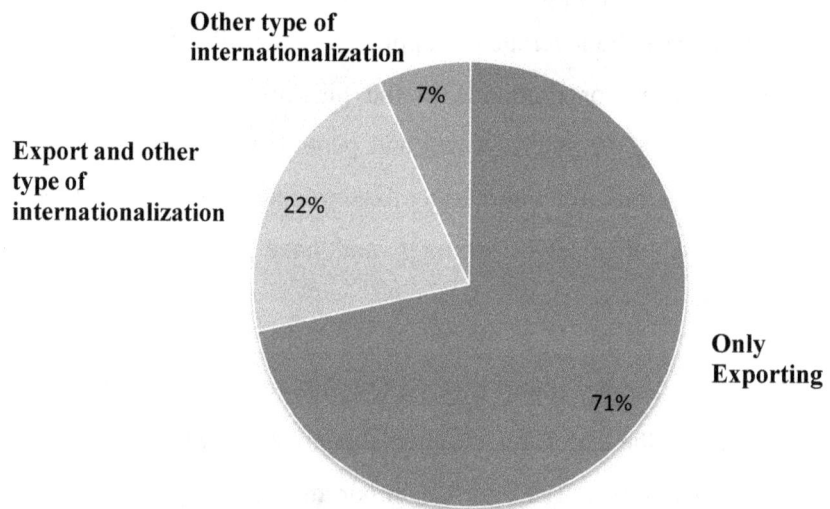

Figure 1.2   Focus of government support programs on SMEs internationalization
Source: (OECD, 2008)

Figure 1.2 shows main focus of government support is on exporting (71.6%), but still the majority of SMEs indicated access to international market as the important barriers for their internationalization (53%) (Figure.1.1 and 1.2).

Other important criteria for internationalizing SMEs were also discovered in the OECD survey. In the survey, economy policy makers, OECD members, and SMEs were asked to identify the most common barriers that they faced in their internationalization experience. The four main barriers that they faced are as below (Table 1.1).

Table 1.1 : Barriers for SMEs internationalization (OECD, 2008)

According to economy policy makers	According to OECD members	According to SMEs
Inadequate quantity of and/or untrained personnel for internationalization(Capabilities)	Obtaining reliable foreign representation (Access)	Shortage of working capital to finance exports (Finance)
Shortage of working capital to finance exports (Finance)	**International opportunity recognition (Access)**	**International opportunity recognition (Access)**
Limited information to locate/analyze markets (Access)	Limited information to locate/analyze markets (Access)	Limited information to locate/analyze markets (Access)
International opportunity recognition (Access)	Maintaining control over foreign middlemen (Access)	Inability to contact potential overseas customers (Access)

Comparison of these four main barriers from the point of views of economy policy makers, OECD members, and SMEs showed that the two barriers of "international opportunity recognition" and "limited information to locate markets" were found as the most common and very important barriers. However, "identify international opportunity" is viewed to be more important than "limited information to locate markets" from the viewpoints OECD members and SMEs. In terms of importance, "identify international opportunity" is recognized as the most important and common barriers in the surveys (See Table 1.1). Therefore, helping SMEs to remove this barrier is essential for SMEs internationalization. This identification wants further research as it would assist SMEs to survive, grow and penetrate the global market.

One of the identified factors required prior to being internationalized is the international opportunity recognition (IOR). This is the first step in an internationalization process and a possible major barrier for SME export development (Jones and Coviello, 2005; Styles and Seymour, 2006; Mathews and Zander, 2007). There have been studies and conferences on opportunity recognition and related topics globally (Hills and Schrader, 1998; Koen and Kohli, 1998; Singh et al., 1999; Zietsma, 1999; Shepherd and Detienne, 2005). Such a topic has emerged as a field of study for entrepreneurship in its own right (Gaglio and Katz, 2001; Venkataraman, 1997; Shane and Venkataraman, 2000). IOR is at the heart of entrepreneurial activity (Vandekerckhove and Dentchev, 2005) and is highly correlated with profitability and growth of a firm (Sambasivan et al., 2009). It is considered as the major success factor in International Entrepreneurship (IE) studies (Dimitratos and Jones, 2005; Julien and Ramangalahy, 2003; Leonidou, 2004; Shaw and Darroch, 2004; Zahra et al., 2005). These studies have shown that IOR merits a more systematic research attention than it has been given because this is the start of a new beginning (Chandra et al., 2009; Park, 2005).

There is no denial on the importance of opportunity recognition within the expansion of SMEs but the literature available on this subject is very limited. There are very few empirical studies focusing on the international opportunity recognition (IOR) process and there is no adequate study that provides an in-depth understanding (Chandra and Styles, 2008). The scarce resources could be to the methodological gaps that exist in the field which have not received much attention (Muzychenko, 2008) and the existing studies on this subject have not been developed further (Park 2005). In another study, Shook et al., (2003) stated that international opportunity awareness subject has never been relevant in IE research since international entrepreneurial firms would act accordingly in any competitive field. Here, speed and promptness in relation to operation of opportunities international become the key success factors (Dana et al., 2008). From another perspective, accessible internationalization theories believe that internationalization is caused by the recognition of opportunity but there is minimal literature and little clarification on this concept (Chandra et al., 2009). Due to the limited research on this specifics concept concerning IOR and its important role for SMEs, thus there should be more research on this subject.

Recognizing the significance of the role of IOR, Etemad (2008) suggested there should be more emphasis on the subject of international opportunity awareness which should study on how managers are going to follow, search actively and finally realize international opportunities (Dana *et al.*, 2008). The question of how opportunities could be identified in international markets remained unexplored because these opportunities are not extensively documented in the IE literature (Singh, 2000; Young *et al.*, 2003). The empirical research about how entrepreneurs identify opportunities in international markets, evaluate and organize the risks, and achieve resources is very limited (Mathews and Zander, 2007). Within the IOR, it is important to study how entrepreneurs are able to recognize opportunities in international markets as there are few empirical studies on it. This is an indication that further exploration on the composite factors of IOR deserves to be given due attention. The study would benefit SMEs at the national and international level.

As mentioned earlier, in the previous studies on IOR, the availability of favorable resources is one of the composite factors that allow a firm to exploit opportunities and reduce threats in competitive environments (Michalisin *et al.*, 1997). Only unique resources could change the firms to become efficient and effective in market (Barney *et al.*, 2001). Most of resources that affected opportunity recognition in the previous studies about IOR are intangible resources. Physical and tangible resources are not necessarily scarce because they can be purchased in the open market (Michalisin *et al.*, 1997) while intangible resources are usually scarce (Peteraf, 1993) as they cannot be easily purchased. According to Andersen and Kheam (1998), only intangible resources were included to constitute capabilities on international markets. Intangible resources are particularly important for predicting growth strategy (e.g. Chatterjee and Wernerfelt, 1991; Grant, 1991; Peteraf, 1993) that most of the SMEs suffer from lack of intangible resources such as market knowledge, experience and information (Coviello and McAuley, 1999; Knight 2000; Hollenstein, 2005). In addition, source of higher performance is believed to be the result of the effect of intangible resources that are difficult to identify, understand and replicate (Fahy *et al.*,2000). International knowledge and experience as the intangible resources are hard to imitate and they could help determine a firm's performance in global competition (Peng and York, 2001). Therefore, the significant role of intangible resources in IOR and internationalization is obvious based on the previous literature due to the obvious problem faced by SMEs due to their lack of intangible resources.

Besides intangible resources, previous studies have also looked into opportunity recognition by focusing on the role and characteristics of individuals and firms. This includes an individual's cognitive limitation and the characteristics of firms as well as looking at the deficiencies or weaknesses of the resources in the firm (Vandekerckhove and Dentchev, 2005). This shows that works from previous researchers about internationalization such as Terjesen and Hessels (2007), who mentioned that the extent of the research in this area largely focuses on the role of owner and firm-specific factors and appears to be the missing resources that SMEs should have for internationalization.

In terms of resources, large manufacturers usually have the necessary resources to handle a wide range of exporting activities in-house while most SMEs do not (OECD, 1997). SMEs are not as well-resourced as the larger firms to face these internationalization challenges or to exploit the market opportunities. SMEs in comparison to large firms are characteristically considered to be resource constrained besides lacking in knowledge, market power, and resources to participate actively in global markets (Fujita, 1995; Hollenstein, 2005). It is noted that the developing countries face many constraints to compete effectively in international markets because of their lack of necessary knowledge, financing, qualified human resources, marketing skills, government support, and information (Fujita,1995; Cviello and McAuley, 1999; Knight, 2000; Hollenstein, 2005). Therefore, it cannot be denied that without these resources and preparation, attempts to export are doomed to fail and may even risk the financial stability of the enterprise as a whole.

It is undeniable that resources for IOR and internationalization in SMEs are crucial and the lack of these resources in SMEs equates with the difficulties faced by entrepreneurs and SMEs on how to compensate their scarce resources and recognize opportunities in international markets. Little is known about the methods used by entrepreneurs on how they compensate their individual and firms limitation in the pursuit of opportunity recognition (Terjesen and Hessels, 2007). Due to these restrictions created by limited or scarce resources, holistically, SMEs and entrepreneurs should pursue innovations to compensate their limitations in terms of resources.

Besides resources, there are other factors to be considered in IOR as the market situation has changed radically these last few decades. The present trend of the related studies is shifting from the individual and firm-specific characteristics to network and relationship between buyers and sellers with multi-polar networks (Dana *et al.,* 2008). This is reflected in the entrepreneurial ways and there is a shift towards a behavioral and process approach that focuses on understanding how opportunities are discovered and acted upon by people and firms (Eckhardt and Shane, 2003; Shane, 2000; Shane and Venkataraman, 2000). In addition, studies about competition in the markets have shifted from companies to networks of companies as well as outsourcing to smaller and specific firms. In this case, control will be divided among independent firms that assist each other in increasing their efficiency and profit. According to Dana *et al.,* (2008), relationships and networking have become important elements for internationalization. Meanwhile the focus of researchers is also changing in their effort by investigating relationships, negotiations, multi-polar networks, and symbiotic entrepreneurship (Dana *et al.,* 2008). Therefore, in the new emerging international economic system, an important contributor to internationalization process is the setting up of a network by the SMEs that would facilitate international opportunities through this symbiotic network.

The reliance on network allows the internationalization of a firm to be facilitated and influenced primarily by its relationships with other business enterprise within their network (Axelsson and Johanson, 1992). In this regard, markets are the systems of industrial and social relationships among suppliers, customers, competitors, friends, family, and other members involved in the network, which is done by exchanging resources (Sharma and Blomstermo, 2003) that lead to compensate their scarce resource. According to Ellis (2003), with a suitable network and potential exchange partner, SMEs would be able to compensate their weakness and recognize the international opportunities. This support system would allow a firm to develop its position in the existing network or by establishing new ties (Johanson and Mattsson, 1988; Kontinen and Arto, 2010). One of the creative ways for SMEs to penetrate the international market is to have entrepreneurs' participation in social and business network because this has been found to be the answer of "why and how people are able to recognize and exploit the opportunities" based on several studies such as the ones by Aldrich and Zimmer (1986) and Arenius and DeClercq, (2005). Therefore, in relation to SMEs scarce resources, they would have to rely on networking with other participants and organizations in the environment by establishing relationships to access the resources thus, paving the way for IOR and internationalization.

Ellis (2003) discussed that SMEs are able to compensate their weakness and recognize the international opportunities by having a suitable network and potential exchange partners. In this context, the definition of networks is based on the exchange of resources. Previous studies about the networking mostly focused on social and business network to acquire information. With reference to the definition of networks based on the resources exchange and previous studies on acquiring the information through the social and business network, it seems essential to pay more attention to acquiring other resources through networking. Another crucial resource is information as one of the intangible resources that affects opportunity recognition and internationalization. Although other resources such as knowledge, experience, marketing and other intangible resources have important roles in opportunity recognition and internationalization, SMEs are still not achieving their goals due to their lack of understanding about them. This is the gap that exists in the current literature, as there is a lack of in-depth understanding in the acquisition of other intangible resources for internationalization. Hence, there is an urgent need to have more research in this area of study because existing literature has neglected to see the importance of acquiring information as one of the resources for internationalization through networking.

Many of the available studies about networking and IOR have not been able to answer the question of "how entrepreneurs recognize opportunities" by responding with the applications of the term "networks". In relation to that, studies should be conducted on the relationship between networking and compensation of scarce resources. Compensating the scarcity of resources is a necessary activity in SMEs due to its role in exploiting the opportunities, neutralizing threats in competitive environments (Michalisin *et al.,* 1997), and in export performance (Leonidou *et al.,*2002). Terjesen and Hessels (2007) stated that there is little known about the method used by entrepreneurs to compensate the limitations of individuals and firms in terms of opportunity recognition. Thus, SMEs should pay special attention to compensate these types of scarce resources that are crucial towards international opportunity recognition and export performance. Therefore, the question of "how entrepreneurs recognize opportunities" which have been addressed in several studies should change towards research on "how entrepreneurs compensate their scarce resources in their attempt to recognize opportunities". More research should be conducted on how SMEs recognize opportunities with reference to the limited resources and how they perform within their cognitive individual limitation and firm resources limitation.

Export is a crucial part of internationalization of SMEs and this study wants to fill this gap by focusing on the export intermediaries networking to acquire the needed scarce resources such as marketing capability, experience and knowledge assets, and relation assets as pre-requisites for opportunity recognition and export satisfaction. This study proposes that one of the solutions to compensate the scarce resources in SMEs is to rely on the ability to network with export intermediaries.

The network cooperation between exporters and export intermediaries is very important due to the exchange of resources. Therefore, SMEs and export intermediaries have a mutual dependence relationship in which the performance of the intermediary depends on the performance of the manufacturer and vice versa. These companies introduce SMEs to the international markets and make them aware of international opportunities. The direction of such an expansion should be a norm for most of these small and medium enterprises. SMEs tend to have a relationship with export intermediaries to gain access to valuable assets and resources of these intermediaries in order to be part of internationalization (Wilkinson and Nguyen, 2003). The motivation for using intermediaries by these small firms is individuality and difficulty of imitating resources and capabilities. When a firm enters a foreign market, a large amount of resources is required and SMEs usually do not have them. Due to the SMEs' scarce resources, they could have access to the resources needed by having a relationship with an export intermediary (Day, 1994). Terjesen *et al.,* (2007) indicated that a manufacturer's success totally depends on the initiative and efforts of the chosen intermediary. It should be mentioned that an OECD survey on "Globalization and SME" recorded that trade company's do 50% of the export on behalf of SMEs (OECD, 2008). Hence, in order to achieve their full potential, exporters must pay special attention to the unique competencies of these various intermediaries (Ling-yee and Ogunmokun, 2001). This shows that the collaborative effort between intermediaries and exporters is crucial for the success of SMEs entry into the international platform

The relationship between SMEs and export intermediaries was developed by Trabold, 2002; Peng, 1998; Root, 1994; Ilinitch *et al.,*1993; Chalmin, 1987; Peng and York 2001; Blomstermo and Sharma, 2006). However, previous studies on the relationship between SMEs and export intermediary, have focused on transactional cost theory (e.g. Karunaratna and Johnson, 1997; Peng and Ilinitch, 1998; Lau, 2008), agency theory (Karunaratna and Johnson, 1997), institutional theory (DiMaggio and Powell, 1983), and resource dependency theory (Hessels and Terjesen, 2008). While internationalization a discussed in the previous sections is fundamentally affected by relationship and networks.

Resource dependency theory focuses on resources, transaction cost focuses on reducing cost, and Hole theory is on the opportunity for other parties in the environment which have the necessary resources. Previous studies have not paid much attention to the relationship between SMEs and export intermediaries based on Network theory. Network theory encompasses the different theories mentioned above because the firms inside a network are able to exchange resources, reduce their cost and also create opportunities for other parties inside the network. Therefore, explaining the relationship among SMEs and export intermediaries based on the network theory is important, as it will create potential beneficial effects of using this network that includes the commonly adopted relation theories used in this field of study.

Existing literature research on SMEs export activity includes the role of owner firm-specific factors such as learning, social capital, ownership, government support, placing less emphasis on the role of the export intermediaries in export development of SMEs and the discovery of international opportunities by SME owners (Spence, 2004). However, independent intermediaries (Mortanges *et al.,* 1999) handle most of the export in the world and most of these related studies examined only the characteristics associated with exporters and intermediaries (Peng and Ilinitch, 1998). Prior research has assumed to some degree that mutual cooperation between producers and export intermediaries is a necessary condition for a high joint performance (Deligonul *et al.,* 2006; Heide and Miner, 1992; Peng and York, 2001; Gençtürk and Kotabe, 2001). These empirical researches have neglected to acknowledge the importance to support the link between effective networks and export intermediaries with SMEs in order to recognize international opportunities and export satisfaction.

Previous studies have reviewed the fact that cooperation and networking increase a firm's success by having a better and positive export performance (Hillebrand and Biemans, 2003; Ambler *et al.,* 1999). On the other hand, using of intermediaries has been argued to lead to higher international performance in the entrepreneurial context (Rabino, 1980; Shepherd and Zacharakis, 1997). SMEs through an intermediary can improve their export performance, profitability, productivity and firm satisfaction (Terjesen *et al.,* 2008; Rabino, 1980; Zacharakis, 1997; Wilkinson and Brouthers, 2006). Wilkinson and Brouthers (2006) stated that using the services of export intermediaries is positively associated with firm satisfaction with export performance (Wilkinson and Brouthers, 2006). However, these previous studies did not analyze this relationship in relation to a network theory.

A number of scholars have theorized about the beneficial effects of networking activities (Birley, 1985; Larson, 1992), or about the effect of export intermediary on export performance (Terjesen *et al.,* 2008; Rabino, 1980; Zacharakis, 1997; Wilkinson and Brouthers, 2006). However, less attention has been given to the understanding of the relationship between effective networks and a firm's performance (Aldrich *et al.,* 1986; Blundel, 2002; Cell and Baines, 2000). Another issue that needs further investigation is supporting link between export intermediary networking and export satisfaction based on the network theory for acquiring resources, which include marketing, experience and knowledge, and relation assets.

This research seeks to contribute towards the understanding of the role of export intermediaries as part of networking to compensate for the scarce resources of SMEs as well as being a part of the international opportunities recognition and export performance. This is due to the fact that our knowledge on the role of export intermediaries in networking for the international opportunity recognition and export performance by SMEs is limited. In addition, previous literatures on IOR have not been given to the importance of networking of intermediaries and its effect on the export behavior of SMEs. The main motivation behind this research is the need to fill this gap that would enable more SMEs to be part of the internationalization process. Based on the previous studies on the relationship among export intermediaries and SMEs which is based on the exchange of intangible resources such as: marketing capability, knowledge and experience, and relationship assets (Theingi, 2008), not much is known about the affecting factors on opportunity recognition in IE literature. Thus, these issues appear to be the requirements that SMEs lack.

Therefore, this study focuses on the network theory and seeks to clarify how a network-based perspective/framework could explain the relationship between SMEs and Export Intermediaries (EIs) to compensate for the scarcity of resources in SMEs. This would include marketing, knowledge and experience, and relation assets as these could lead to international opportunity recognition and export satisfaction in SMEs. The focus on the network ties of export intermediaries is in line with the current call by authors to shift from focusing on agents to their ties based on exchanging of intangible resources such as; marketing, knowledge and experience, and relation assets. Figure 1.3 illustrates the problem statement of this thesis.

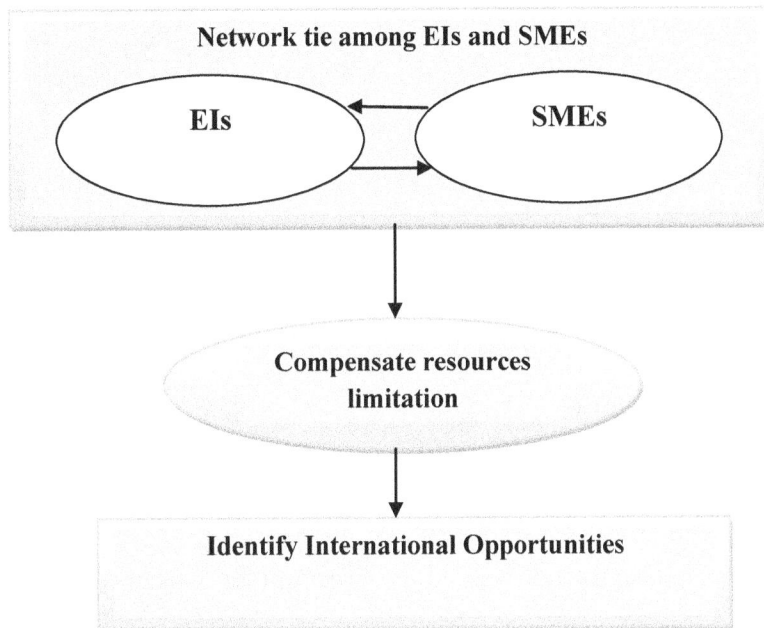

Figure 1.3   The picture drawn from the problem statement

1.3   Scope of the study

This study is conducted in Malaysia, a fast developing country in South-east Asia (Sambasivan and Abdul, 2009).SMEs account for about 80% of total business establishments. Therefore, going forward for Malaysia to achieve a developed nation and high-income status, domestic SMEs are expected to be an important driver of growth (SMIDEC, 2009).

Developing and increasing the SMEs growth via internationalization is the interest and concern of Malaysian government. Regards to this special concern, variety of agencies and ministries are assisting and supporting Malaysian firm different steps of their internationalization (Mahajar and Hashim, 2001). The interest in the SMEs in Malaysia has witnessed a significant growth over the years (SMIDEC, 2009) due to their increasing number in Malaysia (Shankar *et al.*, 2010;

Hashim, 2000). In addition, SMEs in Malaysia have stronger tendency towards exporting activities than large firms and they are looking for broader market for their products (Shanker*et al.,* 2010).

Despite the fact of Malaysian concern on internationalization and its supporting program in Malaysian firm growth, the understanding and access of these programs is difficult for SMEs (Abdullah, 1997). In addition, internationalization can present more beneficial and profitability opportunities that lead SMEs to long-term growth and profitability but Malaysia firms seemed to be lagging in the internationalization, especially in exporting area (Mahajar and Hashim, 2001).

Abdullah (1999) showed that despite of the assistance of Malaysian government, the mass of SMEs do not obtain any government support; the assistance received by the firms is also quite diverse, for example, some firms make advantage of one type of assistance, while some others used more assistance. Therefore, the accessibility of support programs for the development of SMEs is still limited despite the fact that a high policy agenda has been introduced to promote the development of SMEs in Malaysia (Abdullah, 1999).

In Malaysia, 80 percent of the total manufacturing firms are SMEs that they just export about 20 percent of their total output (Mahajar and Hashim, 2001). Malaysian GDP was reported around 750 billion Malaysian Dollar in 2010 and national export reported around 64 Billion Malaysian Dollar (Bank Negara Malaysia, 2011). Thus, SMEs contribution to export revenue is far less than their contribution to GDP. Therefore, SMEs manufacturer in Malaysia have big potential for increasing their exports share. Moreover, they need more incentive and promoting programs in order to increase their export and improve their situation in the global market.

Syed Zamberi and Siri Roland (2010) indicated that government should do more effort for promoting and encouraging SMEs to operate the programs. Mahajar and Hashim (2001) indicated that limited study has examined how Malay firms view the internationalization. In addition, SMEs can survive themselves through internationalization because of limited local market opportunities and maturing markets.

In this regard, a survey was carrying out on small and medium sized enterprises in the manufacturing sector all over Malaysia. However, there are different definitions of SME's in different countries. SMEs are usually considered non-subsidiary, independent firms, which have less than 250 employees. This study used the Malaysian definition for SMEs and can be defined according to size, turnover and activity. SMEs in Malaysia fall into two broad categories (SMIDEC, 2009): 1. Manufacturing, manufacturing-related services and agro-based industries, which have either fewer than 150 full-time employees or an annual sales turnover of less than RM25 million .2.Services, primary agriculture and information and communication technology (ICT), which have either fewer than 50 full-time employees or an annual sales turnover of less than RM5 million.

This research surveys a probabilistic sample of small and medium manufacturers in Malaysia in order to gather data on dependent, independent and intermediating variables of the research. The sample will consist of those SME's that are manufacturer, less than 150 employees, and have used to rely on the services offered by export intermediaries in their export operations. The basic tool for the study is a questionnaire emailed to managers in sample members followed by a telephone call to get the completed questionnaire. The data after preparation were subject to statistical techniques such as multi-regression analysis, correlation analysis, and path analysis.

The study would help SMEs to compensate their resources scarcities by using the export intermediary networking and move to international markets.

1.4   Research Questions

After consideration of previous literature on International Entrepreneurship and international opportunity recognition, this study tries to answer the following research questions:

RQ1: Is there any relationship between export intermediary networking and international opportunity recognition in SMEs?

RQ2: Is there any relationship between export intermediary networking and export satisfaction in SMEs?

RQ3: Is there any relationship between international opportunity recognition and export satisfaction in SMEs?

RQ4: Does international opportunity recognition mediate the relationship between export intermediary networking and export satisfaction?

1.5   Research Objectives

After consideration of previous International Entrepreneurship literature the following research objectives have been developed:

RO1: There is positive relationship between export intermediary networking and international opportunity recognition in SMEs.

RO2: There is positive relationship between export intermediary networking and export satisfaction in SMEs.

RO3: There is positive relationship between international opportunity recognition and export satisfaction in SMEs.

RO4: International opportunity recognition mediates the relationship between export intermediary networking and export satisfaction.

1.6   Research Hypothesis

After consideration of previous International Entrepreneurship literature the following research hypothesis have been developed:

H1: Export intermediary networking by SMEs has relationship with international opportunity recognition in SMEs (RQ1).

- H1.1: Marketing capabilities exchanges between export intermediary and SMEs are positively correlated to international opportunity recognition in SMEs.

- H1.2: Experience assets exchanges between export intermediary and SMEs are positively correlated to international opportunity recognition in SMEs.

- H1.3: Relation assets exchanges between export intermediary and SMEs are positively correlated to international opportunity recognition in SMEs.

H2: Export intermediary networking by SMEs has relationship with export satisfaction in SMEs (RQ2).

- H2.1: Marketing capabilities exchanges between export intermediary and SMEs are positively correlated to export satisfaction in SMEs.

- H2.2: Experience assets exchanges between export intermediary and SMEs are positively correlated to export satisfaction in SMEs.

- H2.3: Relation assets exchanges between export intermediary and SMEs are positively correlated to export satisfaction in SMEs.

H3: International opportunity recognition in SMEs is positively correlated to SME's export satisfaction (RQ3).

H4: There is a mediating effect of international opportunity recognition on the relationship between export intermediary networking and export satisfaction (RQ4).

- H4.1: There is a mediating effect of international opportunity recognition on the relationship between marketing capabilities and export satisfaction.

- H4.2: There is a mediating effect of international opportunity recognition on the relationship between experience assets and export satisfaction.

- H4.3: There is a mediating effect of international opportunity recognition on the relationship between relation assets and export satisfaction.

1.7   Contributions of the Study

This research has two major academic contributions: Firstly, the relationship between firm and export intermediary resources that influence on international opportunity recognition. The findings add to the International Entrepreneurship (IE) literature that export intermediary networking between SMEs and export intermediary for the exchange resources needed, such as experience, marketing capabilities and relationships assets, have a particularly important effect on international opportunity recognition and SMEs can identify more international opportunity. Thus, the understanding and applicability of the network-based view within the relationship between export intermediary and SMEs will further extended.

Secondly, the relationship between firm and export intermediary resources that influence on export performance. The findings add to the export literature in SMEs due to the weakness or lack of resources to go to foreign markets. Thus, the understanding and applicability of the network-based view within the relationship between export intermediary and SMEs will further extended.

The findings also contribute important evidence that establishes the network between SMEs and export intermediary that facilitate more international opportunity recognition. In addition, findings encourage SMEs to overcome SME's external and internal challenges and barriers in their internationalization and their cooperation and relation with other business network.

1.8   Definitions

The definitions provided in this section are only as a preview for which supporting discussions will follow in Chapter 2.

1.8.1   Small and medium-sized enterprises (SMEs)

SMEs are non-subsidiary, independent firms that employ fewer than 150 employees (SMIDEC, 2009).

1.8.2 Internationalization

Internationalization is defined as an entrepreneurial action that starts with the awareness and willingness of the entrepreneur (responsiveness to the conditions) to the necessity of transaction with other countries that is preceded by realization of international activities (entry mode) and location of activities (Beamish, 1990; Miesenbock, 1988).

1.8.3 Entrepreneurship

Neither entrepreneurs nor entrepreneurship is a new concept of human experience. This study have used the definition of Entrepreneurial processes that consist of individual activities such as opportunity identification, resource mobilization, and the creation of an organization (Shane and Venkataraman, 2000).

1.8.4 International Entrepreneurship (IE)

There is no single definition about IE and different researchers stated different definition of IE. In this study IE is the discovery, enactment, and exploitation of opportunities across national borders to create future goods and services(Shane and Venkataraman, 2000).

1.8.5 International opportunity recognition

"International opportunity recognition" is defined as the chance to conduct exchange with foreign market which leads to exchange agreement (Ellis, 2011).

1.8.6　Network-based view

Network –based view is defined as the sets of two or more connected exchange relationships, whichinvolve resource exchange among its different members (Axelsson and Johanson, 1992; Sharma and Blomstermo, 2003).

1.8.7　Export Intermediary

Export intermediary are defined as specialized service firms that connect domestic producers and foreign customers by adding value to the export process (Peng and Ilinitch, 1998) an efficient alternative for SMEs that have limited resources and lack of knowledge regarding foreign markets (Trabold, 2002; Peng, 1998; Root, 1994; Ilinitch *et al.*, 1993; Chalmin, 1987). The term, "export intermediaries" refers to both agents and distributors in this study.

1.8.8　Export managers

Export managers are individuals who are responsible for exporting a product to foreign markets. In SMEs owners, production managers, general managers and marketing managers are often responsible for exporting (Thingi, 2008).

1.8.9　Marketing capability

Marketing capability in this study is one of the export intermediaries' resources and refers to the quality of the firm's customer service, quality of sales force, advertising effectiveness, strength of distributor networks, speed of new product introduction, market research abilities, and ability for differentiation of products (Weerawardena, 2003).

1.8.10 Experience assets

Experience assets is as one of the export intermediaries' resources that includes; knowledgeable about the requirements of potential customers, overall good experience with respect to the market, adequate experience to sell the products, and supply of market information (Theingi, 2008)

1.8.11 Relation assets

Relation assets in this study is one of the export intermediaries' resources and refers to strong trust and fairness, long-term relationship, good communication, helpfulness in emergency case, positive attitude toward any complaints, good reputation, and also keeping promise with customers (Piercy *et. al*, 1997).

1.8.12 Export satisfaction

This study applied subjective measurement instead of objective similar to other studies such as; Robertson and Chetty (2000), Katsikeas *et al.,* (1996). Export satisfaction in this study refers to export manager's satisfaction to sales growth in foreign markets, export market shares, number of countries they are exporting to, and overall export performance (Wilkinson and Brouthers, 2006).

CHAPTER 2

REVIEW OF RELATED LITERATURE

2.1 Introduction

A great deal of significant and extensive research on International Entrepreneurship (IE) has been carried out in the last decades. At the year of 2000, Etemad and Yender have identified IE as a new field or research. They came up with this term by fusion of International Business, Entrepreneurship literatures.IE research raises curiosity all around the globe, and its inevitable outcome had universal attention and recognition during the last decade. IE is defined based on three different factors including; international opportunity recognition; enactment; and exploitation of opportunities.

This study focuses on the first factor, international opportunity recognition, as the initial step of IE researches. Prior studies upon the International Opportunity Recognition (IOR) are categorized into three main questions "Why", "When", and "How" entrepreneurs are able to recognize international opportunities. Current study is conducted based on the last question, which is "how entrepreneurs are able to recognize international opportunities". Previous studies on this particular question mostly examined the influence of individual characteristics and firms' characteristics on IOR while small and medium enterprises (SMEs) are suffering from cognitive individual limitation and firm resources. In conclusion, this study is focused on resource scarcities by examining the Network-Based View (NBV) for IOR.

Figure 2.1 indicated the literature path and focus of this study. The schematic Figure 2.1 indicates the path of current study. The blue boxes represent the particular way that has been chosen to gain the result in this study.

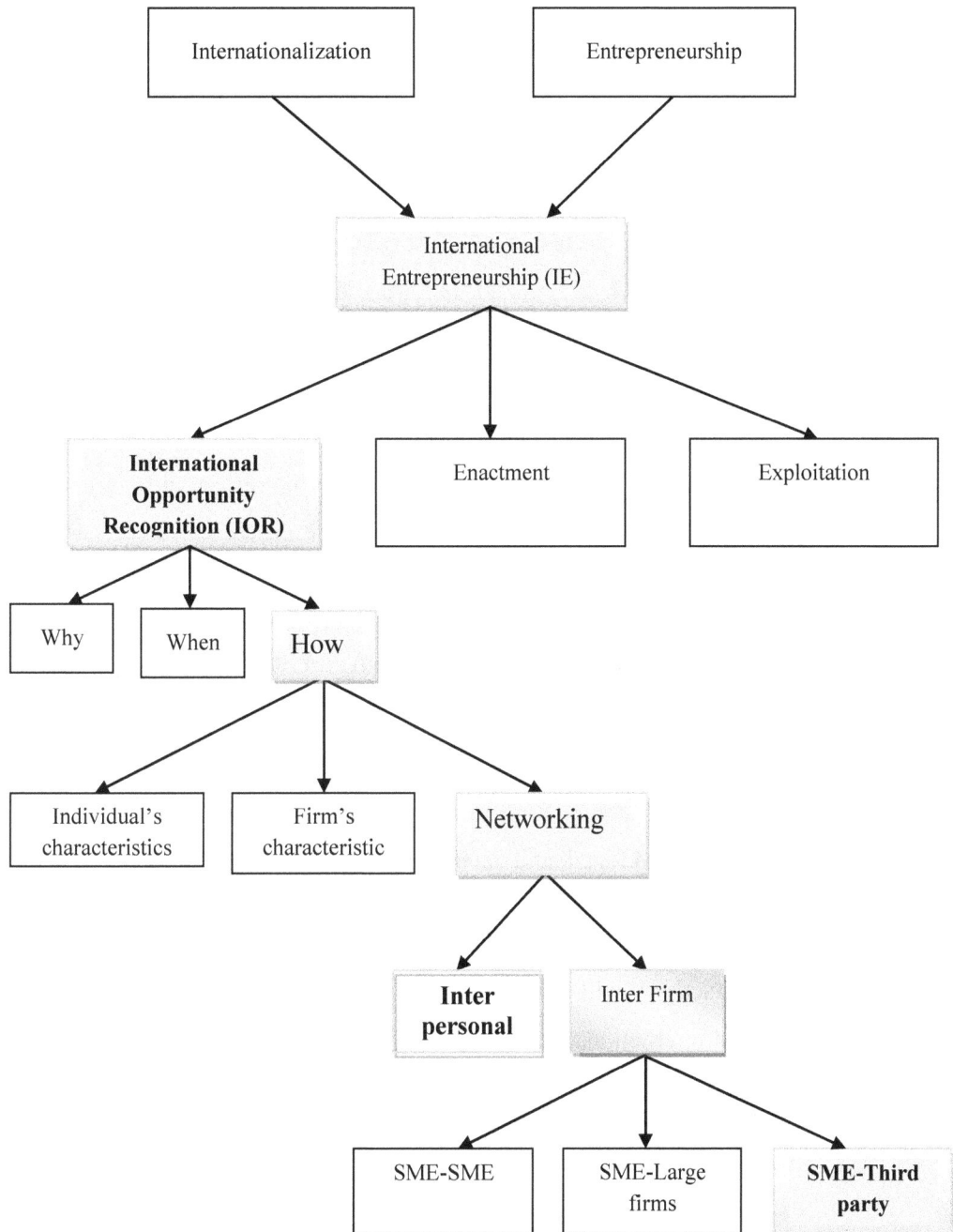

Figure 2.1   Literature path and focus of this study

2.2   Internationalization in SMEs

Internationalization in Small and Medium Enterprises (SMEs) are significant in so many levels. Due to their increasing number, the employment and job creation, and growth opportunities SMEs can be beneficial in regional, national or even international levels (Moen, 2000; OECD, 2000). In fact, according to the importance of SMEs and its working on international levels Small Business Administration of United States of America (SBA) released an interesting statistic. This institute points out that SMEs have a share of 51 percent of private employment in USA and in other countries such as Finland and Ireland, this may increase up to 70 percent (SBA, 2002). In European countries, the average share of SMEs from total employment is appeared to be 66 percent. Also it has been reported that around 53 percent of industrial manufacturing are produced by small and medium enterprises (OECD, 2008). There is a possibility that similar figures could be found in other regions for example other developed or developing countries.

Another reason of the importance of SMEs is their contribution to gross domestic product (GDP) in the country. As the matter of fact Republic of Latvia is a good example in such case. It has been reported that in Republic of Latvia, 63 percent of GDP allocated to SMEs (OECD, 2008). Therefore, it can be implied that small and medium firms are the major contributor for private employment and GDP in most developed, and developing countries.

Furthermore is an arguable issue that any changes in their size, revenue and productivity will have great impact on many levels such as regional, national and even international levels (OECD, 2008). There is a surge in attraction to the small businesses in Asia, which is an inevitable outcome of the success of small businesses experienced by Japan (Nakaoka, *et al.,* 1995).

It is obvious that activities of SMEs in international levels based on contribution that they receive from national economy (OECD, 2004). At present days almost all economies render several services in order to internationalization of small firms. Nevertheless, these programs are not only design to satisfy the smaller firms' requirements (OECD, 2008).

Considering the fact that any changes in SMEs size, revenue and productivity will have great consequences in regional, national and even international levels (OECD, 2008), hence the main debate of development policy of countries is how to facilitate the growth path of SMEs. Several researches and endeavors have been conducted to comprehend SME growth and to develop an understandable theory of SME growth (Davidsson *et al.*, 2006; Garnsey, 1996).As the globalization deepens SME growth is introduced as an interesting topic for further research. Serious concern about SME competitiveness and growth in international markets was created by globalization. Therefore, the relationship between firm growth and firm internationalization becomes an interesting topic for academic research and policymaking. A multidimensional phenomenon like firm growth has a considerable heterogeneity in a variety of variables that possibly are able to affect firm growth (Delmar *et al.*, 2003).

Walking into international scale market, particularly in its simplest form of it which is exporting to abroad considered as one of the important factors for SMEs growth. The previous researches provide evidence that mainly speculate internationalization is focused on large firms. Yet there are proven factor that indicates such positive correlation in the case of SMEs. A major dimension of growth is considered the factor of internationalization of small and medium firms (Peng and Delios, 2006). There are many advantages inside the factor of internationalization for SMEs and economy. For instance exporting has been recognized as a growth factor for SMEs. Also innovation and productivity growth have been known as subsequent of internationalization and exporting behavior for small and medium firms (Harris and Li, 2005; Hughes, 2004). Furthermore, it can be utilized as a competitive weapon for SMEs.

In conclusion, SMEs will be more effective in applying product development and manufacturing process improvement to achieve organizational excellence. Apart from aforementioned advances, internationalization has an extremely positive relationship with SMEs performance. To be clearer about this aspect it can say if SMEs link into the international markets, they will face further improvement in performance (Baldwin and Gu, 2003).

Over the last thirty years, the subject of relationship between SMEs and internationalization has been studied extensively in strategic management and international business fields. There is clear evidence that indicates a statistically significant correlation between internationalization and performance (Bausch and Krist, 2007). Studies in different countries emphasize on this relationship between internationalization and firm performance. For example in Singapore, It is found a positive correlation between them (Pangarkar, 2008). In India, they recognized that there is a U-shaped relation between firm internationalization and performance (Contractor, 2007). Also it was implied that those firms that go earlier to international markets benefit more in terms of performance (Contractor, 2007). Although internationalization and firm performance are related, however the overall internationalization of small and medium firms is remaining limited.

There is plenty of evidence to indicate that the share of SMEs in the international market is usually lower than their share in gross domestic product. A research about GDP indicates that approximately 97 to 99.9 of all business inside an economy are created by SMEs. At the same time statistic shows that share of SMEs in export activities is quite different. This percentage could be only 1% (Republic of Korea) or be as high as 51% (OECD, 2008).Percentage of contribution of SMEs to GDP is estimated around 50% and its contribution to the international level is around 30% of exports, and 10% of foreign direct investment. Asia Pacific region also determined that SMEs share in gross domestic product is 50% and SMEs share in export is 30% (OECD, 1997). The majority of SMEs do not possess the vital means to handle a wide range of exporting activities while large manufacturers do not have this problem (OECD, 1997).

The consequences of this fact is that SMEs will lose this selling opportunity and they need help from domestic or foreign partners or even from public sector organizations to leverage their modest sources (Susman, 2007). Therefore, governments usually support exporting activities of SMEs. Based on a research conducted by OECD government support of SMEs mostly includes various programs to support exporting activities (71.6%). Noticeably lower percentage (21.6 %) of these programs focused on exporting along with other international engagements.

Finally, only 6.9 percent of these programs do not consider exporting activities as the main concern (OECD, 2008)

Internationalization in the small firms has been the subject of research in the last decades. Focus of the many international business literatures involved on the large firms and theories strengthen the idea that firm could be internationalized gradually after a period of domestic experience and growth. Despite of the stage theory in internationalization business literature, scholars in the field of entrepreneurship point out to the incompatibility between the stage hypothesis and the experimental reality of the growing number of entrepreneurially oriented firms. General intendancy for these firms is to adopt a global focus from their conception.

In the response of small firms that are global born from their establishment, international entrepreneurship (IE) seems to have drawn both from international business which traditionally focused on large firms and from entrepreneurship which focused on small firms.

2.3   International Entrepreneurship (IE)

International entrepreneurship considers as a new field of study, which is merger of international business and entrepreneurship studies. Entrepreneurship is looking for recognition and development of opportunities through novel resource recombination (Schumpeter, 1975; Kirzner, 1978). Entrepreneurial processes that has been indicated in published researches include all activities starting with recognition and acting on opportunities and ends to creating of an organization (Shane and Venkataraman, 2000). Therefore based on a definition the way of thinking and making decisions to recognize and exploit the opportunities by entrepreneurs is the significant factor for developing this field (Shane and Venkataraman, 2000; Stevenson and Jarillo, 1990). This definition of entrepreneurship, which is based on opportunity recognition in the literature, has broadly accepted (Brown *et al.,* 2001). On the other hand, this definition of entrepreneurship is matched with the views of Austrian researchers (Kirzner, 1973; Schumpeter, 1975).

Recognition of opportunities is achievable through the recombination of the novel resources in the domestic or global markets (Zahra and Gravis, 2000; Zahra and Dess, 2001).Furthermore,Shane and Venkataraman (2000) have answered three key questions on the entrepreneurship. These questions are how, why and when do these opportunities to make goods and services comes to the reality? How, why and when do only few people discover and develop these opportunities? How, why and when do the various types of action applied to develop entrepreneurial opportunities?

Aforementioned questions are the main structure of IE. As a matter of fact, international entrepreneurship composes of discovering, framing and applying these opportunities as long as international limitations (Zahra *et al.*, 2005). In general, internationalization in firms is an opportunity driven from the perspective of international entrepreneurship (Zahra *et al.*, 2005).

International Entrepreneurship (IE) is defined as *"the discovery, enactment, evaluation, and exploitation of opportunities across national borders to create future goods and services" by* McDougall and Oviatt (2003). Based on this definition, IE was born globally and established firms' center in order to identification and utilization of opportunities (Oviatt and Mcdougall, 2005). Many opportunities are revealed and the rest are the outcome of an enactment process. In conclusion, way of thinking toward the recognition and utilization of the opportunities is the heart of IE studies (Shane and Venkataraman, 2000).

Originally, IE study considers as the firms, which are international from beginning (Oviatt and Mcdougall, 1994). IE research and opportunity recognition is the attraction of universal consideration (Zahra *et al.*, 2005). This has led to more research investigating and how entrepreneurs distinguish or discover new opportunities for international exchange (Dimitratosa and Jones, 2005; Styles and Seymour, 2006). Some studies that has been focused on this topic regarding to this call for more research include (Park, 2005; DeTienne and Cardon, 2010; Ellis, 2011).

2.4   International Opportunity Recognition (IOR)

One of the interesting topics in IE research in international markets is the international opportunity recognition by SMEs. That is because of their importance in the whole economy and role of internationalization on SMEs performance. It was tested by various methods that how and why people and firms recognize opportunities for entering into global markets at the first time (Chandra*et al.,* 2009). The fundamental of opportunity recognition is originally in the classic entrepreneurship study (Park, 2005). How firms and people are able to recognize opportunities for entering to global markets is considered as the beginning of their internationalization (Park, 2005). Many researches in the international entrepreneurship field began to define entrepreneurial behavior in terms of discovering, evaluating and exploiting opportunities (Hills and Schrader, 1998; Shane and Venkataraman, 2000). This definition reflects the fact that a growing observation that entrepreneurs are better defined by their opportunity seeking behavior than by differences in their personality type or risk preferences (Eckhardt and Shane, 2003).

Schumpeter defined five different groups for opportunities. The first group stresses on discovery and making of novel raw materials. Following group is about commencement of new way of production. Third group emphasizes on a new way of organization. Fourth and fifth groups are about introducing of a new product and discovering of a new market, respectively (Schumpeter, 1934). This study focuses on fifth group (opening of a new market for exporting).

Chandler and Jansen (1992) indicated that skills of opportunity identification are positively correlated to ability to take a risk. According to their research, ability to identify opportunities is interrelated to high profitability and ventures growth (Sambasivan *et al,.* 2009). Furthermore, international opportunity recognition has been recognized as the main factor to be successful in IE studies by several researchers (e.g. Zahra *et al.,* 2005; Leonidou, 2002; Shaw and Darroch, 2004; Dimitratos and Jones, 2005; Julien and Ramangalahy, 2003). It also determined as the heart of entrepreneurial activity (Vandekerckhove and Dentchev, 2005).

The grandness of the opportunity identification in the process of entrepreneurial is quite well known (Ozgen and Baron, 2007; Aldrich and Zimmer, 1986; Corbett, 2007; Eckhardt and Shane, 2003; Kirzner, 1979; Venkataraman, 1997; Schumpeter, 1934; Shane, 2000). Although identification of opportunities in foreign markets and the techniques used by entrepreneurs for recognize opportunity remains under explored in the international entrepreneurship literature (Singh, 2000; Young *et al.,* 2003). This subject is still mainly immature (Collarelli-O'Connor and Rice, 2001; Shane, 2000).

As it mentioned before there are very low number of researches, available on this issue. This might be because of various existing methodological gaps (Muzychenko, 2008).Shook *et al.,* (2003), state another reason upon the lack of knowledge in this field. He believed that intention, explore, and finding of opportunities are the stages of opportunity perception process which has never been relevant in the IE study (Dana and Etemad, 2008). In order SMEs to achieve high performance in international level, it has to concentrate more on exploiting, framing and selecting opportunities in foreign markets (Zahra *et al.*, 2005).

Despite the fact that entrepreneurs are well-known as their ability to develop new business ideas, the act of opportunity recognition is initiated to be difficult (Vandekerckhove and Dentchev, 2005; Hisrich and Peters, 1998, p. 39). Although there are various benefits of opportunity recognition in SMEs, they encounter difficulties to recognize the opportunities (Vandekerckhove and Dentchev, 2005; Zahra*et al.*, 2005). Some of researchers have been applied opportunity recognition process as a subject to getting map of its process. However, study on this subject is still mostly undeveloped (Park, 2005). Subjects like identification of opportunity in international markets, evaluate and organize the risks, and achieve resources have a low empirical substantiation (Mathew and Zander, 2007). Presence of international opportunities in extremely complex environments has been proven (Lane and Milesi-Ferretti, 2004; Muzychenko, 2008).

Identification of international opportunity is the first step of internationalization process and deserves more methodical research attention because it leads to activation of the initiates (Chandra*et al.,* 2009). It is an arguable subject that a possibly major barrier for SME export development is failure in opportunity recognition. In addition, several experimental evidence, which was provided in previous sections, supports this argument.

Despite the fact that opportunity recognition is part of the process of internationalization, researchers understand that there are not many researches discuses this subject. Nevertheless the importance of opportunity recognition has been mentioned in several published researches (Jones and Coviello, 2005; Styles and Seymour, 2006; Mathews and Zander, 2007). They mostly agreed that there are very few empirical studies focusing on international opportunity recognition processs (Zahra et al., 2005). As a result of lack of knowledge in this area, this subject has recognized as a field of entrepreneurship study (Shane and Venkataraman, 2000; Gaglio and Katz, 2001; Venkataraman, 1997). Upon the subject of opportunity recognition, several researches were conducted and the results are available through many published papers (Shepherd and Detienne, 2005; Zietsma, 1999; Singh et al., 1999; Koen and Kohli, 1998; Hills and Schrader, 1998).

Despite this fact, the related literature mainly remains sparse (Ardichivili et al., 2003; Zou and Stan, 1998; Shane, 2000). In fact, a few number of researchers followed holistically the method of study, which are mentioned by earlier theorists (Bygrave and Hofer, 1991;Gartner, 1988; 1985).

Opportunity recognition studies in entrepreneurship research have been limited in a domestic context (Corbett, 2007; Shane, 2000; Arenius and DeClercq, 2005; Lumpkin and Lichtenstein, 2005). There are of course several hypothesis about internationalization that believe internationalization is leaded by opportunity recognition but offer few explanation of this (Chandra et al., 2009). Identification of international opportunities is one of the paths to access to the market SMEs barriers in OECD compose of finance capabilities business environment and access to market). In brief, identifying international opportunities is known as a main barrier in SMEs internationalization by OECD survey. Several researches supported this idea. For instance, Dimitratos and Jones, (2005), stated that there should be a study on how international entrepreneurial firms regardless of their size, age, or industrial sector recognize opportunities (Dimitratosa and Jones, 2005). Other researches recommended that there should be larger stress on the issue of international opportunity awareness that is how managers planed to follow, search and finally realize international opportunities (Dana *et al.,* 2008). Therefore it has been suggested that as the intentions model (Krueger, 1993; Krueger and Brazeal, 1994) opportunities search in international markets is required by those who are organized to seize them (Dimitratos and Jones, 2005). For marketing benefits, they must be able to identify international opportunities on time for SMEs and for themselves. Unfortunately, there is not adequate study about identifying international opportunities despite the importance of it for SMEs internationalization and the most important barriers in SMEs. There are several researches about SMEs and export which is focused on the role of firms characteristics and individuals characteristics such as social capital (Yli *et al.*2000), learning (Sapienza *et al.,* 2004) and ownership (George *et al.,* 2005).

The functionality of external factors in opportunity recognition is analyzed in very few cases. Shook *et al., (*2003), mentioned that intention, explore, and finding of opportunities are the stages of opportunity perception process (Dana *et al.,* 2008).Furthermore, SMEs suffer from lack of vital resources for internationalization process. Despite of the large firms, SMEs are considered as lacking resources such as knowledge, marketing and other resources to move to international markets (Hollenstein, 2005; Coviello and McAuley, 1999; Knight, 2000). Their common features are lack the necessary knowledge and lack of financing and qualified human resources other deficiencies such as, lack of marketing skills and limited access to resources, government support and information (Knight, 2000; Hollenstein, 2005; Coviello and McAuley, 1999).

Prior researches about the topic of opportunity recognition have been analyzed role of individuals such as previous knowledge (Shane, 2000) and alertness (Arenius and Clercq, 2005). It is much lesser extent on the importance of network effects (Detienne and Cardon, 2008).

In order to facilitate SME to international markets, there are nearly 10 ministries, 30 government agencies and institutions that support SMEs and to reduce barriers SME beyond the border activities. There is big difference between SMEs share in exporting and gross domestic product despite the fact that 71.6% of the government program is focused on exporting, and 53% of this program is focused on the access to international market. Contribution of SMEs to export revenue is far less than their contribution to GDP.

SMEs face barriers for accessing to international market is one of the reasons mentioned for it. Hence, SMEs should develop their strategies and skills to overcome these barriers and challenges for successful internationalization process (OECD, 2008). International opportunity recognition has been known as the common and important barrier from the point of view of SMEs and OECD member compared to other barriers (OECD, 2008). Further research on the barriers of SME exporting and internationalization is an absolute demand. In this study, international opportunity recognition has been recognized as the main barrier in internationalization that can be executed by referring into academic research concerned with SME internationalization under the IE field as a subfield of entrepreneurship literature. This study is looking for the way to overcome this barrier as the important and main barrier for internationalization.

2.5   Recognizing international opportunities

Previous researches pointed out that there are many potential person and firm related variables that may affect international opportunity recognition in SMEs. As researchers indicated, they can be further divided into individual characteristics and firm characteristics (Figure 2.2).

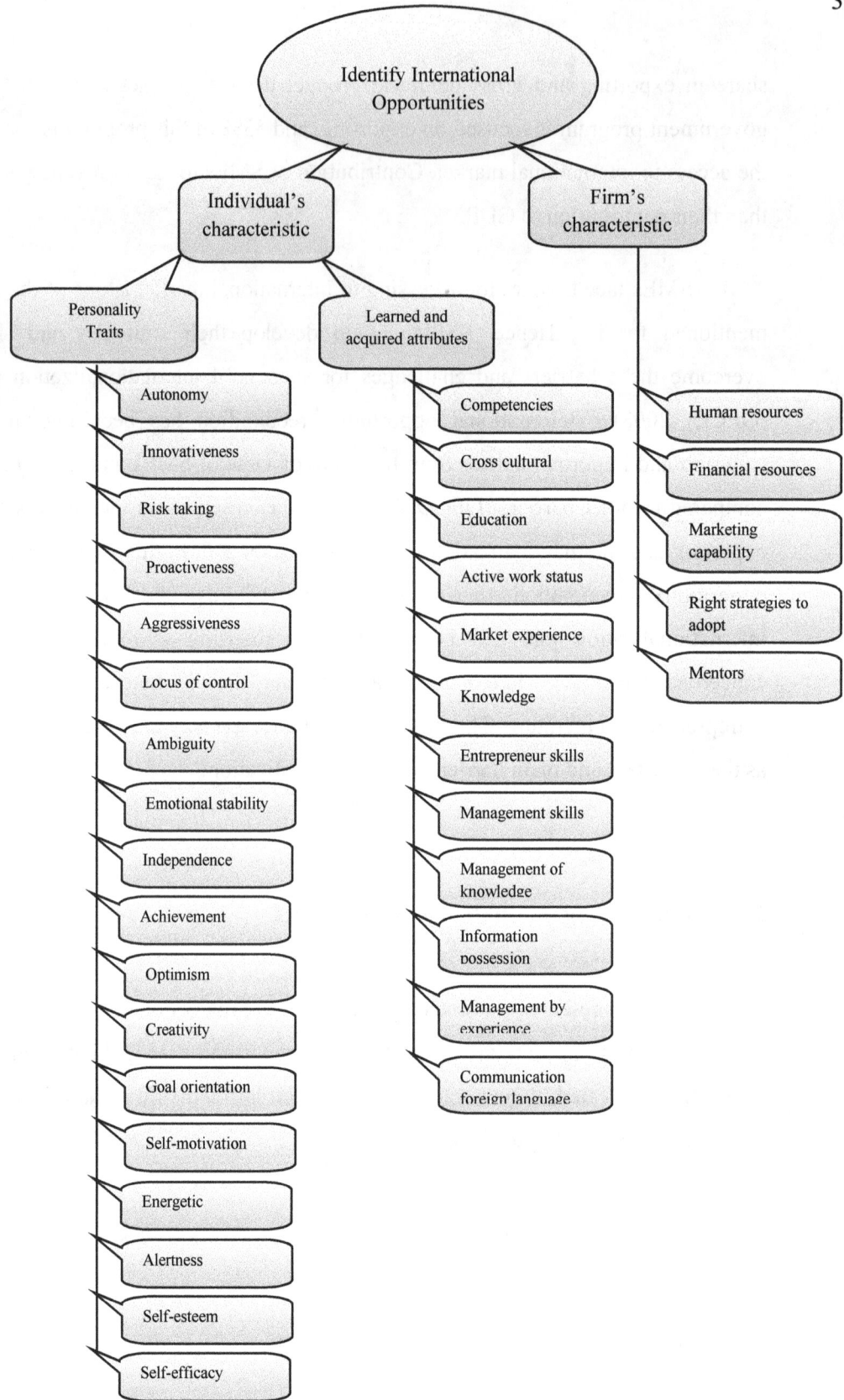

Figure 2.2   Factors affecting IOR according to previous studies

2.5.1 Individuals Characteristics

Individual characteristics have an effect on internationalization and opportunity recognition as the previous studies noted (Bloodgood *et al.*, 1996; Gregorio et al., 2008). Different studies illustrated that opportunity recognition is the role of individuals by organizing the resources. Also those particular individuals control to found viable businesses (Gregorio *et al.*, 2008). Based on the finding of Shane and Vankataraman (2000), there is a positive relationship among individual's characteristics and opportunity recognition skills. It fits with the indication that discovery of opportunities depends on personal characteristics. Individual characteristics can be entrepreneurs personality traits that are stable in entrepreneurs(see Table 2.1).It also can be the characteristic that entrepreneurs learned or acquired during the times (see Table 2.2).

2.5.1.1 Entrepreneur's personality traits

The characteristics of Entrepreneur's personality traits are stable over the time and differ from person to person. Research by Ardichvili et al., (2003) shows that entrepreneur's personality traits are as the antecedents of entrepreneurial alertness that eventually lead entrepreneurs to collect different information and different ways of information analysis. Finally, it guides them to recognize opportunities. Generally, speaking different personal characteristics lead to determine certain entrepreneurial opportunities and also function toward these opportunities in different paths.

To state the matter differently, mental attitude like enthusiasm to take the risks correlated with building new companies and utilize the opportunities (Miller *et al.*, 1982; Miller *et al.*, 1988; Miller and Dröge, 1986; Begley and Boyd, 1987). Hence, the opportunity recognition is limited by the entrepreneur's personal limitations in consulting and analyzing the information (Shane and Vankataraman, 2000). In this study several entrepreneurs' personality traits have been determined as an affecting factor on opportunity recognition. Entrepreneur's personality traits as the variables and their definitions also their references presents at the Table 2.1

Table 2.1 : Entrepreneur's personality traits

Personality traits	References
Autonomy	(Knight, 1997); (Lumpkin and Dess, 1996; 2001); (Zahra *et al.*, 2005)
Innovativeness	(Schumpeter, 1934); (Lumpkin and Dess, 1996; 2001); (Knight, 1997); (Stewart *et al.*, 1998); (Zahra *et al.*, 2005)
Risk taking	(Miller *et al.*, 1982); (Miller and Droge, 1986); (Begley and Boyd, 1987); (Knight, 1997); (Hisrich and Peters, 1998); (Stewart *et al.*, 1998); (Lumpkin and Dess, 1996; 2001); (Miner, 2000); (Zahra *et al.*, 2005)
Proactiveness	(Knight, 1997); (Lumpkin and Dess, 1996; 2001); (Zahra *et al.*, 2005)
Competitive aggressiveness	(Knight ,1997); (Lumpkin and Dess, 1996; 2001); (Zahra *et al.*, 2005); (Sambasivan and Abdul, 2009)
Locus of control	(Rotter, 1966); (Miller *et al.*, 1982; 1986); (Begley and Boyd, 1987); (Hisrich and Peters, 1998); (Miner, 2000)
Tolerance for ambiguity	(Miller and Droge, 1986); (Begley and Boyd, 1987); (Miner, 2000)
Emotional stability	(Miller and Dröge, 1986); (Begley and Boyd, 1987)
Independence	(Hisrich and Peters, 1998); (Sambasivan and Abdul, 2009)
High need for Achievement	(McClelland, 1961); (Miller *et al.*, 1982; 1986); (Begley and Boyd, 1987); (Hisrich and Peters; 1998); (Stewart *et al.*, 1998); (Miner, 2000)
Optimism	(Cooper *et al.*, 1988); (Ardichvili *et al.*, 2003), (Sambasivan and Abdul, 2009)
Creativity	(Ardichvili *et al.*, 2003)
Goal orientation	(Nummela, 2004); (Sambasivan and Abdul, 2009)
Self-motivation	(Herron and Sapienza, 1992); (Sambasivan and Abdul, 2009)
Energetic	(Sambasivan and Abdul, 2009)
Alertness	(Kirzner's, 1973, 1979, 1997, 1999); (McDougall *et al.*, 1994); (Hills and Shrader, 1998); (Zietsma,1999); (Ardichvili *et al.*, 2003); (Baron, 2007); (Sambasivan and Abdul, 2009); (Chandra *et al.*, 2009)
Gender	(Crant, 1996); (Crosa *et al.*, 2002); (Arenius and DeClercq, 2005)
Sense of self esteem and confidence	(Robinson *et al.*, 1991)
Self-efficacy	(Ozgen and Baron, 2007); (Markman *et al.*, 2002)

2.5.1.2 Entrepreneurial learned and acquired attributes

Entrepreneur's skills are actually these characteristics that are gained through the time and thus are subject to more change over time. Output of this study is to determine some entrepreneur's characteristics, which will gain over time by entrepreneurs and has an effect on opportunity recognition. Present study has indicated these variables, their definitions, and their references at the Table 2.2.

Table 2.2 : Entrepreneurial learned and acquired attributes

Entrepreneurial learned	References
Competencies	(Chandler and Hanks, 1994); (Eyre and Smallman, 1998); (Man and Lau, 2002); (Man *et al.*, 2002); (DeTienne and Chandler, 2007)
Cross cultural	(Vincent, 1996); (Zahra, 2005); (Arenius and DeClercq, 2005); (Johanson and Vahlne,2006)
Education	(Clark *et al.*, 1984); (Crant, 1996); (Bates, 1997); (Greene, 2000); (Arenius and DeClercq, 2005); (Evans and Leighton, 2010)
active work status	(Burt, 1992); (Bates, 1997); (Nahapiet and Ghoshal 1998); (Greene, 2000); (Evans and Leighton, 2010)
experience of market	(Hills and Shraders,1998); (Minniti and Bygrave,1999) ; (Shane, 2000); (Ardichivili *et al.*, 2003); (Zahra *et al.*, 2005)
Knowledge	(Kirzner, 1973);(Glaser, 1983); (Christensen and Peterson, 1990);(Venkataraman, 1997); (Hills and Shraders, 1998); (Timmons, 1999);(Cohen and Levinthal, 1999); (Shane, 2000); (Shane and Venkataraman, 2000); (Shepherd and DeTienne , 2001); (Ardichvili *et al.*, 2003); (McKelvie and Wiklund, 2004); (Park, 2005); (Baron, 2007); (Gregorio *et al.*, 2008); (Chandra *et al.*, 2009);(Chandra and Styles, 2009); (Sambasivan *et al.*, 2009)
Entrepreneur's skills	(Ozgen and Minsky, 2006)
Management skills	(Kickul and Walters, 2002); (Ardichvili *et al.*, 2003); (Park, 2005); (Ozgen and Minsky, 2006);
Management of knowledge	(Singh *et al.*, 1999)
Information possession	(Archdvili *et al.*, 2003); (Baron, 2006); (Gaglio and Katz, 2001); (Shane, 2003)
Management of experience	(Park, 2005)
Communication foreign language	(Chandra *et al.*, 2007)

There is an obvious flaw in the personality hypothesis, which is the assumption that the variables characterize the environment and the entrepreneur as static factor. However based on reality environment changes constantly and traits have a little ability to explain behavior and recognition opportunities (Delamar, 2000).The characteristics are not enough to recognize the opportunities due to the typical personal characteristics of entrepreneurs and complexity of environment. For example a car and its driver at the same parallels for enterprise and its entrepreneur will be insightful concept which applied by Etemad (2004).

Etemad stated that:

"Although a driver can accomplish some activities without the car, the car offers flexibility, safety, speed, and power and enables him to achieve even more. While a car is self-propelling, it still needs the driver to give it a directional command, harness its power and control its functions on the road. Similarly, the driver's performance, and possibly freedom of action, is somewhat restricted by what the car can or cannot do. Naturally both have to adapt to each other's capabilities and limitations to function optimally" (Etemad, 2004; p. 19)

Therefore, because of cognitive limitation of entrepreneurs, they need firms and resources for opportunity recognition. If they rely only on their internal characteristics, they may not adopt themselves very well and they fail.

2.5.2 Firm's characteristics

Opportunity recognition has also positive relationship with firms' characteristic. Differences among individuals based on their resources are important to explain differences in opportunity recognition.

Table 2.3 : Firm's characteristics

Firm's characteristic	References
Human resources	(Shane, 2000);(Shane and Venkataraman, 2000).
financial resources	(Park, 2005)
Marketing capability	(Ellis, 2011); (Haar and Ortiz-Buonafina, 1995)
Right strategies to adopt	(Walters, 2002)
Mentors	(Whitely *et al.*, 1991); (Ozgen and Baron, 2007)

It has been shown in several literature review that the availability of firm resources have the significant role in export business, and internationalization of SMEs. It also has an effect on the firm's decision regarding the SMEs international development (Jones, 1999; Zou and Stan, 1998).Superior export performance in exporting firms can be achievable if they allocate and acquire their appropriate resources (Leonidou *et al.*, 2002). Through the unique firm resource, exporting firms are able to become efficient and effective in the market (Barney *et al.*, 2001). The presence of favorable resources leads the firm to exploit opportunities and reduce threats in competitive environments (Michalisin *et al.*, 1997).

Generally, large manufacturers have an access to the necessary resources to handle a wide range of exporting activities in house while most of SMEs have not such accessibility. Due to their lack of knowledge in the foreign markets and their limited resources plus based on the uncertainty that surrounds the international market, several SMEs shy away from exporting (Ilinitch *et al.*, 1993; Ilinitch and Peng, 1994).

Different classifications of firm's resources were provided by the strategic management literature. Divided firm's resources in a simple form included tangible and intangible resources (Michalisin *et al,*. 1997). Due to the fact that they are often purchasable on the open market physical and tangible resources are not necessarily scarce (Michalisin *et al.*, 1997).On the other hand, intangible resources are usually scarce (Peteraf, 1993). Based on the finding of Andersen and Kheam (1998), only intangible resources were included in order to constitute capabilities on international markets. The importances of intangible resource rely on its anticipating growth strategy (Chatterjee and Wernerfelt, 1991; Peteraf, 1993).

As it mentioned before majority of SMEs suffer from intangible resources, for instance, lacking the market knowledge, experience and information (Coviello and McAuley, 1999; Knight, 2000; Hollenstein, 2005). Furthermore, it is general belief that source of higher performance appear to lie more on the intangible resources. Hence it is difficult to identify, understand and replicate (Fahy *et al.,* 2000). Researchers pay more attention to intangible resources (Michalisin *et al.,* 1997; Hall, 1993; Miller and Shamsie, 1996). It is quite hard to stimulate resources such as international knowledge and experience that determine firm performance in global competition (Peng and York, 2001).

In conclusion, as can seen from the literature, most of resources which were affecting on opportunity recognition were intangible resources such as; knowledge, experience, marketing skills and others. Prior researches about the opportunity identification mainly has been consternated on the role of individuals and firms characteristics while they suffer from the individual's cognitive limitation and lack or weakness in the firm's resources (Vandekerckhove and Dentchev, 2005). This gap also was the note of some previous researchers about internationalization such as; (Terjesen and Hessels, 2007) that mentioned the extant research is largely confident the role of firm and owner aspects ignoring the role of external factors.

There had been a shift in research interest in recent times, away from the individual's characteristics (Begley and Boyd, 1987; Brockhaus and Horowitz, 2002; Gartner, 1988) to a behavioral and process approach. This topic focuses on understanding how opportunities are discovered and acted upon by people and firms (Eckhardt and Shane, 2003; Shane, 2000; Shane and Venkataraman, 2000).

2.5.3   Networking

As it clear from prior studies, individuals and firm characteristics had taken most of attention whereas they are suffering from cognitive individual limitation and resources scarcities. Regarding to the resources scarcities in SMEs and their cognitive individual's limitation, how they can recognize opportunities? How they can acquire resources and compensate their resources scarcities?

On the other hand, Dana *et al.,* (2008) pointed out that world is moving toward a focus on relationship with multi-polar instead of focus on firm. Internationalization becomes a function of multi-polar networks including special relationships. Recently, many researchers fulfilled this lack of knowledge. By reviewing of these studies, entrepreneur's participation in social and business network has found as the answer of "why and how people are able to recognize the opportunities" (e.g. Aldrich and Zimmer, 1986; Arenius and DeClercq, 2005; Chen and Chen, 1998; Coviello and Munro, 1997; Johanson and Mattsson, 1988; Komulainen*et al.,* 2006; Loane and Bell, 2006; Meyer and Shak, 2002; Mort and Weerawardena, 2006; Oviatt and McDougall, 2005; Rutashobya and Jaensson, 2004; Sharma and Blomstermo, 2003; Singh, 2000).

Regarding to this answer "participation in social and business network" is the significant factor for recognizing opportunities. However, this question will be raised that they are able to compensate their resources scarcities by their networking. Based on Terjesen and Hessels (2007), research there is little known about the method used by entrepreneurs to compensate their individual and firms limitation for opportunity recognition.

Ellis (2003) stated that they are able to compensate their lack of resources or weakness and recognize the international opportunities with identification of good network and suitable potential exchange partner (Ellis 2003). The importance of networks in international opportunity recognition and exporting was accentuated by Welch*et al.,* (1996). There is less attention to the compensation of SMEs resources scarcities for recognizing opportunities in international markets despite the importance of social and business networking for opportunity recognition.

Considerable number of studies has focused on networking and collecting information for opportunity recognition. Also prior researches mainly examined the resources compensate in SMEs with examining the "resource dependency theory". Hence there is very limited researches on the "network theory" and compensate the resources scarcities for international opportunity recognition. In conclusion, this study focuses on "network theory" and compensates resources limitation in SMEs for recognizing international opportunities

Three ideal types of economy from the past until now exist, stated by Etemad (2008). These three type are included; Bazaar type economy or traditional bazaar, firm-type economy, and new economy. Table2.4 shows these types of economy.

As can see from the table, Bazaar is a traditional, social, cultural and economic system that internationalization is a function of multi-polar networks. In the other word, business can be deeply affected by networks and relationships.

As it seen from the Table 2.4, the emphasis is mainly on relationship and alliances. Both, buyers and sellers seek a relationship. Definition of firm-type economy is an economic institution in which location, consider as a competitive advantage. Internationalization is a sub-branch of uni-polar strategic decision making which centralized at the head office. It is approved that the relationship between consumer and the product is more important than the relationship between the consumer and the seller.

Table 2.4 : Comparing economies (Dana *et al.,* 2008, Pg. 121)

Bazaar economy	Firm-type economy	New economy
Focus on personal relations, alliances and networks	Focus on impersonal transactions	Focus on relationship marketing, alliances and networks
Geographical clustering facilitates information search	Exclusivity clause replaces clustering, complicates comparative shopping	Web allows for easy information search
Flexible prices are negotiated and preferential pricing is based on status and relationships	Prices are indicated by the vendor and buyers are treated as equals	Flexible prices are negotiated and preferential pricing is based on status and relationships
Would-be competitors cooperate, re-enforcing relationship networks	Competition takes place between sellers	Former competitors cooperate for mutual gain, thus re-enforcing relationship networks
Brand loyalty is influenced by preferential treatment; brand loyalty – based on relationships – exists even for commodities	Brand loyalty is a function of product differentiation; therefore, not applicable to commodities	Brand loyalty is influenced by preferential treatment; brand loyalty – based on relationships – exists even for commodities
Effective unit is network	Effective unit is individual firm	Effective unit is network
Decisions influenced by relationships with members of network; power and control thus de-centralized in multi-polar networks	Strategic decisions centralized at Head Office; power and control centralized in uni-polar fashion, with Head Office central to strategic decision-making	Decisions influenced by relationships with members of network; power and control thus de-centralized in multi-polar networks
Internationalization takes place along networks of relationships, resulting in a multi-polar, decentralized, distribution of power (Dana, 2000b)	Internationalization takes place under the directives of a centralized Head Office, enabling hierarchic decision-making (Buckley and Casson, 1976; Cavusgil, 1980; Dunning, 1973; etc.)	Networks facilitate internationalization, resulting in a multi-polar, decentralized distribution of power

However, a significantly different set of norms were set in the 21st century. World backed to the past which relationship is important. The new economy defines as an economic system plus cultural phenomenon in which the virtual clustering of vendors facilitates the consumer's comparative information search by relationship. In addition, internationalization describes an act of multi polar networks, which involve in the special relationship. Multi-polar internationalization consider as a novel field of study (Dana *et al.*, 2008).

Recently, studies are changing from the focus on individual and firm-specific characteristics to network and relationship between buyers and sellers. As Dana *et al.*, (2008) believe alliances and relationships are quite important. This fact is matched in situations like bazaar, buyer and seller negotiate price. Hence, the interaction inclination has to be between seller and buyer rather than interaction between buyer and product (Dana *et al.*, 2008).

In bazaar type as it described by Dana *et al.*, (2008) entrepreneurs searched the new information about new products for supplying or demanding. In order to take the new position they updated themselves quickly about new information and knowledge.

In addition, some of buyers and suppliers acted as intermediaries in order to gain profit from arbitrage. Entrepreneurs of the bazaar form the alliances and they engaged in mutual bargaining. The bazaar agents resembled modern-day agents or intermediaries. According to Etemad, in all types of economies, which include, bazaar-type economy, firm-type economy and new economy the mutual factor is relationships. That is why multi polar networking is reemerging. These days accentuate of internationalization is mainly on price discussion, status relationship, multi polar networks and symbiotic entrepreneurship. All the aforementioned factors are able to be facilitated by networks (Dana *et al*, 2008).Table 2.4 presents the three types of bazaar comparison. Based on the table presented by Dana *et al.* (2008), the effective unit in new economy is network and networks facilitate internationalization. The interest in new economy, congregate in alliances, networks, and relationship marketing.

Ellis (2011) indicated that the opportunity identification is fundamentally influenced by network structure. Network research is concerned upon the understanding of how "networks determine firm's strategic opportunities" (Meyer and Shak, 2002, p.181). Although the role network for SMEs to internationalization is highly important, it appears that there is very limited attention to discover of entrepreneurial and finding opportunities. Number of studies, recently have been addressed this limitation and examine how entrepreneurial managers to compensate their personal networks to acquire information about foreign market opportunities (Loane and Bell, 2006; Meyer and Shak, 2002; Rutashabya and Jaensson, 2004; Zain and NG, 2006).

Extracted from a network perspective, the internationalization of the firm is facilitated and influenced primarily by its relationships with others in its network (Axelsson and Johanson, 1992). As the matter of fact the network perspective was originally advanced in part as a framework for analyzing sources of information about foreign market opportunities (Johanson and Hallén, 1989; Sharma and Johanson, 1987), prompting scholars to analyze foreign market entry decisions through a network lens (Chetty and Holm, 2000; Blankenburg, 1995; Axelsson and Johanson, 1992; Covielloand Munro, 1997; Johanson and Vahlne, 1992; Meyer and Skak, 2002; Loane and Bell, 2006).

The main debate in network theory is that business networks of firms which coordinated by relationship governance are better suited than multi-level hierarchy governance or market governance or other forms of governance because of today's demanding environments (Snowet al., 1992). Briefly, such networks are the chains functionality that starts from manufacturers, through export intermediaries and end with end users (Ha°kansson and Johanson, 1992).

Internationalization through a network proposes strategic advantages in going to international market (Kogut and Kulatilaka, 1994). Furthermore, the network characteristics influence the process of getting more quantity of information. Diverse networks could be more effective than small networks (Burt, 2000). The size of network has an effect on the quantity of information, while diversity of network influences the quality of information (Birley *et al.,* 1991; Aldrich and Zimmer, 1986).

Initially when a firm walks in a foreign markets, having a background knowledge about that particular market also a large amount of fund are required (Ohmae, 1989; Eriksson *et al.,* 1997) which in general SMEs lack these resources. It is impossible that a firm be excellent at all activities required for process because of to the scarceness of these resources (Porter and Fuller, 1986).

Firm can concentrate on the various behaviors that they are perfect at with division of work. They will be able to gain and store various capabilities and knowledge and ultimately will become more efficient in the whole process (Kogut, 2000; Porter, 1990; Achrol and Kotler, 1999).

Second function of a network is that has a positive effect on flexibility that is quite valuable when market is unpredictable (Peng and Ilinitch, 1998; Kogut and Kulatilaka, 1994). Once a firm concentrates on doing just one unit within a network, it is able to allocate all aspects of its organization to this single task.

Third, risks and uncertainly are inseparable from an international market. By applying a network these risks and uncertainly spread and reduces. For instance if a firm do on activity, it not cause to risk and high cost (Root, 1994). Forth through the networking, making decision is rapidly therefore answering time will be shorter (Johnson and Lawrence, 1988). Fifth, economies of scale and learning by concentrating on a special activity unit within a chain will be acquired by operating through a network (Porter, 1986). Finally, a network is able to provide safeguard against market instability (Achrol and Kotler, 1999). According to the network literature, the main debate in network can be on an inter-firm (Easton and Hakansson, 1996; Johanson and Vahlne, 1992) and inter-personal relation (Blankenburg, 1995; Johanson and Vahlne, 1992; Meyer and Shak, 2002). Either of these topics have an effect on international opportunity recognition (Aldrich and Zimmer, 1986; Arenius and DeClercq, 2005; Chen and Chen, 1998; Coviello and Munro, 1997; Johanson and Mattsson, 1988; Komulainen*et al.,* 2006; Loane and bell, 2006; Meyer and shark, 2002; Mort and Weerawardena, 2006; oviatt and

McDougall, 2005; Rutashobya and Jaensson, 2004; Sharma and Blomstermo, 2003; Singh, 2000). Figure 2.3 illustrates the division of networking in the previous literature.

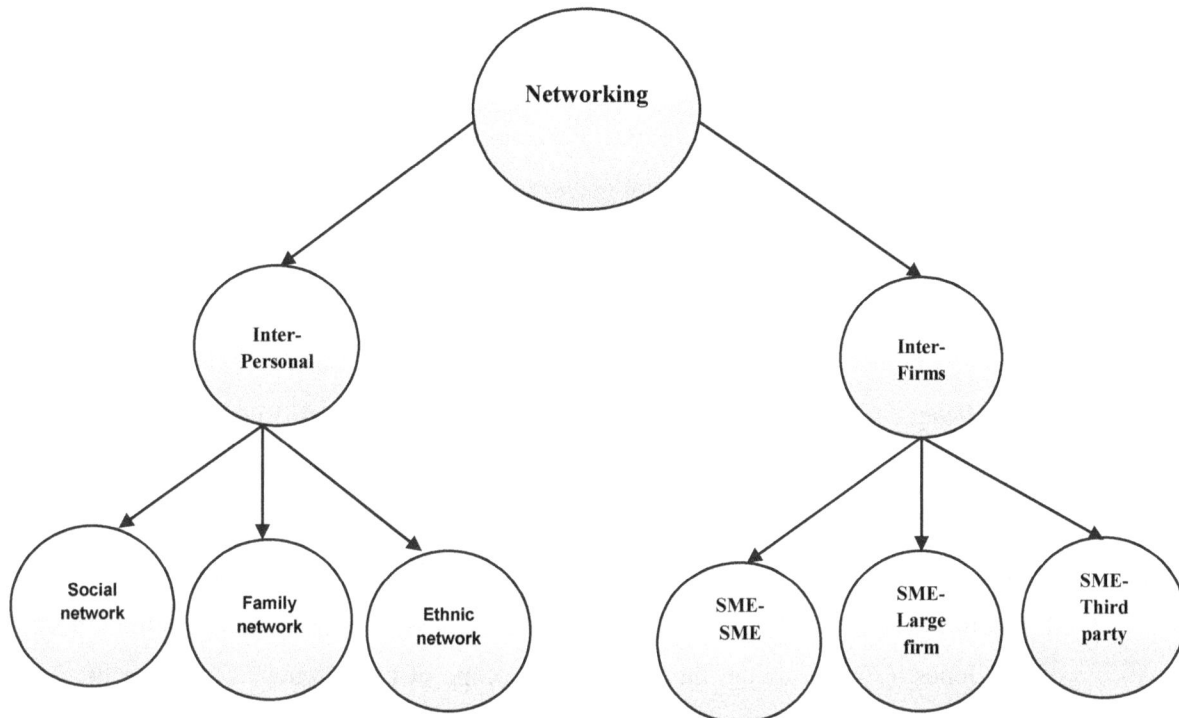

Figure 2.3   Division of networking in the previous literatures

2.5.3.1 Inter-personal network

One of the important factors in opportunity recognition is interpersonal networks (Singh *et al,.* 1999). Entrepreneurs who are open to the concept of network and apply it have more chance to recognize the opportunities (Aldrich and Zimmer, 1986). In addition, entrepreneurs can gain more information and knowledge that lead them to recognize potential (Nahapiet and Ghoshal, 1998; Arenius and DeClercq, 2005). According to Nahapiet and Ghoshal (1998), knowledge and information can be exchanged among entrepreneurs by interpersonal network and they can recognize international opportunities. Basically, interpersonal network is able to facilitate the process of gaining information and knowledge for entrepreneur in which information is not presently available that ultimately will lead to a potential for opportunity recognition (Arenius and Clercq, 2005). In addition, the relationship between entrepreneurs and their network contact could be a significant source of new opinion (Christensen and Peterson, 1990). Apparently a network has been linked with the different number of new opportunities which perceived by entrepreneurs (Singh *et al.*, 1999). Symbiotic benefit gained by the members in a network from each other's (Acs and Yeung, 1999). Previous researches implied that inter-personal network could be divided to; social networks, family networks, and ethnic networks.

- **Social network**

Number of authors have designated social and business networks as the significant factor for recognition opportunities (e.g Aldrich and Zimmer, 1986;Arenius and DeClercq, 2005; Chen and Chen, 1998; Coviello and Munro, 1997; Johanson and Mattsson, 1988; Komulainen*et al.,*2006; Loane et al., 2002; Mort *et al.,* 2006; Oviatt and McDougall, 2005; Rutashobya and Jaensson, 2004; Sharma and Blomstermo, 2003; Singh, 2000; Ellis, 2011). Also based on Dimitratosa and Jones, (2005) finding, the quality, and scope of entrepreneur's social networks influence the opportunity recognition and its growth (Dimitratosa and Marina, 2005).

In addition DeTienne, (2008) pointed out that entrepreneurs' social network with known others have a direct attitude on both opportunity recognition and following patterns of firm internationalization. Developing social and business networks contribute with the firm and entrepreneur to be recognized and providing for them, international opportunity to access to new and different types of information and ideas than would otherwise be encountered (Wilkinson *et al.*, 2003).

Networking also helps entrepreneur and firms to develop and exploit entrepreneurial opportunities and a way of managing the risks and uncertain environment (Wilkinson and Young, 2005). According to the Ellis (2003), social network is a significant foundation for innovative ideas and it influence the numeral of perceived opportunities for some reasons (Arenius andDeClercq, 2005; Ellis, 2003; Singh *et al.*, 1999).Firstly, cognitive methods have limited ability to understand the information. Secondly, analytical processes are subjective

(Vandekerckhove and Dentchev, 2005). Clearly, social network is the important firm's resource (Johanson and Mattson, 1988).

It seems that international entrepreneurial opportunity development is a discovery process rather than searching via strategic process, normal processes, or methodical information gathering (Coviello and Munro, 1997; Styles and Ambler, 1994). Strong and weak tie as a social network are designated in entrepreneurship research as an individual or firm social network (Elfring and Hulsink, 2003; Christensen and Peterson, 1990; Aldrich and Zimmer, 1986). Previous literatures of network pointed out weak ties as an important source for SMEs in process of opportunity recognition and firm internationalization (Crick and Spence, 2005; Harris and Wheeler, 2005; komulainen *et al.,* 2006; Sharma and Blomstermo, 2003; Zain and Ng, 2006).

Figure 2.4 illustrates the Butler and Brown model that indicated the relationship between social tie and business network on international opportunity recognition and performance (Butler*et al.,* 2003).

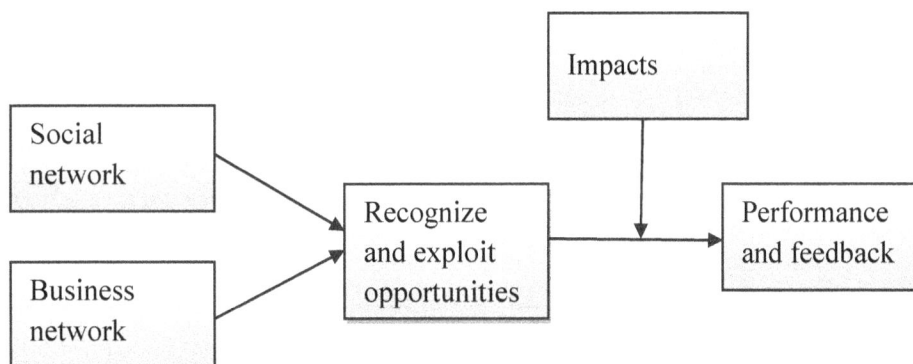

Figure 2.4   Model of Butler (Butler *et al.,* 2003)

A model of Butler and Brown has implied that, business and social network provide more information for recognize and exploiting of opportunities, which influence on firm's performance. A social network could exist among various sorts of people such as friends, suppliers, customers, stakeholders etc. According to the prior researches various types of social networks that influence on opportunity recognition have been shown in Table 2.5

Table 2.5 : Types of social networks

Types of Social Networks	Reference
Networking between Malaysian SMEs	(Senik *et al.*, 2010)
Relation with previous customers, friends and relatives living in foreign	(Rutashobya and Jaensson, 2004)
Relationship between customers-suppliers	(Johanson and Mattsson, 1988; Chetty and Holm, 2000; Majkgard and Sharma, 1998)
Relation between stakeholder management	(Vandekerckhove and Dentchev, 2005)
Relation with employment and the manager having experience	(Bell, 2006)
Relation between personal ties with extended family	(Kotkin, 1992; Rauch, 1996)
Relation between distribution channels and	(Hsing , 1999)
Relation between local government	(Barrett , 1997)
Relation between military	(Peng , 1998)
Relationships with other traders, suppliers and consumers	(Fafchamps and Minten, 1999)
Relation between social network and business network	(Bulter *et al.*, 2003)
Relationship between entrepreneur and her network contacts	(Christensen and Peterson, 1990)
Social network with known others	(DeTienne, 2007)
Social networks	(Johanson and Mattsson, 1988); (Styles and Ambler, 1994) ; (Coviello and Munro, 1995); (Ellis , 2011; 2003) ; (Wilkinson and Young, 2005).
Weak tie	(Crick and Spence, 2005; Harris and Wheeler, 2005; Komulainen *et al.,.* 2006; Sharma and Blomstermo, 2003; Zain and Ng, 2006).
Previous employment and the manager having experience in the foreign market	(Loane and Bell, 2006)
Participation in professional forums	(Ozgen and. Baron, 2007)

- **Family network**

One type of interpersonal networking is family network. It leads entrepreneur to recognize opportunities. The estimation of presence of family firms in US and EU shows a high percentage of 85 (IFERA, 2003). Management has been recognized as an important factor in order to internationalization process of a family firm (Kontinen and Ojala, 2010; Claver*et al.,* 2008).

Family firms based on finding of Sirmon and Hitt, (2003), can keeptheir trading even during economic recession. Some of studies that have been conducted about family network are Kontinen and Ojala, 2010; Lee, 2006. Obviously, number of researches on family networks is quite limited. This reflects the fact that this issue needs to be probed and further studies are necessary.

- **Ethnic network**

Another type of networking which is mentioned in the literatures is Ethnic network. Ethnic network described as a network that could be exist between marriage systems, religion, common language, credit associations, etc (Light, 1972). As an example for ethnic network we can pointed at Asians who brought their networks to the West countries when they moved there as the immigrant entrepreneurs (Light, 1972). Furthermore, there are literature reviews that imply how business contacts established through ethnic or extended family ties can resolve the problem of trust in international transaction (e.g., Curtin, 1984).

Despite the fact that several immigrant groups that arrived in their new countries have little technical business expertise, they apply their personal networks to uncover information about the commercial success of fellow immigrants' business. Their network provided the personal support and it motivates them to walk into various profitable industries within their immigrant community (Granovetter, 1985; Butler*et al.,* 2003). Hence this sort of network has been determined as the important source of information about potential buyers or sellers (Rauch, 1996). Table 2.6 presents the studies about ethnic networks in previous studies.

Table 2.6 : Types of ethnic networks

Types of Ethnic Networks	Reference
Chinese in Mississippi	(Loewen, 1971)
Han Chinese in New York	(Wong, 1987)
Han Chinese entrepreneurs in Calgary	(Ray *et al.,* 1988)
Han Chinese entrepreneurs in Canada	(Brenner and Toulouse, 1990)
Han Chinese in Vietnam	(Dana, 1994)
Turkish entrepreneurs in West Berlin	(Blaschke and Ersoz,1986)
Surinamese entrepreneurs in Amsterdam	(Boissevain and Grotenbreg,1987)
Minority entrepreneurs in the sub-Arctic	(Dana, 1995; 1996)
Turkish Cypriots in London	(Ladbury, 1984)
Koreans in Atlanta	(Min and Jaret, 1985)
Pakistanis in Manchester and United Kingdom	(Werbner, 1984)
Chinese entrepreneurs	(Kotkin, 1992)
Indian entrepreneur in Hong Kong	(Kotkin, 1992)
Sogo Shosha	(Rauch, 1996)
Korean immigrants in the U.S.	(e.g., Aldrich and Waldinger, 1990; Bonacich and Light, 1988; Light, 1972),
Chinese immigrants in Thailand	(Butler and Chamornmarn, 1995),
Pakistan in India	(Misra and Rumar, 2000)
Immigrant entrepreneurs	(Aldrich *et al.,* 1984)
Small firms in Amsterdam succeed within a social support network	(Boissevainand Grotenbreg, 1987)
Guanxi network between Chinese	(Tsang, 1998)

2.5.3.2 Inter-firm network

Definition of inter-firm network is the existing network one firm and other external firms in the national or international environments. Having this relationship and networks with external parties is a significant strategy of many companies in different industries (Gulati, 1995; Beamish and Killing, 1997; Ling-yee and Ogunmokun, 2001). Clearly long term relationship among firms can be potentially beneficial and also it leads to drop negative side of competition (Ganesan, 1994).

Exchanging resources that firm need for internationalization such as experiential knowledge about a market composed the basic of the inter-firm relationship and cooperation (Johanson and Vahlne, 1977). Despite all of the aforementioned, there is only a little experimental evidence of the strategic impact of resources and capabilities that can be shared and exchanged in marketing's cooperative relationships (Ling-yee and Ogunmokun, 2001; Morgan and Hunt, 1999).

"Invisible College" is a term that Best (1998) came up with. In this sort of network, in order to develop the quality of products and achieve more market share, ideas and knowledge could be exchange and shared in a cooperative effort (Ceglie and Dini, 1999).

Three types of inter-firm relationship have found through the reviewing previous studies. They are included; SME-SME, SME-Large firm, and SME-Third party relationships.

Although the path that correspondent factors influence competitive advantage in an export setting remains unknown. The relational capability of a firm has been theoretical supported by several researches alike, the resource based view of the firm (Morgan and Hunt, 1999; Barney, 1986), the knowledge based view of the firm (Grant, 1991; Connor and Prahalad, 1996) and the export channel literature (Jap and Ganesan, 2000; Ambler *et al.*, 1999) put forward their explanations on how interfirm relationships build up potential competitive advantageous (Ling-yee and Ogunmokun, 2001).

- **SME-SME network**

There is a network among the SMEs, which usually suffer from the limited resources. This network has a significant role in internationalization (Hadjikhani*et al.*, 2005; Ellis, 2011; Crick and Spence, 2005).This network has been mentioned in various research (e.g. Ghauri*et al.,*2003; Crick and Spence, 2005; Coviello, 2006). It is a major factor in initiating the internationalization process and it can act as a link into the foreign market (Johanson and Mattsson, 1988; Kontinen and Ojala, 2010). Internationalization will be facilitated by joining SMEs with limited resourcees together.

- **SME-Large firms**

Some of previous studies examined the networking between SMEs and large firms. SMEs will be able to conquer the global market much more faster if they collaborate with larger firms (Harrison, 1997).This question that how SMEs can rely on large firms for their internationalization activity has been explained by many researchers like Dana and Etemad (1994; 1995) and Bonaccorsi (1992).

SMEs can elevate their network resources in the short time and reduce the risk and cost of their internationalization by this 'scaling' up process. In addition, small firms will be able speed their learning and act competitive at the international level by having relationship with large firms. Hence, internationalization is a symbiotic relationship among small and large sized firms.

The competitiveness of large and small sized firms could be improved by presence of the network among these types of organizations. The small firms have the ability of getting their own economies of scale by providing of a vital resource for the bigger firms. Capturing scale economies for small firms will not be practical without relationship with large firms. On the other hand, in return, large firms will gain competitiveness by mingling those economies into their own value chains. Furthermore there is other advantage for large firms through the relationship with small firms for example large firms will improve in ability to tailor products or even process to fit local demand or content requirements. Also large firms will gain flexibility and economies of scope by accessing to the number of highly specialized small firms which each of them producing a small range of components at very substantial scale economies (Dana *et al.* 2008).

An example of presence of the networking among large and small firms is the small-scale entrepreneurs in the agro-food sector in Philippines. They link into a network with larger firms another network of small and large sized firms is Villasis Mango Growers Association. Federation of Cooperatives has brought several networks of mango-growers together for Pangasinan. In the same region, Ilocos Norte Federation of Agribusiness Cooperatives does the same for vegetables. Also as a smaller network we can mention Christian Farmers Kilusang Bayan which is for credit and allied services(Dana, 2001).

Eventually through the cooperation with large firms, small firms will be able to acquire to an adequate size and ability to move into international markets and to compete internationally (Dana, 2001).

- **SME-Third Party networking**

SME-Third party networking designated as another source for information, which has the ability to facilitate the recognition of international opportunities. SME-third party also known as intermediary and an example of that would be like professional forums (Ozgen and Baron, 2007). There is no trace of transaction exists between the buyer and the seller in the intermediary tie (Ojala, 2009).

Although in some cases, there is interaction in these two levels in intermediary. For example, organizers of exhibition or promotion organizations, which facilitate the establishment of a network, tie between the seller and the buyer. Hence such a third parties could initiate international activities between the buyer and the seller (Kontinen and Ojala, 2010; Oviatt and McDougall, 2005).

Based on the finding of Welch *et al.* (1996), the relationship between SMEs and export intermediaries may be good choice for entrepreneur to exchange information and resources for identify international opportunities (Welch *et al.*, 1996).

Majority of the researches upon the networking and international opportunity recognition pointed out that networking and acquire information is vital for going into international market. Although there is a little attention, about the acquiring resources to identify international opportunities while the basic of the inter-firm relationship and corporation is exchanging resources that firm need for internationalization such as market experimental knowledge (Johanson and Vahlne, 1977) and other resources. However, the amount of experienced evidence is not substantial about the influence of resources, which can be exchange and share in marketing's cooperation relationship (Morgan and Hunt, 1991; Ling-yee and Ogunmokun, 2001).

Firm resources, based on available literatures are important factor in influencing the internationalization of SMEs (Jones, 1999).Also it allows firm to exploit international opportunities and neutralize threats in competitive environments (Michalisin *et al.*, 1997). The characteristics, capabilities and resources of the firm are the basic items regarding to international expansion of SMEs (Jones, 1999). Majority of the SMEs do not possess the resources to handle a wide range of exporting activities in house while large manufacturers do not suffer from this deficiency. SMEs in compare with large firms are known to lack of resources such as knowledge, experience and other resources to move into international markets (Fujita, 1995; Coviello and McAuley, 1999; Knight, 2000; Hollenstein, 2005).

This feature of their resource-constrained form of SMEs amplified in developing countries since they often lack the necessary knowledge, financing, qualified human resources, marketing skills, limited access to resources, government support, information (Fujita,1995; Coviello and McAuley, 1999; Knight, 2000; Hollenstein,2005). Hence, several SMEs are not able to be active in field of exporting due to their limited resources and also it is hard for them to imitate resources such as international knowledge and experience that determine firm performance in global competition (Peng and York, 2001) and attempts to export are doomed to failure. Export intermediaries, especially those located in the export markets can be an essential link in an export network due to the network advantages and resource scarcities in SMEs (Gadde and Hakansson, 1992).

According to Ellis (2011), direct links with suppliers and customers is not the only beneficial way for firms. They can make profit also through their indirect relations with suppliers' suppliers and customers' customers (Johanson and Mattson, 1988). Therefore the network could be particularly suited to those, which require a certain level of cooperation between exchange parties (e.g., for product development and marketing) (Johanson and Vahlne, 1992).

Prior researches indicated that export intermediary resources have an effect on the internationalization and firm's export performance (Peng and York, 2001). Based on this fact, identification of a suitable exchange partner is quite significant in process of international opportunity recognition. Research of Ellis (2011) showed that after identifying an exchange partner and intermediaries such as a distributor or wholesaler in the foreign market an entrepreneur who perceives an opportunity will be able to exploit it. To be clearer, identification of potential exchange partners and international opportunity recognition are synonymous (Ellis 2011). SMEs that apply intermediaries are able to overcome their gaps of knowledge, find more opportunities and customers, and even decrease the risks to operate in international markets (Terjesen *et al.,* 2008).

According to several published papers, a mediatory can act as a catalyst to assist the emergence of clusters and networks that can result to significant decrease in the high transaction costs and risk (Ellis, 2011). SMEs which have lack experience in international markets if start to apply network connection, they will be beyond the boundaries into foreign markets (Johanson and Vahlne, 1992; Sharma and Johanson, 1987). Internationalization could be difficult regarding to various aspects such as cultural, geographic and locating customers in foreign country, which is economic uncertainly. This uncertainly could be reduced through mediating and developing international trade flows (Kojima and Ozawa, 1984), viewpoint of agency theory (Jensen and Meckling, 1976; Eisenhardt, 1989) and transaction cost analysis theory (Williamson, 1996; Williamson, 1975; Williamson, 1985; Coase, 1937; Rindfleisch and Heide, 1977; Heide, 1994; Bello and Lohtia, 1995;Kim and Nugent, 1997).

The relation between export performance and the types of the relationship between the manufacturing exporter and its intermediaries is one of the growing bodies of literature (Ellis, 2003a). Definition of an export intermediary can be as an entrepreneurial service that would connect the manufacturers and end users (Peng, 1998).

An export intermediary could be capable alternative to connect and discuss with foreign customers due to the resources limitation in SMEs and also uncertain and risks that is surrounded them to act internationally (Root, 1994; Chalmin, 1987; Ilinitch*et al.,* 1993). Generally speaking SMEs have deficiency of the necessary resources to engage in a direct exporting. Intermediaries have provided alternatives for SMEs to export through the connecting manufacturers of one country and customers of another country (Lee and Danusutedjo, 2000).

Valuable assets and resources of intermediaries such as their market knowledge, skills and networks is being probed by exporters (Wilkinson and Nguyen, 2003). The value, uniqueness, and difficulty of imitating resources and capabilities provide a rationale for the existence of export intermediaries (Peng and Ilinitch, 1998). Exporters of small and medium sized who have deficiency in skills, financial resources and international marketing experience tend to depend on export intermediaries, making them particularly important for SMEs (Ford and Rosson, 1982; Peng and Ilinitch, 1998).

Inadequate information about foreign markets in small manufacturing firms could have been overcome by choosing partners, who possess such knowledge and resources (Inkpen and Beamish, 1997). Intermediaries export can help their costumers to recognizing clients, funding and distribution infrastructure providers (Balabanis, 2000). There are some large firms that despite the fact that they have no interest to commit to a certain market, they also rely on export intermediaries (Peng and York, 2001). Therefore, exporters must pay special attention to the distinctive competencies of intermediaries, in order to achieve their full potential (Ling-yee and Ogunmokun, 2001).

SMEs with export intermediary connection can overcome their gap of knowledge, decrease risks to operate in international markets, marketing search, negotiations and searching new customers' costs (Peng and York, 2001).

Furthermore they are able to identify new customers, finance and credit sources. Firms are intended to apply intermediaries while entering to foreign markets and they need to less control to exporting (Blomstermo *et al.*, 2006). Due to the fact that intermediaries can act exporting better based on their specific knowledge (Li, 2004). SMEs may use intermediaries in order to discuss and barging with foreign customers, achieve experience and knowledge of foreign markets (Terjesen *et al.*, 2006).

An issuing bunch of research discusses that how SMEs become internationalization through indirect path (e.g. Acs *et al.*, 1997; Peng and York, 2001; Terjesen et al., 2006; Acs and Terjesen, 2006) or applying intermediaries in the form of local or foreigner to introduce and trade their products and services to foreign markets. In order to overcome knowledge gaps (Terjesen *et al.*,2008), insufficient information limitations about international markets (Inkpen and Beamish, 1997), find customers, discuss with foreign customers, reduce uncertainties, risks and costs of trading in foreign markets (Terjesen *et al,.* 2008; Zacharakis and Meyer, 1998) reducing costs for example marketing research, reducing negotiation costs (Peng and York 2001), access to experience and knowledge of international markets (Susman 2007; Terjesen *et al.*, 2008; Root, 1994), access to the flow of ideas and unexpected rent appropriation, SMEs are more likely to use intermediaries.

Identification of customers, credit sources and financial activities are some of other acts that SMEs could find themselves able to do them with the help in export intermediaries (Balabanis, 2000). According to Feenstra and Hanson (2001) export intermediary participated significant role in ancient, medieval (Greif 1993) and modern world trade (Jones, 1999) while they were not exist in the pure theory of international trade.

Therefore, due to possession of required resources and increase the internationalization speeding process, intermediaries could act as the agent to increase the export performance of SMEs manufacturers. The potential of export intermediaries is just beginning to be explored in the literature. Thus far, the majority of studies on small producers and export intermediaries have addressed following issues (see Table2.7).

Table 2.7 : Focus of the majority of intermediary studies

Studies about the relation between small producers and export intermediaries	References
Commitment to export intermediaries by manufacturers	(Peng and Ilinitch; 1998; Gilliland and Bello, 2002; Trabold, 2002; Schroder *et al.,* 2003; Deligonul and Cavusgil, 2006; Peng *et al.,* 2006)
Export performance of manufacturers using intermediaries.	(Bello and Gilliland, 1997; Gencturk and Kotabe, 2001; Bello *et al.,* 2003);
Performance of export intermediaries	(Bello *et al.,* 1991; Peng *et al.,* 2000; Peng and York, 2001; Balabanis, 2001).

Despite the fact that the majority of world trade is handled through independent intermediaries (Mortanges and Vossen, 1999), most of published literatures only covered the characteristics associated with exporters, and consequently, export intermediaries have become a omitted link in the literature of markets (Peng and Ilinitch, 1998). There has been little theoretical and empirical research about the export intermediary networking despite the importance of it. The advantages of applying export intermediaries are summarized in the Table 2.8.

Table 2.8 : the benefit of using Export Intermediary (EI) based on the past studies

Advantages of EI	References
Identify new customers,	(Balabanis, 2000)
Help their client to financing , credit sources and distribution infrastructure providers	(Balabanis, 2000)
Reducing uncertainties and other risks associated	(Trabold, 2002; Peng, 1998; Root, 1994; Ilinitch *et al.,* 1993; Chalmin, 1987; Peng and York, 2001; Zacharakis, 1998; Terjesen *et al.,* 2008)
Negotiate with foreign customers, negotiate contracts	(Terjesen *et al.,* 2008; Zacharakis, 1998; Terjesen *et al.,* 2008)
Overcome experience gap	(Zacharakis, 1998; Terjesen *et al.,* 2008)
Overcome foreign market information	(Inkpen and Beamish, 1997)
Successful communication in geographically different markets	(Trabold, 2002; Peng, 1998; Root, 1994; Ilinitch *et al.,* 1993; Chalmin, 1987)
Overcome knowledge gap	(Peng and York, 2001; Terjesen *et al.,* 2008; Root, 1994)
Reducing marketing search	(Peng and York, 2001)
Reducing searching new customers costs	(Peng and York, 2001)
Less control in exporting	(Blomstermo and Sharma, 2006)
Control and resource commitment	(Johanson and Wiedersheim-Paul, 1975; Blomstermo *et al.,* 2006)

The relationship between SMEs and export intermediary is base on their exchange of intangible resources for example exporters seek to gain access to the valuable assets and resources of intermediaries such as their market knowledge, skills and networks to improve their business processes (Wilkinson and Nguyen, 2003).

Furthermore, export intermediaries expect certain contributions from their exporters such as their commitment; consistent product quality and marketing support (Hocutt, 1998).Various types of theoretical perspectives make different assumptions about the nature of relationship between SMEs and export intermediary. The affinity between SMEs and intermediaries has been analyses from the viewpoint of different theories. Table 2.9 presents different types of theories that these relationships have been analyzed. In this study, the relationship between export intermediaries and SMEs is analyzed by applying the network and exchange theory.

Table 2.9 : The focus of the relationship between manufacturer and intermediaries base on theories in the previous studies

Theory used in the previous studies	References
Transaction cost analysis theory	(Coase, 1937; Rindfleisch and Heide, 1977; Williamson, 1975; 1985; 1996)
Resource dependency theory	(Zahra *et al.*, 2005; Salancik and Pfeffer, 1978; Sherer and Lee 2002;Theingi, 2008)
Structural Hole Theory	(Burt, 1992; Nahapiet and Ghoshal, 1998)

2.6 Theoretical Framework

2.6.1 Network Theory

The basic of network thinking can be appeared first time at the early 20th century and even further (Ritter and Gemunden, 2003). Definition of a network is "sets of two or more connected exchange relationships" (Axelsson and Johanson, 1992). The term of Network has been applied in several ways within the literatures to represent the link between players that can be organizations or individuals (Coviello and Cox, 2006). According to Ellis (2011), researchers that utilized internationalization network model contributed to explore the interaction between organizations (Kontinen and Ojala, 2010).

Markets are the systems of industrial and social relationships among suppliers, customers, competitors, friends, family, and others, according to network theory. Members of a network can be involved in exchanging resource (Sharma and Blomstermo, 2003). In the network model, internationalization defines as developing network links with other firms which they have connection with a foreign market (Johanson and Mattsson, 1988; Kontinen and Arto, 2010). It facilities foreign market entry as the bridges between firms in different markets (Johanson and Vahlne 1990; Chetty and Holm, 2000; Kontinen and Arto, 2010).

Internationalization is development of a network that links to other firms, which they are member of foreign market network. This is called internationalization network model (Johanson and Mattsson, 1988).These links and relations among firms in various different markets act as bridges facilitating foreign market entry (Johanson and Vahlne, 1990; Chetty and Holm, 2000).

A firm can develop its situation in the networking, which is exist or by creating new ties to compensates resource scarcities, according to network model (Johanson and Mattsson, 1988, Kontinen and Ojala, 2010). While they could not easily attain with acting alone this relationship helps each firm to achieve goals. Mutual benefit is the common interests in network theory that encourage firms to growth and preserve network tie together (Johanson and Vahlne, 2003; Johanson and Mattson, 1988).

Different sort of resources can be absorbed by firms based on their relationship with different resource elements. These resources could be tangible or intangible, which in both cases small firms demand it. Even companies that are able to confront and combine resources need to have relationship with each other. Overtime the interaction between the resources of the two companies can become both broad and deep; it can embrace different types of resources and activate these to various degrees.

Companies become specifically oriented towards each other, that is, various resource ties will emerge and eventually the resources of the two companies will be tied together that will be the effect on the resources.A relationship develops in such cases could be like a resource combinations. Two companies constitute resources of new quality, as different elements of the two companies, tangible as well as intangible, become integrated. Two companies can also consider themselves as resources and their relationships are valuable bridges to access resources. A relationship could be a resource that ties together various resource elements. The process of developing a business relationship is quite similar to investment process. Various opportunities will be available by providing resources and ultimately it gives the company freedom to undertake their limitations.

One of the significant points to collect the available resources for a company is its developing relationship with others. It influences the mobility and accessibility of the resources of others for a company's own purposes and advantage. Within a certain context, there are some resource ties among most of the interacting actors (resource providers). The conclusion will be sort of an aggregated resource structure or as it known as a resource gathering (Ha°kansson and Snehota, 1995).

According to the network theory, the affinity between SMEs and export intermediaries will be crucial network for internationalization particularly for young SMEs because of their lack of resources and unknowing networks for internationalization. Export intermediaries networking for internationalization can be supported by following reasons.

2.6.1.1 Complement the internal firm resources

The resources of smaller manufacturing firms for potential international opportunities play an important role in order to be successful in the international market (Andersen and Kheam, 1998; Bloodgood et al., 1996; Crick and Batstone, 2001). It is a fact that, entering to a foreign market requires particular knowledge about the host country and financial resources (Ohmae, 1989; Eriksson et al., 1997).However, most of SMEs normally lack these necessary internal resources(Acs, Morck et al.,1997; Alvarez, 2004; Ramaswami and Yang, 1990; Wolff and Pett, 2000).

Deficiency in such resources is important barrier in going to international markets (Seringhaus and Rosson, 1989). According to Wilkinson and Brouthers (2006), by developing external and internal resources, SMEs could be able to overcome these barriers in international market. This complement of internal resources could be through export intermediaries' resources (Day, 1994).

2.6.1.2 Decreasing Transaction Cost

In order to internationalization each firms have the potential costs associated with transactions such as costs of export activities including such ex ante costs as negotiating contracts and such ex post costs as monitoring and enforcing agreements (Peng, 1998; Williamson, 1985). Intermediaries are able to do with the lesser transaction costs related to export activities such as monitoring, enforcement, negotiation, plus bundling product lines of several manufacturers in order to create goods synergies (Lilien 1979; Peng and Ilinitch, 1998; Schroder and Trabold, 2003).

With better country-specific, knowledge about the export market, closer contacts with end users and shorter psychic distance in foreign export intermediaries, It facilitates to reduce the possibilities of bounded rationality by manufacturers and opportunism by end users (Rindfleisch and Heide, 1997) and reduce directly costs of information gathering and processing, negotiation, and monitoring (Peng and Ilinitch, 1998). Hence, the relationship between SMEs and export intermediaries can be pursued due to its benefit of transaction cost for SMEs (Peng and Ilinitch, 1998).

2.6.1.3 Division of work

One firm solely will not be able to fine at the all behaviors in the process of internationalization because of the scarcity of internal resources (Porter and Fuller, 1986). Hence firms must concentrate on the functionalities that they are excellent at acquire various knowledge and resources and increase the efficiency of all process (Achrol and Kotler, 1999; Kogut, 2000; Porter, 1990) or even they can combined and emerge their resources. The conclusion of aforementioned combination could be a new quality of resources suited to internationalization (Ha°kansson and Snehota, 1995). Better quality of resources to internationalization could be acquired through the relationship between export intermediaries and SMEs. As the matter of fact, firms will be able to obtain new knowledge, experience new opportunities and take profit from various resources by the help of network (Wang, 2008).

Furthermore, other advantages support the relationship between SMEs and export intermediaries that showed in published literatures. Here is presented some of those advantages, gathering and exchanging the information (Meyer and Shak, 2002), assists firms to spread from domestic to global markets by introducing them to new customers and their positions within those markets (Naughton, 2000), internationalization will be easier and faster and there is no need to follow a staged progression to internationalization compared to large firms (Coviello and Munro, 1997), providing SMEs to acquire information and necessary strategy to internationalization, reducing risk and uncertainty in the foreign markets (Root, 1994), getting quick decision through existing network by SMEs (Johnston and Lawrence, 1988), achieving resources, which both manufacturers and end users require but do not have (Day, 1994; Sharma and Blomstermo, 2003), and helping SMEs to combine resources drawn from diverse national locations (Dimitratos and Jones 2005; Oviatt and McDougall 2005a; Zahra *et al.*, 2005). Based on the network theory, there is an export intermediary because of the resources possession and their unequaled place at the player relations (Burt, 1992).In addition, this kind of networking is as the safeguard for SMEs against market instability (Achrol and Kotler, 1999).

2.6.2   Exchange theory

The vital conception for the entrepreneurship study is exchange theory plus it consider as the significant element in the internationalization field (Steenkamp, 2001). Definition of exchange is transferring of value such as intangible or tangible resources, symbolic or actual among more than two parties, with the implication that all exchanged parties receive and give the value (Houston and Gassenheimer, 1987). One of the different ways that people satisfy their needs is exchanges (Houston and Gassenheimer, 1987). Psychological, social or other intangibles goods are also exchangeable (Bagozzi, 1975; Levy, 1977). Based on the exchange theory, affinity between SMEs and export intermediaries exists. The reason of presence of such relationship is that they both need exchanging resources. In order to be more transparent we can say that manufacturer should be good at product quality and intermediaries should be good at intangible resources such as knowledge, information and experience (Theingi, 2008). Hence, internationalization for SMEs will be facilitated by these theories.

2.7   Research Gap

To conclude from literature review it can be argued that while the need for progress in SME internationalization is fully understood and appreciated in literature, our knowledge on the drivers of SME internationalization is limited in the sense that different theoretical approaches and frameworks have been adopted to explain SME internationalization. As international opportunity recognition is the important and main barrier faced by majority of small and medium firms in international markets and also is the first and most important step in internationalization, more research is needed to explore this issue.

While the traditional theories of firm internationalization are not suitable for the study of small and medium firms, entrepreneurship studies and especially international entrepreneurship as a subfield of it could assist us to understand SME internationalization. As seen from the literature, most of resources, which were affecting on opportunity recognition, were intangible resources instead of tangible. Physical and tangible resources are not necessarily scarce because they are often purchasable on the open market (Michalisin *et al.*, 1997) while intangible resources are usually scarce (Peteraf, 1993). According to Andersen and Kheam (1998), only intangible resources were included to constitute capabilities on international markets. Intangible resources are particularly important for predicting growth strategy (e.g. Chatterjee and Wernerfelt, 1991; Grant, 1991; Peteraf, 1993) while most of SMEs suffer from intangible resources, for example lacking the market knowledge, experience and information (e.g. Coviello and McAuley, 1999; Knight, 2000; Hollenstein, 2005). In addition, source of higher performance is believed to lie more on the intangible resources that are difficult to identify, understand and replicate (Fahy *et al.*, 2000). It is hard to imitate resources such as international knowledge and experience that determine firm performance in global competition (Peng and York 2001). In addition, previous studies about the opportunity recognition has focused on the role of individuals and firms characteristics while they suffer from the individual's cognitive limitation and lack or weakness in the firm's resources (Vandekerckhove and Dentchev, 2005). This gap also was the note of some previous researchers about internationalization such as; (Terjesen andHessels, 2007) that mentioned the extant research is largely confident the role of owner and firm-specific factors, ignoring the role of external factors.

SMEs in comparisons to large firms are typically regarded as resource-constrained, lacking the market power, knowledge and resources to operate in international markets. Therefore, the question of "How entrepreneur recognize international opportunity" which was indicated by some of researchers is still under explored.

However, SMEs and entrepreneurs should pursue innovations to compensate their resource's limitation. The market situation has changed radically during the last decades. The existence and the role of relationships between companies have received growing attention. The literature shows that opportunity recognition is influenced by entrepreneurs' participation in networks. Entrepreneur's participation in social and business network has found as the answer of "why and how people are able to recognize and exploit the opportunities" (e.g Aldrich and Zimmer, 1986; Arenius and DeClercq, 2005; Chen and Chen, 1998; Coviello and Munro, 1997; Johanson and Mattsson, 1988; Komulainen *et al.,* 2006; Loane and Bell, 2006; Meyer and Skak, 2002; Weerawardena and Mort, 2006; Oviatt and McDougall, 2005; Rutashobya and Jaensson, 2004; Sharma and Blomstermo, 2003; Singh 2000).

From a network perspective, the internationalization of the firm is facilitated and influenced primarily by its relationships with others in its network (Axelsson and Johanson, 1992). Regarding to SMEs resources scarcities, they have to rely to networking with other actors and organization in the environment and establish relationships to access the resources for international opportunity recognition and their internationalization. Besides resources, there are other factors to be considered in IOR as the market situation has changed radically these last few decades. The present trend of the related studies is shifting from the individual and firm-specific characteristics to network and relationship between buyers and sellers with multi-polar networks (Dana *et al.,* 2008). This is reflected in the entrepreneurial ways and there is a shift towards a behavioral and process approach that focuses on understanding how opportunities are discovered and acted upon by people and firms (Eckhardt and Shane, 2003; Shane, 2000; Shane and Venkataraman, 2000).

As seen from the literatures the network and international opportunity recognition most of studies focused on the social and business network to exchange the information for internationalization while information is just one of the intangible resources that affect on opportunity recognition and internationalization. Since other resources such as, knowledge, experience, marketing and other intangible resources have the important role in opportunity recognition and internationalization, and also SMEs are suffering from their lackness. Therefore studies cannot easily answer to the question of "how entrepreneurs recognize opportunities" by answering "networks". Studies should be making deeper toward the relation between networking and compensate resource scarcity. Therefore, the question of "how entrepreneurs recognize opportunities" should change to how entrepreneurs compensate their resources scarcities for recognizing opportunities regarding to the resources scarcities and their cognitive individual's limitation.

As the literatures (part of networking) markets are the systems of industrial and social relationships among suppliers, customers, competitors, friends, family, and others and members involve in the network are able to exchange resource (Sharma and Blomstermo, 2003) and also to compensate resource scarcities, a firm can develop its position in an existing network or by establishing new ties (Johanson and Mattsson, 1988; Kontinen and Arto, 2010). According to Ellis (2003), with the suitable network and potential exchange partner, SMEs are able to compensate their weakness and recognize the international opportunities. Regarding this definition of networks base on the resources exchanging and also the focusing of networking studies on the social and business network to collect the information, there has been big gap because existing literatures has ignored acquiring other resources for internationalization. Terjesen and Hessels (2007), stated that there is little known about the method used by entrepreneurs to compensate their individual and firms limitation for opportunity recognition.

Compensating resources scarcities is the necessary activity in SMEs due to its role with exploiting the opportunities, neutralizing threats in competitive environments (Michalisin *et al.*, 1997), and in export performance (Leonidou *et al.*, 2002b). SMEs should pay special attention to compensate resources scarcities towards international opportunity recognition and export performance. Despite of the importance of resources for internationalization, export literature has not paid much attention to the role of resource in internationalization (Srivastava *et al.*, 2001).

In this regard, this study attempt to fill this gap by focusing on the export intermediaries networking to acquire resources scarcities including (marketing capability, experience and knowledge assets, and relation assets) for opportunity recognition and export satisfaction. The network cooperation between exporters and export intermediaries is considered very important (Ling-yee and Ogunmokun, 2001) due to the resources exchange.

Based on the literature review, SMEs tend to make relationship with export intermediary to gain access to valuable assets and resources of intermediaries to internationalization (Wilkinson and Nguyen, 2003). The motivation for using intermediaries by small firm is individuality, and difficulty of imitating resources and capabilities. When a firm enters a foreign market, a large amount of resources are required which SMEs lack or weak. Due to the scarceness of these resources, it could be able access to the resources needed by relationship with export intermediary (Day, 1994). Terjesen *et al.*, (2008), indicated that the manufacturer's success totally depends on the initiative and efforts of the chosen intermediary. Hence, in order to achieve their full potential, exporters must pay special attention to the unique competencies of intermediaries (Ling-yee and Ogunmokun, 2000).Therefore, SMEs and export intermediary have a mutual dependence relationship in which the performance of the intermediary depends on the performance of the manufacturer and vice versa.

The relationship between SMEs and export intermediaries was developed by Trabold, 2002; Peng and Ilinitch, 1998; Root, 1994; Ilinitch *et al.,* 1993; Chalmin, 1987; Peng and York, 2001; Blomstermo and Sharma, 2006. Previous studies about the relationship between SMEs and export intermediaries have addressed the resource dependency theory, transaction cost theory and Hole theory. Resource dependency theory is focused on resources, transaction cost is focused on reducing cost and hole theory is focusing on the opportunity for other parties in the environment which have necessary resources. Previous studies have not much attention to the relationship between SMEs and export intermediaries based on Network theory and Exchange theory. Network theory and Exchange theory as discussed in the part of 2.7.1 and 2.7.2 can cover all these theory, because firms inside of network are able to exchange resources, reduce their cost and also can make opportunities for other parties inside of network. However, independent intermediaries (Mortanges *et al.,* 1999) handle most of exporting in the world; most studies examined only the characteristics associated with exporters, and intermediaries (Peng and Ilinitch, 1998). Prior research has assumed that some degree of mutual cooperation between producers and export intermediaries is a necessary condition for a high joint performance (Deligonul *et al.,* 2006; Heide and Miner, 1992; Peng and York, 2001; Gençtürk and Kotabe, 2001). However, there is some empirical research to support the link between effective networks between export intermediaries and SMEs to recognize international opportunities and export satisfaction.

Therefore, this study focused on the network theory and seeks to clarify how network based view explain the relationship between SMEs and export intermediaries to compensate resource scarcities for IOR. Based on the previous studies the relationship among export intermediaries and SMEs is based on the exchanging intangible resources such as, marketing capability, knowledge and experience, and relationship assets (Theingi, 2008).

2.8   Conceptual Framework Development and Hypothesis

2.8.1   Export intermediary networking and IOR

According to previous studies, the cooperation networking increases a firm's success and better and positive export performance (Hillebrand and Biemans, 2003; Ambler *et al.*, 1999).

In other hand, using of intermediaries has been argued to lead to higher international performance in the entrepreneurial context (Rabino, 1980; Shepherd and Zacharakis, 1997). SMEs through intermediaries can improve export performance, profitability, productivity and firm satisfaction (Terjesen *et al.*, 2008; Rabino, 1980; Zacharakis, 1997; Wilkinson and Brouthers, 2006). Wilkinson and Brouthers (2006) stated that using services of export intermediaries is positively associated with firm satisfaction with export performance (Wilkinsonand Brouthers, 2006). However, previous studies did not analyze this relationship through network theory.

A number of scholars have theorized about the beneficial effects of networking activity (Birley, 1985; Larson, 1992), or about the effect of export intermediary on export performance through other theories (Terjesen *et al.*, 2008; Rabino, 1980; Zacharakis, 1997; Wilkinson and Brouthers, 2006). There is less attention to the relationship between effective networks and firm performance (Aldrich *et al.*, 1987; Blundel, 2002; Cell and Baines, 2000) and less attention to supporting the link between export intermediary networking and export satisfaction base on the network theory for acquiring resources including marketing, experience and knowledge, and relation assets. Therefore, this study propose that;

H1: Export intermediary networking by SMEs has positive relationship with international opportunity recognition in SMEs.

2.8.1.1 Marketing capabilities and IOR

Marketing is an activity of searching for opportunities by structuring an organization through a formal search, participating at trade shows, advertising and relying on networks. Marketing capability gives firms the competitive advantage in any competitive environment and there are different definitions for marketing capabilities(Weerawardena, 2003). This study uses Weerawardena's definition that marketing capability refers to the quality of the firm's customer service, quality of sales force, advertising effectiveness, strength of distributor networks, speed of new product introduction, market research abilities, and ability for differentiation products. Marketing capability is a crucial resource in firms that is used to penetrate the markets (Theingi, 2008).

According to Ellis (2011)states, that marketing is the firm's resource, which contributes towards opportunity recognition. Thus, marketing capabilities for exporting firms is an important resource for opportunity recognition in international markets and SMEs should develop their own marketing capabilities (Haar and Ortiz-Buonafina, 1995). Furthermore, an emerging marketing and entrepreneurship interface paradigm suggests that entrepreneurs should possess marketing capabilities (Hills and La Forge, 1992; Carson and Grant, 1993).

As discussed earlier in the literature review presented in this chapter, the lack of marketing capabilities in most SMEs on export suggests that export intermediaries do play an important role in the marketing of many manufacturers' goods in the export markets (Munroand Beamish, 1987; Rosson and Ford, 1982). Therefore, this study proposes that exchanging marketing capability as part of the relationship between SMEs and export intermediaries would guide SMEs to recognize international opportunities. Therefore, it leads to the following hypothesis;

- H1.1: Marketing capabilities exchanges between export intermediaries and SMEs is positively correlated to international opportunity recognition for SMEs.

2.8.1.1 Experience Knowledge Assetsand IOR

Knowledge and experience are part of a firm's intangible resources as they enhance the familiarity of SMEs with the export markets that broadens marketing capabilities (Theingi, 2008). Knowledge and experience of a firm are widely recognized in the literature as common and important factors in the opportunity identification process (Ardichivili *et al.,* 2003; Shane, 2000; Park, 2005).Without experience and knowledge, making decisions would be not easy for entrepreneurs, firms will fail in the market (Baron, 1998), and international opportunity discovery does not occur simply through chance.

Prior experience will lead entrepreneurs to gather and analyze certain types of information quickly and recognize opportunities (Zahra *et al.,* 2005) and at times, could even restrict the evaluation of opportunities (Muzychenko, 2008). Therefore, prior experience, particularly about the markets plays a prominent role in successful opportunity recognition (Ardichivili *et al.,* 2003; Shane, 2000; Zahra *et al.,* 2005).

Chandra *et al.,* (2009) say that prior knowledge is also as one of the main drivers of the opportunity recognition process that has been identified in the literature. Individuals typically discover opportunities based on their prior knowledge and thisis profitable based on how they perceive the external stimuli (Gregorio *et al.* 2008). Previous knowledge mixed with novel information deduced from different sources such as social and business networks has the ability of revealing the opportunities worthy to pursuit(Chandra *et al.,* 2009).

In order to recognize opportunities, prior knowledge could be helpful because they have relevant information that can help them identify the opportunities unlike those who do not have (Shane and Venkataraman, 2000; Chandra *et al.,* 2009; Venkataraman, 1997). In a research project of technological innovations at Massachusetts Institute of Technology (Shane, 2000) It was pointed out that differences in prior knowledge such as ways to serve markets, customer problem, markets and etc have an effect on the basis for those who could discover entrepreneurial opportunities. Also apart from that, various entrepreneurs see various opportunities for themselves.

This fact shows that prior knowledge has a particular and important role for customers and markets in the identification of opportunities. Based on the research of Ardichvili *et al.* (2003), prior knowledge of markets and customers has the ability to direct his/her possession successful opportunity recognition and eventually, successful ventures.

He also imply the tem of ''knowledge corridor'' as a symbol that makes the one whom has prior knowledge walks through and allows him/her to recognize certain opportunities (Venkataraman,1997; Ardichvili et al., 2003, p. 114).The way entrepreneurs interpret, comprehend, extrapolate is influenced by prior knowledge (Roberts, 1991).

Also it leads to the facts that entrepreneurs can be appreciable from receiving new information. Furthermore ability to make new connections among pre-existing ideas and an individual's willingness are affected by this knowledge that eventually allowing them to recognize opportunities (Chandra *et al.*, 2009).

As it mentioned by Timmons (1999) proposed that successful entrepreneurs have the knowledge and capacity to see what others do not. Based on the studies of Shane (2000), discovering opportunities by an entrepreneur can only possible through his/her prior knowledge. It s proposed by Kirzner (1973) that entrepreneurs possess or obtain specialized knowledge and could use these to create or exploit opportunities.

In pursuit of business opportunities, one only can identify an opportunity when they possess prior knowledge. In addition, they must have cognitive abilities that will enable them to value and use such knowledge (Shane and Venkataraman, 2000).

Several published papers indicate that prior knowledge of a industry, market or customer needs can be a major advantage for entrepreneurs. Possessions of this knowledge have the ability of recognizing potentially profitable opportunities thus these it is crucial this information studied further in order to assist SMEs identify opportunities.

Recognition of a first time international opportunity by means of discovery rather than through deliberate search is more likely happens in firms with no prior international experience and knowledge (Chandra and Styles, 2009).

SMEs in comparison to large firms are typically regarded as resource-constrained in terms of knowledge and experience. Without significant knowledge and experience, attempts to export would be doomed to failure. Therefore, lack of knowledge and experience in most of SMEs is the gap proposed in this study because knowledge and experience exchange between SMEs and export intermediaries could lead SMEs to recognize international opportunities. Therefore, this study proposes that: H1.2: Experience and assets exchange between export intermediaries and SMEs is positively correlated to international opportunity recognition in SMEs

2.8.1.2 Relation Assets and IOR

The relationship with customers has found to facilitate SMEs participation in IOR (Rutashobyaand Jaensson, 2004). Besides that, the significant role of the relationship between supplier and customers on internationalization has been examined in numerous previous studies (Bradley *et al.,* 2006; Leavy, 1990; Fawcett and Birou, 1992; Holland *et al.,* 1992; Monczka and Carter, 1988; Kalwani and Narayandas, 1995; Paliwoda and Bonaccorsi, 1994; Schonberger, 1986; O'Neal and Bertrand, 1991; Johanson and Mattsson, 1988; Chetty and Holm, 2000; Majkgard and Sharma, 1998).

With reference to the relevant literature, interaction between the buyer and the product is deemed to change due to the importance of the relationship between buyers and sellers. Internationalization becomes the setting for multi-polar networks that involve special relationships between buyers and sellers (Etemad and Paul, 2008). There is literature in this field of study which views customer relationships in terms of trust and commitment as part of the important firm resources needed for IOR (Luo et al., 2004).

Despite the importance of the role of the relationship between buyer and seller, SMEs lack this type of relationship. This is because most SMEs are new and small and do not want to undergo the various stages of development in order to achieve internationalization. Hence, they may be referred to indirect relationship as the third parties with customers. An intermediary, for example, through their relation with customers and manufacturers bring customers and manufacturer together and is instrumental in a new market entry and international opportunity recognition. Therefore, this study proposes that networking between export intermediaries and SMEs will help SMEs compensate for their lack of relation assets and to recognize international opportunities. (H1.3)

H1.3: Relation assets exchange between export intermediaries and SMEs is positively correlated to international opportunity recognition in SMEs.

2.8.2 IOR and export performance

Previous studies have reviewed the fact that cooperation and networking increase a firm's success by having a better and positive export performance (Hillebrand and Biemans, 2003; Ambler *et al.,* 1999). On the other hand, using of intermediaries has been argued to lead to higher international performance in the entrepreneurial context (Rabino, 1980; Shepherd and Zacharakis, 1997). SMEs through an intermediary can improve their export performance, profitability, productivity and firm satisfaction (Terjesen *et al.,* 2008; Rabino, 1980; Zacharakis, 1997; Wilkinson and Brouthers, 2006). Wilkinson and Brouthers (2006) stated that using the services of export intermediaries is positively associated with firm satisfaction with export performance (Wilkinson and Brouthers, 2006). However, these previous studies did not analyze this relationship in relation to a network theory.

A number of scholars have theorized about the beneficial effects of networking activities (Birley, 1985; Larson, 1992), or about the effect of export intermediary on export performance (Terjesen *et al.,* 2008; Rabino, 1980;

Zacharakis, 1997; Wilkinson and Brouthers, 2006). However, less attention has been given to the understanding of the relationship between effective networks and a firm's performance (Aldrich*et al.,* 1986; Blundel, 2002; Cell and Baines, 2000). Another issue that needs further investigation is supporting link between export intermediary networking and export satisfaction based on the network theory for acquiring resources, which include marketing, experience and knowledge, and relation assets (H2). Therefore, this study proposes that networking between SMEs and export intermediaries will affect the level of export satisfaction in SMEs.

Therefore, export intermediary networking by SMEs has a relationship with export satisfaction in SMEs (RQ2).

2.8.2.1 Marketing Capability and Export Satisfaction

Previous empirical studies found that marketing capability were found to be directly responsible for export profitability (Wang*et al.,* 2002; Pope and Ralph, 2002) and successful export business operation (Constantine *et al.*, 1996).The literature on export suggested that exporting firms for internationalization should develop their own marketing capabilities (Haar and Ortiz-Buonafina, 1995). Moreover, marketing knowledge, promotional efforts and assessment of export market developments are found to have a positive relationship with export performance (Leonidou and Katsikeas, 1996).

With reference to the lack of marketing capabilities in most SMEs, this study proposes that SMEs are able to achieve marketing capability based on their relationship with export intermediaries that would lead SMEs to achieve export satisfaction (H2.1).

- H2.1: Marketing capabilities exchange between export intermediaries and SMEs is positively correlated to export satisfaction in SMEs.

2.8.2.2 Experience Knowledge Assets and Export Satisfaction

Madsen (1987) concluded based on 17 empirical studies that there was support for positive impacts of export experienced by firms in terms of export performance, particularly, export sales. Similarly, firms that are internationally active for a longer time displayed higher export intensity (Baldauf *et al.*, 2000). Atuahene-Gima (1995) and Kirpalani and Macintosh (1980) also found that international market experience has a strong impact on export performance. These various experience knowledge assets do have an impact on the export performance. Therefore, this study proposes that knowledge and experience exchange between SMEs and export intermediaries would lead SMEs to achieve export satisfaction (H2.2).

H2.2: Experience assets exchange between export intermediaries and SMEs is positively correlated to export satisfaction in SMEs.

2.8.2.3 Relation Assets and Export Satisfaction

The effect of external buyer–seller relationships in influencing export performance has been examined by many researchers (Ambler *et al.*, 1999; Anderson and Narus, 1987; Heide and John, 1988; Rosson and Ford, 1980). A strong association between skills in building and maintaining customer relationships and achievement of export competitive advantages was discovered by Piercy *et al.* (1998). Furthermore, between customer relationship skills and high export performance there is a significant correlation

Based on the research of Hsieh (1994), there is a long term relationships with foreign buyers and suppliers is a critical component of doing business among Chinese businesspersons in Taiwan. This study proposes that relation assets between export intermediaries and SMEs will help SMEs compensate its lack of relation assets and export satisfaction (H2.3).

H2.3: Relation assets exchange between export intermediaries and SMEs is positively correlated to export satisfaction in SMEs.

2.8.2.4 IOR and Export Satisfaction

Internationalization for small and medium firms is considered as a major dimension of growth (Peng and Delios, 2006) and if these firms are engaged in international markets, they will face further improvement in performance (Baldwin and Gu, 2003).

The relationship between a firm's internationalization and performance has been subject to extensive research in strategic management and international business fields over last thirty years. It is argued that there is strong evidence showing a statistically significant correlation between firm internationalization and performance (Bausch and Krist, 2007). Participating in international markets, especially in its simplest form by exporting products abroad is considered as a competitive weapon of SMEs. This mode tends to be more effective in utilizing product development and manufacturing process improvement to achieve organizational excellence. There is surge in the theoretical development in international entrepreneurship in academic world (Steenkamp, 2001).

As discussed in the previous section, (international opportunities recognition) IOR is the first and most important step in internationalization. According to Chandler and Jansen (1992), opportunity recognition skills are optimistically interrelated to venture performance. Profitability and growth of the ventures are highly related to recognition of international opportunities. A relationship between opportunity recognition skills and firm's growth has been found by Baum et al. (2001). The relation between IOR and export performance in the literature is well established and SMEs can recognize more international opportunities that could lead to increase their performance. According to the literature presented earlier in this chapter, SMEs are able to recognize opportunities in international markets based on several factors such as: individuals' characteristics, firms' characteristics and networking. Ability to possess opportunities recognitions highly correlated with profitability and a firm's growth (Sambasivan *et al.,* 2009).

However, there is no study about the relationship between international opportunity recognition by intermediaries and export activity. Therefore, this study proposes that international opportunities recognized by export intermediaries networking have a positive relationship with export satisfaction in SMEs (H3). **H3:** International opportunity recognition in SMEs is positively correlated to SME's export satisfaction (RQ3).

2.8.3 The Mediating role of IOR

International opportunity recognition is the first and most important step in internationalization and networking work although many other factors do impact venture performance such as opportunity recognition skills. There is empirical research to support the link between effective networks and firm export performance in entrepreneurship research (e.g. Aldrich*et al.,* 1987; Blundel, 2002; Cell and Baines, 2000; Hillebrand and Biemans, 2003; Hunt *et al.,*1985; Ambler *et al.,* 1999). In addition, there are studies that have shown there is a link between opportunity recognition and performance (Baum *et al.,* 2001).

Opportunity recognition in entrepreneurship research with influence of mediating has been considered in only very few studies. Some of this few researches include, the study of Sambasivan *et al.,* (2009) which shows that the mediating affect of opportunity recognition skills as the mediator between the qualities skills and venture performance. Also in another study Kickul and Walters (2002) pointed to the role of opportunity recognition skills as a mediator between strategic orientation of the entrepreneurial firm and e-commerce innovations in Internet companies. Butler *et al.* (2003) have examined that opportunity recognition has mediated the relationship between social and business network, and performance.

More specifically, previous studies have shown that there is a strong link between networking and export performance and this is in relation to their important role in the international opportunity recognition, this study predicts that greater export intermediaries networking by SMEs would lead to more recognized international opportunities leading to a higher export satisfaction among the SMEs. Therefore, this base relationship between export intermediary networking and export satisfaction should be affected by the degree of international opportunity recognition.

However, since the international opportunity recognition is a process oriented variable (first step in internationalization process) and is not an outcome oriented variable, thus, it is considered as the mediating factor. In other words, international opportunity recognition would mediate the relationship between export intermediaries networking and export satisfaction.

Another potential mediator of international opportunity recognition is between the marketing capability and export satisfaction relationship. Marketing capabilities is one of the important resources which would lead SMEs to internationalization and this is the missing factor among the SMEs. Therefore, this study predicts that SMEs are able to acquire marketing capabilities by networking with export intermediaries, as this would lead to the recognition of international opportunities and export satisfaction. In addition, following this relationship, this thesis would review IOR as having a mediating role from another dimension of export intermediary networking (marketing capability, experience capability, and relation assets) and export satisfaction. This understanding leads to hypothesis 4. H4: There is a mediating effect of international opportunity recognition on the relationship between export intermediary networking and export satisfaction (RQ4).

This research proposes that SMEs, which have relationships with export intermediaries, are able to access marketing capabilities, knowledge and experience, and relation assets. This relationship could help identify international opportunities and increase the export performance of SMEs. The Network Theory will be used to examine the relationships discussed in this section. The research proposes a model to study the various relationships that would increase the possibilities of SMEs being part of the internationalization community based on the following:

- H4.1: There is a mediating effect of international opportunity recognition on the relationship between marketing capabilities and export satisfaction.

- H4.2: There is a mediating effect of international opportunity recognition on the relationship between experience assets and export satisfaction.

- H4.3: There is a mediating effect of international opportunity recognition on the relationship between relation assets and export satisfaction.

Thus this research propose that SMEs with the relationship with export intermediary are able to access marketing capabilities, knowledge and experience, and relation assets which this relation affect on identify international opportunities and export performance of SMEs. Network Theory was used to examine this relationship. Based on these discussions, the following Figure 2.5was developed as the research proposed model could for this study.

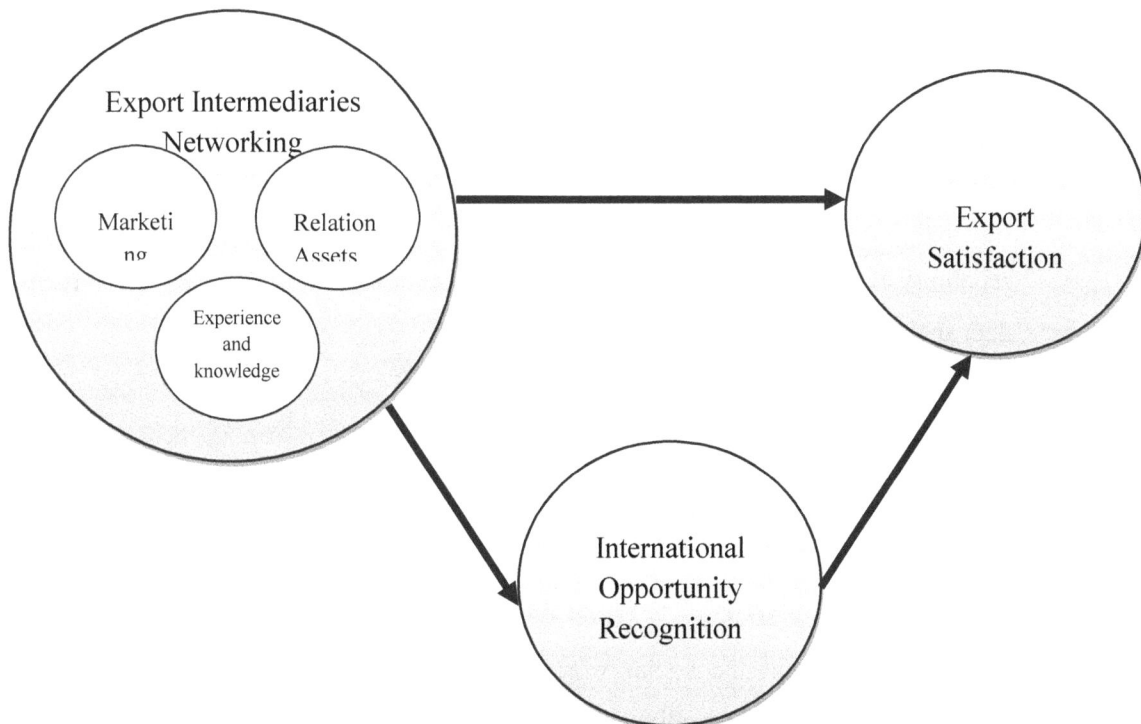

Figure 2.5   Conceptual framework and development of thesis

CHAPTER 3

RESEARCH METHODOLOGY

3.1 Introduction

Chapter three presents an argument about methodology used for this study. Even though there are increasing numbers of international entrepreneurship research, there are relatively fewer studies compared to the research conducted in the international opportunity recognition especially in Malaysia. Since SMEs suffer from the individuals and firm's resources limitation for IOR and focusing of prior studies on individuals and firm resources, this study expects to raise some methodological issues, which are base on the networking with external factors such as export intermediaries. The main aim of this present chapter is to show the research methodology. The chapter presents the research paradigm, design and research type. In addition, research instrument, unit of analysis, validity and reliability of research tool, sampling design is also described in this chapter. Finally, data analysis is also explained in this chapter.

3.2 Research Paradigm

A research strategy is based on hypotheses that describe the researcher's point of view about the social world. Quantitative and the qualitative are two different standpoints of paradigms. Quantitative researches focus on the analysis and measurement of fundamental relationships between variables. On the other hand, qualitative researches look for answers to questions that clarify how social experience is given meaning and created (Denzin *et al.*, 1994). This present study principally focuses on quantitative techniques concerning to the nature of the research that examines the relationship between variables and wants to generalize the findings based on an acceptable sample size of firms.

Quantitative techniques comprise of two main types: experiment and survey (Creswell, 1994). Survey method is described as a technique of collecting data based on conveying information with a representative sample of individuals. On the other hand experiment technique is a research method that has a controllable condition therefore it is possible that several variables can be adjusted in order to test a hypothesis (Zikmund, 2003). In this research, survey method has been applied.

Among different types of survey techniques, a structured survey was chose as it reduced a researcher's bias during data collection and analysis (Sayre, 2001; Skinner *et al.*, 2000). It provides an efficient, relatively inexpensive and accurate means to examine data about the respondents (Zikmund, 2003).

3.3   Research design

A cross-sectional analysis of Malaysian SMEs was conducted and provided a snapshot of the variables of interest at a single point in a moment. Although many researchers recommended the use of longitudinal studies, they are rarely carried out because it is difficult and expensive to administer due to the need to find the same respondents (Boyce, 2002). Maintaining the same respondents is extremely difficult because some respondents might decide not to continue and some companies might have closed down or have changed their addresses.

Cross- sectional surveys is a significant subject since it represents the most common type of empirical research in many fields such as sales force management, marketing strategy and marketing channels and thus provides a vital basis for much of the knowledge on these topics (Jap and Anderson, 2004, Theingi, 2008). Rindfleisch*et al.*, (2008) indicated that 178 survey based Journal of Marketing

Research articles, 94% are cross-sectional in nature (Rindfleisch et al, 2008). Cross-sectional approach is less costly means of reducing common method variance bias and boosting fundamental deduction under certain situation (Rindfleisch *et al.,* 2008).

Therefore, a design of cross-sectional used due to the limited time and budget. Many studies in export literature used a similar approach (see Katsikeas *et al.,* 1997; Baldauf*et al.,* 2000; Prasad*et al.,* 2001;Theingi, 2008). However, the adoption of a cross-sectional design limits the potential to detect cause-effect inferences (Katsikeas *et al.,* 1997).

3.4   Research Type

Stempel (1981) categorize research in three different types; pure, applied, and developmental. Basic research is applied primarily to test the theory. Its main aim is to found general principle without known practical appliance of the findings. On the other hand, applied research is regarding to the application of theory to the problems or solution. Applied research is conducted for the reason of applying, testing theory, and estimating its value.

This study is an applied research. In other words, it helps SME's managers to select their networking to compensate resources scarcities and recognize more international opportunities.

3.5   Research Instrument

Questionnaire is developed as the data-gathering tool because of the operational model of research aforementioned. The questions are adapted from prior studies.

3.5.1 **Questionnaire Design**

Based on the previous studies, the questionnaire was developed. The survey questionnaire includes two cover letters, a copy of official university letter to FMM, and a copy of questionnaire. Questionnaire layout was designed to enable the respondents to participate and fill the questionnaire simply. Respondents were offered an outline of the research results as a motivation to complete the questionnaire. The close-ended questions are designed and prepared to facilitate, and speed up the survey processes (Alerck and Settle, 1985).

3.5.1.1 **Measurement format and scales**

The marketing literature has placed significant consideration on survey measurement over the past 25 years (Churchill, 1979; Diamantpoulous and Winklhofer, 2001; Gerbing and Anderson, 1988). This concentration has focused primarily on procedures for refining and constructing scale items instead of how these items should be scaled. Likert format and a five- to seven-point scale have known as the most appropriate means of assessment by authors, editors, and reviewers (Rindfleisch *et al.*, 2008). This format has employed, two-thirds (62 of 93) of the measures listed in the Hand-book of Marketing Scales (Bearden and Netemeyer, 1998; Rindfleisch *et al.*, 2008). Granovetter (1973) has claimed that in the social science, the strength of network ties is categorized as either strong or weak but this study is not measuring the weakness or strength of network. This present study is trying to show the resource exchanges between firms and SMEs through their networking. Therefore, the questionnaire used a scale of Likert that is very popular and simple to administer (Zikmund, 1999). Most interval level scales have either 3 or 5 or 7 or 9 anchor points. Many researchers use items with 5 or 7-point rating scales (Maxim, 1999). The respondents were asked to indicate their attitudes by rating how far they disagree or agree with the mentioned statement. This study used a 5-point Likert scale similar to previous research conducted in the export studies (see Baldauf *et al.*, 2000; Nakos *et al.*, 1998; Prasad *et al.*, 2001; Sangsuwan,

1992). All questions in the questionnaire were statement structure and respondents were requested to specify the level of their agreement with every statement by clicking response in web-based questionnaire or by circling a response in the paper questionnaire. The overview of the questionnaire development is discussed in the section of 3.5.1.2 and 3.5.1.3

3.5.1.2 Language of questionnaires

Two versions of questionnaires (Malay version and English version) were developed as some Malay export managers preferred to answer the questionnaire in Malay. Four steps were followed in the development of the Malay questionnaires. Firstly, the questionnaire was first written in English and then translated into Malay by a translator who was lecturer in business and management. Secondly, a consultant working in the export and marketing field translated the Malay questionnaire back into English. Thirdly, to ensure its validity, the modified questionnaire was again read concurrently in Malay and English by a Malay lecturer in business studies. Finally, two lecturers teaching Malay language and literature proof read the questionnaire. Similar back translation and follow-up discussion techniques have been used previously (see Herkenhoff, 2000; Li, 1998; Theingi, 2008).

3.5.1.3 Questionnaire division

The questionnaire consisted of six parts and included 48 questions. The 6 parts of the questionnaire are as follows: Part 1) Research's criteria; Part 2) Respondent's background; Part 3) Firm's background Part 4) Export intermediaries networking (including; 4.1 Marketing capabilities, 4.2 Experience assets, and 4.3 Relation assets), part 5) International opportunity recognition, and part 6) Export satisfaction.

- **Part1. Research Criteria**

The purpose of this section is to understand which firm had research criteria to answer the questionnaire. This part was added after pretesting. Firm should have following research criteria to participate in the filling of questionnaire.

1. The respondents must be manufacturing exporters

2. They must employ 150 or less than 150 employees (the definition of SMEs that was used for the present study was based on the SMIDEC definition in Malaysia)

3. They must be independent business firms

4. They must use export intermediary for their exporting

When all answers were "Yes" and firms met the above criteria, they (owner-manager, general- manager, sales and marketing manager, export manager, and production or product manager) were asked to fill the rest of questionnaire. Respondents were offered results of the research as an incentive to complete the questionnaire.

- **Parts 2 and 3 (General Information)**

The questionnaire begins with general and simple questions as the first questions are crucial and respondents should not find them threatening in any way (Churchill, 1995). General information was divided into two parts (part 2 and 3).

Questions in Part 2 started with general information on the respondent's background including gender, ethnic, age, education, total working experience in this firm (Q5 to Q9, see Table 3.1). Question 6 regarding to the ethnic group was based on the most current population in Malaysia (Malay, Chinese and India). The purpose of this question is indicating the using of networking in which ethnic group is most popular because the result of study of Ling-yee and Ogunmkun (2001) stated China compared with US has the higher level of relational orientation. Chinese people are more likely to used different types of networking such as Guanxi network between

Chinese (Tsang, 1998), Chinese immigrant in Tailand (Butler and Chamornmarn, 1995), and other countries.

Part 3 is about firm's background including: age of firm, number of employees, engaging in export, percentage of firm's total export sales and sales agreements which comes from export intermediary, their product category, countries to export, type of export intermediary used, type of exporting product, number of countries exported to (Q10 to Q19, see Table 3.1).

Question 11 regarding the number of employees was based on the definition of SMEs in SMIDEC, which divided small firms into 1 to 50 employees, and medium sized firms into 50 to 150 employees. Question 15 regarding the products category was based on the FMM division for product category, which divided products to 24 categories. Question 13 and 14 were added after pretesting. Because the definition of international opportunity recognition is recognized opportunities in foreign markets, which have led to the development of exchange agreements or new ventures (Ellis, 20011) therefore, some IE expert and professional suggested that the percentage of firm's total export sales and sales agreement should recognize in this study. Therefore, question 13 and 14 were added according to their suggestion.

The items in the part 2 and 3 of questionnaires and their measurement scales could be found in Table 3.1. These two parts was adapted from previous export studies such as (Theingi, 2008; Hessels and Terjesen, 2008; Ellis, 2011).

Table 3.1 : Questions of General Information in the questionnaire (part 2 and 3)

PART 2: RESPONDENT'S BACKGROUND		
No	**Constructs**	**Measurement scale**
Q5	Gender	Male, Female
Q6	Ethnic group	Chinese, Malay, Indian, others
Q7	Age	1= 21–30; 2=31–40; 3=41–50;4=51–60; 6= More than 60
Q8	Educational Status	1=Primary school; 2=Secondary school; 3=Diploma; 4=Bachelor; 5=Master; 6=Higher than master
Q9	Experience in exporting	1=1–5 years; 2=6–10 years; 3=11–15 years; 4= 16–20 years; 5=Over 20 years

PART 3: FIRM'S BACKGROUND		
Q10	Age of firm	1 =1 –5; 2 =6 –10; 3 =11–15; 4 =16 –20;5 =More than 20
Q11	Number of employees	1=1–4; 2=5–50; 3 =51–100; 4 = 101–150
Q12	Experience of exporting	1=1–5; 2=6–10; 3=11–15;4=16 – 20; 5=More than 20
Q13	Firm's total export sales from export intermediary	1=1% –20%; 2=21% –40%; 3=41% –60%; 4 = 61% –80%; 5=More than 80%
Q14	Firm's foreign sales agreements from export intermediary	1=1% –20%; 2=21% –40%; 3=41% –60%; 4 = 61% –80%; 5=More than 80%
Q15	Type of product category	Divided to 24 product category (according to FMM directory category)
Q16	Countries most exported	1=North America; 2=South America; 3=Central America; 4=Eastern Europe; 5=Western Europe; 6=Southern Europe; 7=Northern Europe; 8=Oceania; 9=Eastern Asia; 10=Southeast Asia; 11=Africa; 12=Mid East
Q17	Type of most export intermediary used	1= Foreign intermediary based in Malaysia; 2= Malaysian private intermediary (based in Malaysia); 3= Foreign intermediary based in foreign market; 4= Government agency
Q18	Type of product category	1=Business goods; 2=Consumer goods
Q19	Number of countries exported to	1 =1–5; 2=6–10; 3=11–15 ; 4=16–20; 5=More than 20

- **Part 4 (Export intermediary networking)**

Despite the fact that Network-Based View is accepted to a larger scale in international entrepreneurship literature and as important factor to recognize international opportunities, there is lack of networking studies in international opportunity recognition. Most of network studies have focused on acquiring information to recognize international opportunities. Since SMEs lack other resources to identify international opportunities, Part 4 of the questionnaire were designed to investigate whether resources exchange through export intermediaries networking influenced the international opportunity recognition in SMEs.

Previous research about the relationship between SMEs and export intermediary, have mentioned about; 1) marketing capabilities, 2) experience assets, and 3) relationship assets that could be exchanged among SMEs and export intermediaries. Therefore, this study also followed the prior studies and divided part 4 into 3 main dimensions including; 4.1) Marketing capabilities, 4.2) Experience assets, and 4.3) Relation assets.

- **Part 4.1 (Marketing Capabilities)**

The measurement that used for marketing capability is an adaptation that was developed originally by Atuahene-Gima (1993).He developed10 items and accounteda 0.78.forAlpha.Several studies also used this measurement (e.g. Weerawardena, 2003; Weerawardena *et. al.,* 2004).Therefore, this study used Atuahene-Gima scale for measuring marketing capabilities. These items are as below:

- The quality of the firm's customer service
- Advertising effectiveness
- Quality of sales force
- Strength of distribution networks
- Advertising expenditure as percentage of sales
- Market research ability
- Speed of new product introduction
- Ability to differentiate products
- Number of market segments served
- Diversity of product line

The managers were requested to rate their agreement degree by 5-point Likert rating scale (1= Highly disagree, 2=Disagree, 3= Natural, 4= Agree, 5= Highly agree). Items 8 and 10 were eliminated after pretesting.

- **Part 4.2 (Experience assets)**

The measurement that used for experience assets is an adaptation that was developed by Theingi (2008).These items are as below:

- Knowledgeable about the requirements of potential customers

- Overall good experience with respect to the market
- Adequate experience to sell the products
- Supply of market information

The managers were requested to rate their agreement degree by 5-point Likert rating scale (1= Highly disagree, 2= Disagree, 3= Natural, 4= Agree, 5= Highly agree).

- **Part 4.3 (Relation Assets)**

The measurement that used for relation assets in this study is an adaptation of Piercy*et al.,* (1997). On the investigating of the relationship between buyer and seller in the export performance, he developed 7 items for measuring the relation assets. Some other researcher such as Theingi (2008) also used this measurement. Therefore, this study also followed the Piercy measurement for relation assets factor. These items are as below:

- Fairness and trustworthiness
- Ability to keep promises
- Helpful in emergencies
- Positive attitude toward complaints
- Continuous long-term supply
- Regular communications
- Company reputation

The managers were requested to rate their agreement degree by 5-point Likert rating scale (1= Highly disagree, 2= Disagree, 3= Natural, 4= Agree, 5= Highly agree).

- **Part 5 (International opportunity recognition)**

According to Johanson and Mattsson (1988), active networking means that the initiative taken by the sellers. In reactive networking, by contrast, the initiation comes from the buyer. This thesis is focused on the initiation of sellers, which manufacturers should have innovation to sell their products. Therefore, the questions should ask from the manufacturers that find international opportunities through their networking with export intermediaries.

According to the entrepreneurship literature, there are several techniques for opportunity recognition. Some of these methods include, counting the number of perceived opportunities in the immediate past (Singh, 2000), guessing the possibility of opportunities recognition in the immediate future (Arenius and DeClercq, 2005), and estimating the level of awareness to new opportunities in common (Ozgen and Baron, 2007; Hills and Schrader, 1998). Based on the Ellis (2011) research, an opportunity is as executable as another is however, several potentially lucrative opportunities cannot be recognized because they suffer from measurement ambiguity.

Another approach to recognize the opportunities is to validate only opportunities that caused formation of exchange agreements or new ventures (Shane, 2000; Ellis and Pecotich, 2001; Collarelli-O'Connor and Rice, 2001; Sharma and Blomstermo, 2003; Mort and Weerawardena, 2006). This explanation match the belief that when creative entrepreneurs offer solutions that match unfulfilled market needs, those needs become opportunities (Collarelli-O'Connor and Rice, 2001).

This method was regarded to be more suitable based on this study's aims because reducing the chance of misinterpreting of definition of opportunities by entrepreneurs in different location (Ellis, 2011).

Therefore international opportunity recognition measurement in this research is an adaption of Ellis (2011) that is recognized opportunities in foreign markets, which have led to the development of exchange agreements or new ventures via export intermediary including following dimension:

- Recognized opportunities in the more different countries
- Recognized opportunities in more different cultures
- Recognized opportunities in more different languages
- Greater foreign sales volumes

- Greater foreign market share
- Greater sales agreements volumes

The managers were requested to rate their agreement degree by 5-point Likert rating scale (1= Highly disagree, 2= Disagree, 3= Natural, 4= Agree, 5= Highly agree).

- **Part 6 (Export satisfaction)**

In most of studies performances measurement are perceptual evaluations or subjective which made by the manager responsible for export activities. That is why subject to many sources of bias. Many scholars are supported applying subjective instead of objective for example Robertson and Chetty (2000), Katsikeas *et al.,* (1996).

Although in the strategic management, there are several evidences in literature that points out to the general reliability of subject, self-reported performance data (Venkatraman and Ramanujam, 1986; Dess and Robinson, 1984; Woodcock *et al.,* 1994).

Hence, in order to avoid the distinctive secretiveness of respondents who are required to give financial information, perceptual measures used instead of financial measures. According to some previous research, perceptual measures are highly correlated with 'objective' financial data (Geringer and Hebert, 1991; Dess and Robinson, 1984). In addition, this method has been applied in several studies (e.g. Nitisch *et al.,* 1996; Woodcock *et al.,* 1994; Luo *et al.,* 2001; Brouthers and Xu, 2002).

Therefore, export performance measurement in this research is subjective and an adaption of Wilkinson and Brouthers (2006) that is export satisfaction with four measures including of following dimension:

- Sales growth in foreign markets
- Export market share
- Number of countries exporting to

• Overall export performance

The managers were requested to rate their satisfaction of those top items through export intermediaries by 5-point Likert rating scale (1= Highly disagree, 2= Disagree, 3= Natural, 4= Agree, 5= Highly agree).

All the constructs and dimensions in part 4, 5, and 6 of the questionnaires and their associated reference could be found in Table 3.2.

Table 3.2 : Summary of dimension's variables

Construct	Dimension	Items	Adapted from	Similar measures in previous studies
Export intermediary networking	Part 4.1 Marketing Capabilities Q20-Q27	The quality of the firm's customer service Advertising effectiveness Quality of sales force Strength of distribution networks Market research ability Speed of new product introduction Ability to differentiate products Number of market segments served	(Atuahene - Gima,1993)	(e.g. Weerawardena, 2003; Weerawardena et. al., 2004)
	Part 4.2 Experience Assets Q28-Q31	Knowledgeable about the requirements of potential customers Overall good experience with respect to the market Adequate experience to sell the products Supply of market information	(Theingi, 2008)	(e.g. Aaker, 1989; Hitt and Ire land, 1985; Katsikeas and Morgan 1994)
	Part 4.3 Relation Assets Q32-Q37	Fairness and trustworthiness Ability to keep promises Helpful in emergencies Positive attitude toward complaints Continuous long-term supply Regular communications Company reputation	(Piercy et. al, 1997)	(Katsikeas and Piercy, 1993; Theingi, 2008;Luo et al., 2004; Shipley,1989;Purchase and Phungphol, 2007)

International opportunity recognition	Part 5 Q38-Q43	Opportunities in the more different countries Opportunities in more different cultures Opportunities in more different languages markets Achieve greater foreign sales volumes Achieve greater foreign market share Achieve greater sales agreements volumes with foreign customers	(Ellis, 2011)	(Ellis and Pecotich 2001; Weerawardena and Mort 2006; Collarelli-O'Connor and Rice, 2001; Shane, 2000; Sharma and Blomstermo, 2003)
Export satisfaction	Part 6 Q44-Q47	Sales growth in foreign markets Export market share Number of countries exporting to Overall export performance	(Wilkinson and Brouthers, 2006)	(Francis and Collins-Dodd, 2004; Robertson and Chetty, 2000; Wilkinson and Brouthers, 2006)

3.6   Unit of Analysis

Many studies on exporting have been conducted at the overall firm level (see Bijmolt and Zwart, 1994; Chan, 1992; Katsikeas and Morgan, 1994; Leonidou et. al., 2002). This research studied individual export ventures rather than the firm as a unit of analysis similar to researchesconducted by Cavusgil and Zou (1994), Myers and Harvey (2001), Piercy et al.,(1998), and Theing (2008).

The rationale is that export channel relationship, competitive positioning, and performance vary across new export ventures within the same firm. It would be erroneous and difficult to examine a common pattern of channel relationship, competitive positioning and performance among all new export ventures managed by the same firm (Li and Ogunmokun, 2001) and individual product-market export venture allows a more precise measurement of the factors that influence export performance (Cavusgil and Zou, 1994). A firm level of analysis provides a useful macro view of the relationships between determinants and export performance but it also potentially involves an averaging effect over the different product-market settings of individual firms (Prasad et al., 2001). Hence, it is argued that venture-level analysis rather than firm-level analysis would provide more reliable data (Matthyssens & Pauwels, 1996; Cavusgil & Zou, 1994; Li and Ogunmokun, 2001).

In this study, the questionnaire was designed for the manufacturer SMEs that had less than 150 employees and have been exported at least one of their products through export intermediaries. Therefore, the questionnaire instructed respondents to focus on the company's products that were exported through export intermediary and to use that export venture as the source of reference when answering the questions.

This study is on the perception of managers in independent manufacturing exporters SMEs. Because this study is measuring resource available in export intermediary which, leads to recognize international opportunities in SMEs. Therefore, SMEs are more knowledgably about their opportunities, which have found through their export intermediaries. The basic tool for the study is a questionnaire emailed to managers in sample members followed by a telephone call to get the completed questionnaire.

3.7   Validity of research tool

Validity of a test is defined as the issue of what the test measures and how well it does so. It also indicates what outcome can be drawn from the results. Validity must be identified with reference to the specific use for which the test is being measured. Any data rejecting or supporting the created hypothesis represent suitable evidence for validation.

For the validity of the survey instrument of the research that is adapted from the previous studies, examined by the scholars and project professionals for thevalidation.

3.7.1   Distribution among experts

To do such a test a copy of questionnaire distributed among individuals who were experts of the field. Also the questionnaire was sent to some of IE experts through the email and they gave back some comment and suggestion. IE expert are authors and professors who have article about International Opportunities and this study used their article as studies' references. In addition, the purpose, method and conceptual model of research attached to questionnaire. They asked for the consistency and validity of research as a whole and data gathering tool. They mentioned the problems related to questions and the structure of research. Problems mentioned by experts were edited. This is the base for the validity check of the tool.

3.7.2 Pretesting

Pretesting was conducted to identify ambiguity or bias in the questions (Zikmund, 1997) and to ensure that respondents understood the questionnaire, and are familiar with terms used in the questionnaires (Mortanges and Vossen, 1999). Pretesting for long and complex questionnaires strongly is recommended (Kumar *et al.*, 1999).

Kumar et al., (1999), considered due to time and budget limitation, a pretest sample size of 25 as a reasonable size. Therefore, 30 exporting firms were chosen for the pretesting. The respondents were asked to complete structured questionnaires followed by design, wording and length of questionnaire (Kumar *et al.*, 1999). The research criteria for choosing the respondents were the same as those in the sample size (see Section 3.5.1.3, Part 1, Research criteria).

Pretesting firms were chosen from firms that were participated in the "Information and Communication Technology (ICT) and "Business Opportunity and Networking" seminars which were organized by Federation Malaysian Manufacture (FMM) at Jun and July, 2010. Attendance to the seminar was arranged by email before participation. Short interview about the questionnaire also has done since the questionnaires were filling by managers.

3.8   Reliability of research tool

For the measuring of internal consistency and reliability, Cronbach's alpha was used   (Hair *et al.*, 1998). According to Sekaran (2003), Cronbach's Alpha shows that how well the items in a set are positively correlated to one another. Cronbach's alpha is computed in terms of the average inter correlations among items measuring the concept.

The closer Cronbach's alpha is to 1, which demonstrating the higher internal consistency reliability. It was suggested that the lower limit for Cronbach's alpha is 0.70 although it may decrease to 0.60 in exploratory research (Hair *et al.*, 1998). Due to time and effort constraints in conducting this research, the reliabilities of 0.7 or higher should suffice (Nunnally, 1978).

Table 3.3 presents the Cronbach's alpha values for the whole questionnaire is 0.927, which indicates that the reliability of the instrument is significantly high. Also the Cronbach's alpha values for the five factors ranged from 0.819 to 0.950, represents high internal consistency reliability.

Table 3.3 : Cronbach's Alpha for all constructs

All constructs in the questionnaire	Cronbach's Alpha
Marketing capabilities	0.819
Experience assets	0.844
Relation assets	0.847
International opportunity recognition	0.865
Export satisfaction	0.950
Cronbach's Alpha for all constructs in the questionnaire: **0.927**	

- **Result of pretesting**

The pretest results suggested some minor changes. Respondents suggested writing the research criteria at the beginning of the questionnaire rather than asking one by one. Therefore, part 1 was added at the beginning of the questionnaire. The purpose of part 1 is to select right manufacturer and right person to fill the questionnaire according to the research criteria. If all answers were "Yes", related managers were asked to fill the rest of questions.

Some countries also were added to the question 16 after pretesting.In addition, Question 17 was changed after pretesting because respondents were not familiar with the answers of this question. They suggested to change intermediary categories into 4 types including; Foreign intermediary based in Malaysia; Malaysian private intermediary (based in Malaysia); Foreign intermediary based in foreign market; Government agency (based in Malaysia).

Part 4 is related to marketing capabilities, which is adapted from previous studies. The questions of "Ability to differentiate products" and "Diversity of product line" were incomprehensible for respondents. Therefore, respondents suggested eliminating these questions because most of respondent did not have idea about these questions. In addition, in the result of Cronbach's Alpha for marketing capability, they had the lowest correlation with other items and if these itemswould be deleted, Cronbach's Alpha increases in the highest level. Therefore, these questions were eliminated after pretesting for the final data collection.

The above-mentioned changes were again back translated into Malay and the revised version of the questionnaire was used for final data collection. The following section presents the sampling design and data collection procedures.

3.9   Sampling Design and procedures

Study population was independent exporting manufacturers with 150 or less than 150 employees whom they were using export intermediary for exporting their products. It was impossible to get the list of the whole population. Thus, Federation Malaysian Manufacture (FMM) Directory of Malaysian Industries (2009) which is cooperated with Malaysia External Trade Development Corporation (MATRADE) was chosen as a sampling framework that is believed to be the most reliable manufacturer list in Malaysia. Most researchers on Malaysian SMEs used this directory as a sampling framework for their research such as Mahajar and Hashim, 2001; Seow and Liu, 2006; Thurasamy *et al.,* 2009; Nee and Wahid, 2010 etc. Therefore, export ventures of manufacturing companies in the FMM (Federation Malaysian Manufacturers) list were considered as the study population.

Based on FMM Directory (2009), SMEs in Malaysia are divided into manufacturing related services and agro-based industries as the first category and services, primary agriculture and ICT as the second category of SMEs. The number of employees in the first category is 150 or less than 150 employees and in the second category is 50 employees and less. This study is based on the first category.

According to FMM Directory (2009), 2175 manufacturers companies were listed base on Alphabet in all over Malaysia. The list provides the names of manufacturer, years of incorporation, addresses, contact information, products manufactured, current export market, future export market, number of employees, brand name, quality standard achieved and annual sale. 859 manufacturers inside of the list had 150 employees or less and they had current export market. There was not information about their independent business and about direct or indirect exporting. Therefore, base on FMM Directory, population of this thesis is 859 manufacturers.

In addition, this book categorized products into 10 main categories products as below:

Table 3.4 : Products Manufactured

Products
1. Fabricated Metal Products, Except Machinery and Equipment(22)
2. Machinery and Equipment(33)
3. Office, Accounting and Computing Machinery
4. Electrical Machinery and Apparatus
5. Radio, Television and Communication Equipment and Apparatus
6. Medical, Precision and Optical Instrument, Watches and Clocks
7. Motor Vehicles, Trailers and Semi-Trailers

8.	Other Transport Equipment(13)
9.	Manufacture of Furniture
10.	Recycling

(FMM Directory, 2009, pg: A103)

However, the following three main issues arose from the utilization of the FMM's Directory (2009):

1) Most companies listed were firms with more than 150 employees

2) The list was not updated regularly because the researcher found that some companies have been closed down, have changed their email addresses or their phone number when contacting these companies

3) A few companies listed in the FMM' Directory (2009) was not independent manufacturer for example they were based on other countries and have branch in Malaysia.

4) A few companies listed in the FMM' Directory (2009) were mentioned about current export market but they were not exporter.

3.9.2 Phase I. Random sampling

According to FMM Directory, population of this thesis is 859 manufacturers. Krejcie and Morgan (1970) sampling size model were used to estimate the sample size. Table shows the Krejcie and Morgan sampling size.

Table 3.5 : Table for Determining sample size from a Given Population

N	S	N	S	N	S	N	S	N	S
10	10	100	80	280	162	800	260	2800	338
15	14	110	86	290	165	850	265	3000	341
20	19	120	92	300	169	**900**	**269**	3500	246
25	24	130	97	320	175	950	274	4000	351
30	28	140	103	340	181	1000	278	4500	351

108

35	32	150	108	360	186	1100	285	5000	357
40	36	160	113	380	181	1200	291	6000	361
45	40	180	118	400	196	1300	297	7000	364
50	44	190	123	420	201	1400	302	8000	367
55	48	200	127	440	205	1500	306	9000	368
60	52	210	132	460	210	1600	310	10000	373
65	56	220	136	480	214	1700	313	15000	375
70	59	230	140	500	217	1800	317	20000	377
75	63	240	144	550	225	1900	320	30000	379
80	66	250	148	600	234	2000	322	40000	380
85	70	260	152	650	242	2200	327	50000	381
90	73	270	155	700	248	2400	331	75000	382
95	76	270	159	750	256	2600	335	100000	384

Note: "N" is population size
"S" is sample size.

(Krejcie, and Morgan,1970)

Based on the Krejcie, and Morgan(1970) sampling size table, for 900 populations, 269 is the sample size.

Firms were drawn randomly from the manufacturer's list in the FMM directory. Those selected firms were ranked according to their alphabet to facilitate the field researchers to organize and collect the data efficiently. The firms were contacted by phone. Those firms which met the research criteria were asked for their willingness to participate in the study by explaining the length of questionnaire and purpose of the survey.

Based on the web-based questionnaire, one scan of the university letter was sent to them through email. In some cases that managers were not available to answer the questionnaire, an appointment was made to meet them that were mostly in the upcoming trade show and exhibition in Kuala Lumpur.

3.9.3   Procedure of Data Collection

In order to deliver to the export managers or managers who were responsible for exporting decisions, the structured questionnaire was designed. The web-based survey method, among the different methods of quantitative research, was found to be the principal data collection method.

Popularity of this method of collecting data has become much more effective based on several advantageous. Some of its preferable features are mentioned in following: first accessibility of internet allows data to be entered directly into a central database. Second, this method needs less dependency on specific types of equipment for entering data. Third it allows for instant editing checks as responses are entered also allows for several traditional techniques for inputting responses such as dropdowns, textboxes, checkboxes or other styles (Cooper, *et al.,* 2006). Fourth in term of time and location, it permits individuals to send data to a researcher at their convenience (Smith and Leigh, 1997; Schmidt, 1997). Fifth, it is efficient in terms of time and the resources it requires also it allows to automatic transformation of raw data into an analyzable format (Schmidt, 1997; Davis; 1999; Kieley, 1996; Schmidt*et al.,* 1997). Furthermore, the Web-based survey lead to minimizing any interruptions, creation of interest from the participant and keeping the participant focused.

Several researchers apply this approach of collecting data, and it is considered as an effective tool for data collection (Hsiu Mei, 2002; Morrel Samuels, 2003; Cobanoglu and obanoglu, 2003).Therefore based on all aforementioned advantageousness this study applied web-based questionnaires.

Although in order to gain response rate, current study applied "drop-in-questionnaire" which is characterized by a personal request for cooperation in advance, the handing over the questionnaire through field researchers at the beginning of the survey, and his/her presence during the completion of survey (Theingi, 2008; Holzmüller and Stottinger, 1996). High commitment by the respondents as they were asked for cooperation in advance is the advantages of this method.Also it helps to keep the originality of the replies and eventually make a standard data collection. To state the matter differently, the outcome of this procedure has a highly quality and a great respond rates (Holzmüller and Stottinger, 1996). Furthermore, the respondents have an option of asking question about unclear questions in the field from researchers.

Hence, the whole members of MATRADE and FMM were listed out from FMM directory book. This list compile of manufacturers, having export to international market and less than 150 employees. Afterward the questionnaire's link and scan of the university letter to FMM were distributed by e-mail. The sample of email and link can be found in the appendix.

3.9.4 Dealing with Non-Response

In order to gain the respondents' cooperation and attract higher response, the University letter that was organized to ask the FMM's participate and assistance to the survey and also to certify the researcher's degree in UTM, was emailed to the respondents. In addition, one briefly email, which was, described the purpose of the research, the important role of respondents participation in this research, and length of the questionnaire were sent to them.

Moreover, email stressed that their data will not disclosed to any third party. For getting more motivation to their cooperation, a summary of the findings and the results of the study were offered to send them at the end of the study upon their request. The email was sent after calling and persuading them on the phone. The two web-based questionnaires designed (Malay and English version) could easily achieve by respondents just with one click on "English Language" or "Bahasa Language". For people who were arranged to meet them directly, questionnaire had two cover letters. One was university letter and another one was same email content.

3.10   Data analysis

For analyzing the data, inferential and descriptive statistical methods were used in this research. The proposed model in this thesis is including the independent variables, mediate variable, and dependent variable. According to Baron and Kenny (1986), the basic casual chain that is including the dependent, independent and mediating variable should be diagrammed same as picture of 3.1.

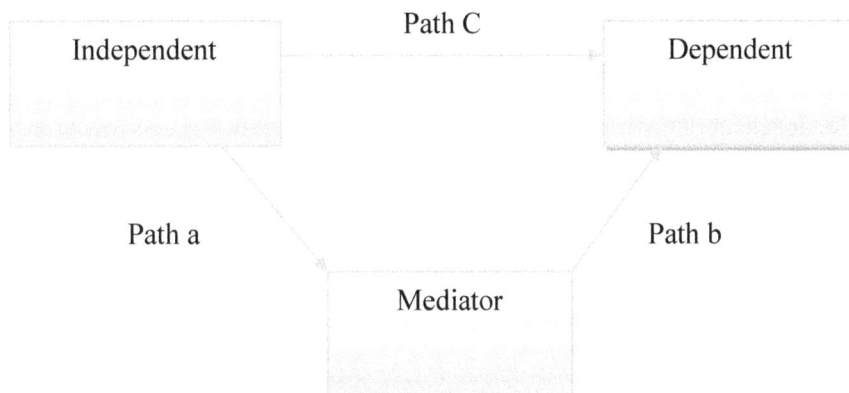

Figure 3.1   The basic casual chain of dependent, independent and mediating variable (Baron and Kenny, 1986)

Based on the finding of MacKinnon *et al.,* (2002), for testing mediation the most common way is actually developed by Kenny and his colleagues (Kenny *et al.,*1998; Judd and Kenny, 1981; Baron and Kenny, 1986).According to them four following regression equation should be estimated in order to test for mediation:

1- It must be shown that there is an extremely important link between the independent and the dependent variable (path c).

2- It must be indicated that the independent is related to the mediator (path a).

3- It must be shown that the mediator is related to the dependent variable (path b).

4- Finally it must be indicated that the intensity of the relation between the dependent and independent is highly reduced when the mediator is added to the model.

The computer software MedGraph -Iprogram (Jose, 2003) was ruled out to test whether mediate factor will mediate the relationship between independent and dependent variables (hypothesis H3). MedGraph is a program to graphically represent mediation among three variables. Recently most of studies have used MedGraph-I for describing mediation among three variables (e.g. Godos-Dı'ez *et.al,* 2011; Kuvaas, 2009) because user is able key in statistical information about covariance relationships among three variables quickly and easily; obtain rapid feedback about whether a proposed mediation process has occurred or not (Jose, 2003). In addition, it shows the mediation role by (Baron and Kenny, 1986) at the same time and in one process.

Bivariate correlation test was used to test the relationships between two variables (hypothesis H1.1, H1.2, H1.3, H2.1, H2.2, and H2.3). Multiple regressions were used to evaluate the effects of two or more independent variables on a single dependent variable (For testing hypothesis H2 and H3). Frequency tables and statistical measures like mean, standard deviation, and mode, median were used to describe the personal background and firm background of the respondents.

CHAPTER 4

DATA ANALYSIS

4.1   Introduction

This chapter presents the findings of the study. The identified factors were tested through statistical analysis. The discussion is divided into some main sections. The first part is on the reliability and factor analysis of the questionnaire. The second part is descriptive analysis. This is followed by analysis on the research criteria, respondent's background and firm's background. The third part is on the normality and linearity that are assumptions of correlation and multiple regression analysis. The forth part is on the testing hypothesis, which is followed by Bivariate and Multiple regressions. Finally, the last part is on the mediating test that is followed by the mediating test of international opportunity recognition between export intermediary networking and export satisfaction.

4.2   Reliability of research tool

In order to measure internal consistency and reliability, Cronbach's alpha value was applied   (Hair *et al.,* 1998). Based on the research of Sekaran (2003), definition of Cronbach's Alpha was presented as a reliability coefficient that indicates how well the items in a set are positively correlated to one another.

In terms of the average inter correlations among items measuring the concept Cronbach's alpha is computed. The higher internal consistency reliability is represented by the closer Cronbach's alpha to (1).The Lower limitation for Cronbach's alpha proposed to be (0.70). However, in exploratory research it might be decreased to 0.60 (Hair *et al.,* 1998).The reliabilities of 0.7 or higher should suffice, due to time and effort constraints in conducting this research (Nunnally, 1978).

Some of the attributes are recommended to be deleted because of their smaller than 0.7 value.Based on the fact that the Cronbach's alpha value is larger than 0.7, none of the items should be removed (Rasli, 2006).Cronbach's alpha for all constructs could be found in the Table 4.1 to 4.6.

4.2.1   Cronbach's alpha for the Marketing capabilities

Cronbach's alpha for the Marketing capabilities showed "0.511" since it was less than "0.7" that indicated lower internal consistency reliability of marketing capabilities constructs. As it is presented in the appendix if "Differentiate the products" item was deleted, reliability would increase to "0.743" and if "Firm's product line diversity" item were eliminated, reliability would increase to "0.740".

That means these items are not clear and not suited to this research. Also respondents suggested eliminating these items. Therefore, according to Rasli (2006), these items were suggested to delete.

Therefore, in this construct "Differentiate the products" and "Firm's product line diversity" were deleted. After eliminating these items, Cronbach's Alpha had done again and reliability increased significantly to "0.921" that indicates higher reliability of marketing capabilities construct (see Table 4.1).

Table 4.1 : Cronbach's Alpha for items under Marketing capabilities

Items under Marketing capabilities	Corrected Item-Total Correlation	Cronbach's Alpha if Item Deleted
Quality of customer service	.625	.919
Effective advertising in gaining market share	.741	.910
High quality sales person	.838	.902
Effective distributor networks	.838	.902
Advertising expenditure	.628	.919
Strong market research	.776	.907
Introduce new products very fast	.842	.901
Serve different market segments	.604	.921

Cronbach's Alpha for whole items under Marketing capabilities: **0.921**

4.2.2 Cronbach's Alpha for experience assets

Table 4.2 shows Cronbach's alpha for the items under experience assets "0.844" since is more than "0.7" indicates high reliability of experience assets construct.

Table 4.2 : Cronbach's Alpha for items under experience assets

Items under experience assets	Corrected Item-Total Correlation	Cronbach's Alpha if Item Deleted
Knowledgeable about the requirements of potential customers	.856	.747
Overall good experience with respect to the market	.512	.843
Adequate experience to sell the products	.735	.785
Supply of market information	.524	.844

Cronbach's Alpha for whole items under experience assets : **0.844**

4.2.3 Cronbach's Alpha for Relation assets

Table 4.3 shows Cronbach's alpha for the items under Relation assets "0.847" since is more than "0.7" indicates high reliability of Relation assets construct.

Table 4.3 : Cronbach's Alpha for items under Relation assets

Items under Relation assets	Corrected Item-Total Correlation	Cronbach's Alpha if Item Deleted
Trust and fairness	.391	.859
Keeps the promise	.389	.858
Helpfulness in emergency case.	.591	.828
Positive attitude toward any complaints	.789	.798
Long-term relationship	.649	.819
Good communication	.727	.807
Good reputation in the foreign market	.761	.804
Cronbach's Alpha for whole items under Relation assets : **0.847**		

4.2.4 Cronbach's Alpha for International opportunity recognition

Table 4.4 shows Cronbach's alpha for the elements under International opportunity recognition "0.865" since is more than "0.7" indicates high reliability of International opportunity recognition construct.

Table 4.4 : Cronbach's Alpha for items under International opportunity recognition

Items under International opportunity recognition	Corrected Item-Total Correlation	Cronbach's Alpha if Item Deleted
Foreign opportunities in the different countries	.736	.827
Foreign opportunities in the different cultures	.718	.832
Foreign opportunities in the different languages	.633	.847
Greater sales volumes	.677	.839
Greater foreign market share	.512	.865
Greater sales agreements volumes with foreign	.696	.837

Cronbach's Alpha for whole items under International opportunity recognition: **0.865**

4.2.5 Cronbach's Alpha for Export satisfaction

Table 4.5 shows Cronbach's alpha for the items under Export satisfaction "0.950" since is more than "0.7" indicates good reliability of Export satisfaction construct.

Table 4.5 : Cronbach's Alpha for items under Export satisfaction

Items under Export satisfaction	Corrected Item-Total Correlation	Cronbach's Alpha if Item Deleted
Satisfied with the sales growth	.902	.934
Satisfied with the firm's export market share	.892	.932
Satisfied with number of countries exporting to	.855	.942
Satisfied with the overall export performance	.893	.930

Cronbach's Alpha for whole items under Export satisfaction: **0.950**

4.2.6 Cronbach's Alpha for all constructs

Table 4.6 presents the Cronbach's alpha values for the whole questionnaire is 0.927, which indicates that the reliability of the instrument is significantly high. Also the Cronbach's alpha values for the five factors ranged from 0.819 to 0.950, represents high internal consistency reliability.

Table 4.6 : Cronbach's Alpha for all constructs

All constructs in the questionnaire	Cronbach's Alpha
Marketing capabilities	0.819
Experience assets	0.844
Relation assets	0.847
International opportunity recognition	0.865
Export satisfaction	0.950
Cronbach's Alpha for all constructs in the questionnaire: **0.927**	

4.3 Factor Analysis

To verify the dimensionality of the export intermediaries networking construct in the IOR and export satisfaction, a factor analysis, using the principal components extraction technique, was performed on Malaysian SMEs, calculated by perception-minus-expectation mean scores (see Table 4.7).

For quantifying the degree of inter-correlations among the variables, Kaiser-Meyer-Olkin (KMO) measure of sampling adequacy was computed. KMO measure of sampling adequacy provides an index (between 0 and 1) of the proportion of variance among the variables that might be common variance. The SPSS software package suggests that a KMO near 1.0 supports a factor analysis and that anything less than 0.5 is probably not amenable to useful factor analysis (Rasli, 2006). The results of KMO in this study indicated for marketing capability (0.944), experience assets (0.849), relation assets (0.931), international opportunity recognition (0.924), and for export satisfaction (0.837).In addition, high KMO value for all the variables is achieved (0.954). Since all KMO values are more than 0.5 and near to 1.0, means the dataset is suitable for factor analysis (Rasli, 2006).

The reason for high KMO could be validity and reliability, which have done carefully before distributing questionnaire to sample size. The scholars and project professionals examined validity. A copy of questionnaire distributed among individuals who were experts of the field. They asked for the consistency and validity of research as a whole and data gathering tool. They mentioned the problems related to questions and the structure of research. Problems mentioned by experts were edited. In addition, pretesting was conducted to identify ambiguity or bias in the questions and to ensure that respondents understood the questionnaire, and are familiar with terms used in the questionnaires. The respondents were asked to complete structured questionnaires followed by design, wording and length of questionnaire (Kumar et al., 1999). In addition, for the measuring of internal consistency and reliability, Cronbach's alpha was used. It shows that how well the items in a set are positively correlated to one another. The pretest results suggested some minor changes, which, all was edited before sending questionnaire to the sample size. Therefore, the result of KMO in factor become high and near to 1.

The construct validity is confirmed by reviewing the communality values. Communality refers to total amount of original variable variance shares with all other variables included in the analysis. According to Hair et al. (1998), factor analysis arrives at essential identical result if the communalities exceed 0.60 for most variables. Since all the variables values are more than 0.86, means all the questions have validity.

In addition, the results report its cumulative variance greater than 80.76 percent (marketing capability: 87.77%; experience assets: 90.36%; relation assets: 91.47%; International opportunity recognition: 80.76%, and export satisfaction: 83.36 %.).

Table 4.7 : Principal component analysis of the networking and IOR

No	Statement	Factor Loadings				
		1	2	3	4	5
Q22	High quality sales person	.955				
Q25	Strong market researches	.952				
Q20	Quality of customer service	.951				
Q24	Advertising expenditure	.949				
Q27	Serve different market segments	.930				
Q21	Effective advertising in gaining market share	.927				
Q23	Strong market research	.916				
Q26	Introduce new products very fast	.913				
Q28	Adequate experience to sell the products		.958			
Q30	Overall good experience with respect to the market		.957			
Q29	Supply of market information		.947			
Q31	Knowledgeable about the requirements of potential customers		.941			
Q38	Good reputation in the foreign market			.972		
Q33	Keeps the promise			.968		
Q32	Trust and fairness			.967		
Q34	Helpfulness in emergency case			.956		
Q37	Good communication			.955		
Q36	Long-term relationship			.945		
Q35	Positive attitude toward any complaints			.931		
Q40	Foreign opportunities in the different cultures				.916	

Q43	Greater foreign market share				.913	
Q42	Greater sales volumes				.905	
Q39	Foreign opportunities in the different countries				.901	
Q41	Foreign opportunities in the different languages				.893	
Q44	Greater sales agreements volumes with foreign				.864	
Q46	Satisfied with the firm's export market share					.935
Q47	Satisfied with the sales growth					.925
Q48	Satisfied with the overall export performance					.904
Q45	Satisfied with number of countries exporting to					.888
% of variance explained		87.77	90.36	91.47	80.76	83.36
Cronbach's alpha		0.921	0.844	0.847	0.865	0.950
KMO for each constructs		0.944	0.849	0.931	0.924	0.837
KMO for all constructs		0.954				

4.4 Descriptive analysis

All demographic questions were used to conduct a descriptive analysis for the characteristics of sample organizations, which is followed, by the research criteria questions, respondents' background, and the firm's background questions.

4.4.1   Research Criteria Question (Q1-Q4)

The questions 1 to 4 are initially asked to a related manager to find out if the responding firms meet with research criteria. If the answer of all questions were "yes", they met the research criteria and they were requested to fill the whole of questions otherwise firms did not meet the criteria and they were not requested to fill the rest of questions.

The questionnaires were distributed to 500 SMEs which 338 of them responded to the questions. 265 out of 338 respondents answered positively to these research criteria questions and then asked them to answer the rest of questions.

4.4.2   Respondent's Background Questions (Q5-Q9)

Questions 5 to 9 are respondent's background questions (See Table 4.1 to 4.5). The results of this section provided the gender, ethnic group, age, education level and experience of managers, which gives a general idea on demographic characteristics of managers of exporting manufacturer SMEs.

123

Table 4.8 : Gender

Ethnic group	Frequency	Percent
Male	221	83.4
Female	44	16.6
Total	265	100.0

Table 4.9 : Ethnic group

Ethnic group	Frequency	Percent
Malay	48	18.1
Chinese	191	72.1
Indian	23	8.7
Others	3	1.1
Total	265	100.0

Table 4.10 : Age of Respondents

Age	Frequency	Percent
20 - 30	50	18.9
31 -40	104	39.2
41 - 50	94	35.5
51-60	17	6.4
Total	265	100.0

Table 4.11 : Level of Education

Education	Frequency	Percent
Primary school	1	.4
Secondary school	10	3.8
Diploma	112	42.3
Bachelor	112	42.3
Master	20	7.5
Higher than master	10	3.8
Total	265	100.0

Table 4.12 : Experience in exporting

Experience	Frequency	Percent
1-5 years	102	38.5
6-10 years	115	43.4
11-15 years	32	12.1
16-20 years	10	3.8
Over 20 years	6	2.3
Total	265	100.0

The results of respondent's background illustrate that 83.4% of respondents were male (Table 4.8). Majority of managers (72.1%) were Chinese (Table 4.9). Most of managers were young between 31 to 40 years old or less (Table 4.10). Regarding the highest level of education attained, Table 4.11 indicates that 42.3% of managers held a bachelor degree and diploma. In addition, Table 4.12 shows that 43.4% of managers had between 6-10 years export experience. Therefore, the above findings indicate that most managers are male, Chinese, young, less experienced and bachelor degree held.

4.4.3 Firm's Background Questions (Q10-Q19)

Questions 10 to 19 are firm's background questions (See Table 4.13 to 4.22). The results of this section provide age, size, level of export experience, the percentage of export sales, sales agreements with foreign customers, product category of product export venture, countries most exported to, market entry distribution most used, type of the product category exported, and the number of countries that firms were exported to. This section gives a general idea on demographic characteristics of exporting manufacturer SMEs.

Table 4.13 : Firm's age

Firm's age	Frequency	Percent
1 - 5 years	79	29.8
6-10 years	145	54.7
11 - 15 years	24	9.1
16-20 years	9	3.4
Over 20years	8	3.0
Total	265	100.0

Table 4.14 : Number of employees

Number of employees	Frequency	Percent
1 - 4 employees	4	1.5
5 - 50 employees	137	51.7
51 - 100 employees	98	37.0
101-150 employees	26	9.8
Total	265	100.0

Table 4.15 : : Firm's exporting experience

Firm's exporting experience	Frequency	Percent
1 - 5 years	145	54.7
6 - 10 years	109	41.1
11 - 15 years	7	2.6
More than 20 years	4	1.5
Total	265	100.0

Table 4.16 : percentages of firm's total export sales

firm's total export sales	Frequency	Percent
1 %- 20%	3	1.1
21% - 40%	131	49.4
41 %- 60%	55	20.8
61% - 80%	29	10.9
More than 80%	47	17.7
Total	265	100.0

Table 4.17 : percentages of firm's total sales agreement with foreign customers

firm's total export agreement	Frequency	Percent
1 %- 20%	3	1.1
21% - 40%	129	48.7
41 %- 60%	56	21.1
61% - 80%	29	10.9
More than 80%	48	18.1
Total	265	100.0

Table 4.18 : Product category of respondent's firm

Products category	Frequency	Percent
Agricultural products & machinery	33	12.5
Automotive parts & components	13	4.9
Building material, machinery &related products	22	8.3
Cement & concrete products	7	2.6
Ceramic & tiles	9	3.4
Chemical & adhesive products	16	6.0
Electrical & electronics products	34	12.8
Food & beverage	7	2.6
Furniture & wood related products	22	8.3
Gifts, stationery & office supplies	4	1.5
Household products & appliances	13	4.9
Industrial, engineering products	13	4.9
Iron & steel products	11	4.2
Laboratory equipment, fittings & services	3	1.1
Paper, packaging, labeling & printing	8	3.0
Pharmaceutical, medical equipment & cosmetics	33	12.5
Plastic products & resins	3	1.1
Rubber products	24	9.1
Total	265	100.0

Table 4.19 : Countries most exported

Countries most exported to	Frequency	Percent
1=North America	11	4.2
2=South America	2	.8
4= Eastern Europe	6	2.3
5= Western Europe	56	21.1
6= Southern Europe	1	.4
7= Northern Europe	9	3.4
8= Oceania	5	1.9
9= Eastern Asia	5	1.9
10= Southeast Asia	115	43.4
11= Africa	5	1.9
12=Mid East	50	18.9
Total	265	100.0

Table 4.20 : Export intermediary most used

Export intermediary most used	Frequency	Percent
Foreign intermediary based in Malaysia	7	2.6
Malaysian private intermediary (based in Malaysia)	44	16.6
Foreign intermediary based in foreign market	59	22.3
Government agency (based in Malaysia)	155	58.5
Total	265	100.0

Table 4.21 : Type of exported products

Type of exported products	Frequency	Percent
Business goods	139	52.5
Consumer goods	126	47.5
Total	256	100.0

Table 4.22 : Number of countries exported

Number of countries exported to	Frequency	Percent
1 - 5 countries	81	30.6
6 -10 countries	113	42.6
11 - 15 countries	13	4.9
16-20 countries	46	17.4
More than 20 countries	12	4.5
Total	265	100.0

The results show that (54.7%) of firms were new established between 6 to 10 years old (Table 4.13). Majority of firms (51.7%) are small firms, which had 5 to 50 employees (Table 4.14).Table 4.15 indicates that most firms (41.1%) had 6 to 10 years exporting experience. Regarding the percentage of firm's total export sales and firm's total sales agreement with foreign customers, Table 4.16 and Table 4.17 indicates that most of SMEs achieved 21% to 40 % through export intermediary.

Table 4.18 indicates that 12.5% of SMEs were pharmaceutical and medical equipment producer. Table 4.19 shows that 43.4% of SMEs were most exported to Southeast Asia. Table 4.20 indicates that 58.5% of SMEs introduces government agency as the most export intermediaries that have used for their exporting.

Table 4.21 shows that most of product type of SMEs was business products (52.5%) and finally Table 4.22 indicates that most of SMEs were exporting into 6 to 10 countries (42.6%). Therefore, the above findings indicate that most of manufacturers SMEs were young, small, less exporting experience, which introduced government agency as their export intermediaries used to foreign markets.

4.5 Assumption before analysis

Linearity, normality and co-linearity are the assumptions before doing regression and correlations.

4.5.1 Normality

The normal P-P plot is considered as the most reliable approach to examine the assumption of normality in the multivariate analysis (Hair *et al*, 2010). It is seen that the observed residuals are not far above or far below the normal line. As can be seen on the Figure 4.2, the normal plot of regression standardized residuals for the IOR also indicates a relatively normal distribution. Normal probability plots for the other variables are examined and found to indicate support for the normality assumption for all of the variables. Therefore, the assumption of normality has not been violated.

Histogram

Dependent Variable: IOR

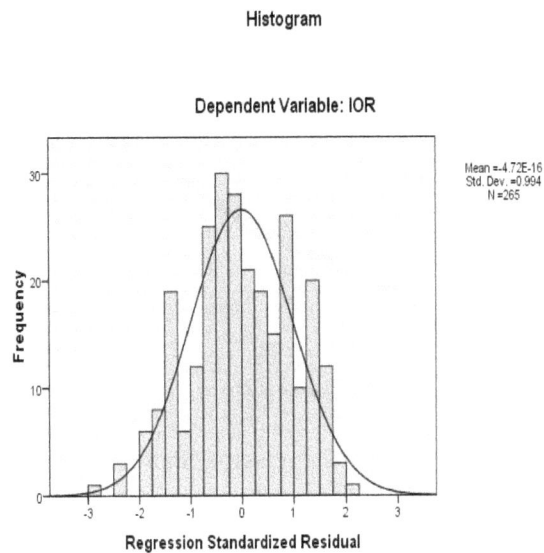

Figure 4.1   Residual histogram of MC, EA,RA and IOR

In the histogram given above, the distribution seems normal. It is evident that the majority of scores are plotted in the histogram' middle and it demonstrates that IOR is following the assumption of normality not violating it. Histograms for other variables were examined in the same way. Generally, all the histograms indicated a normal distribution of the residuals suggesting that the normality assumption of the data is met.

The normal P-P plot is considered as the most reliable approach to examine the assumption of normality in the multivariate analysis (Hair *et al*, 2010). It is seen that the observed residuals are not far above or far below the normal line. As can be seen on the Figure 4.2, the normal plot of regression-standardized residuals for the IOR also indicates a relatively normal distribution. Normal probability plots for the other variables are examined and found to indicate support for the normality assumption for all of the variables. Therefore, the assumption of normality has not been violated.

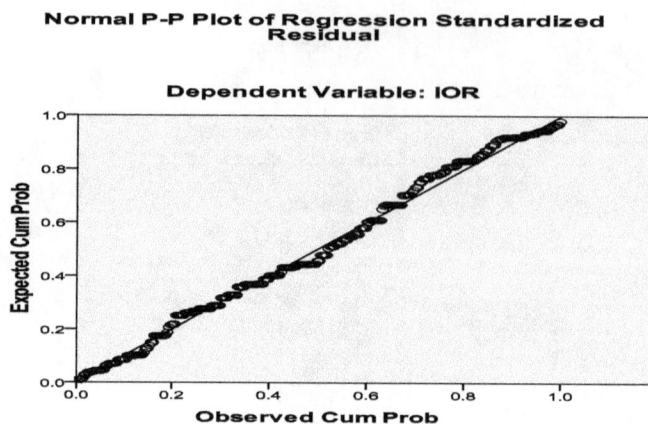

Figure 4.2   Normal Probability Plot Regression Standardized Residual of histogram of MC, EA, RA and IOR

4.5.2   Linearity

Linearity indicates the linearity of the relationship between independent and dependent variables. For the linearity assumption observation, one of the methods is scatter plots. Figure 4.3 illustrates the tendency of the plots that starts low on the left and going to the right side and become higher that indicates that there is a positive and linear relationship among IOR and marketing capabilities. The results prove that there is a linear and positive relationship among all independent and dependent variables.

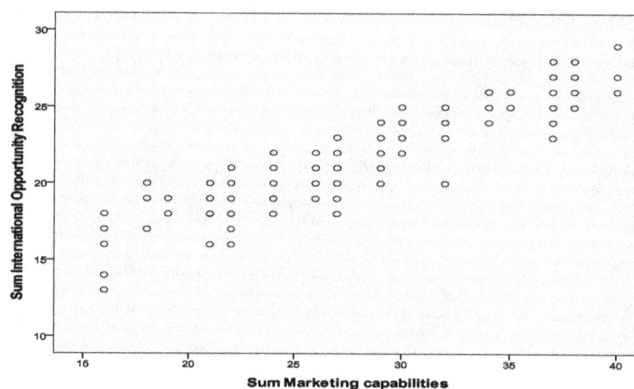

Figure 4.3   Linearity

4.5.3 Co-Linearity

The values of the regression coefficients for the correlated variables may change drastically when there is co-linearity. It depends on which independent variables are involved in the model. The Variance Inflationary Factor (VIF) is the method that selected for evaluating co-linearity for each independent variable. Amount of variability of the specified independent variable has been referred to as tolerance which is not described by other independent variables.The possibility of multicollinearity has been suggested whether tolerance value is less than 0.10, or a VIF value more than 10 (Pallant, 2007).Table 4.5 presents the outcome of co-linearity of independent variable on dependent variables.

Table 4.23 : Co-linearity

Model	Collinearity Statistics	
(Constant)	Tolerance	VIF
Marketing Capabilities	.545	1.835
Experience Assets	.559	1.789
Relation Assets	.689	1.452
IOR	.321	3.113

4.6 Testing Hypothesis

As it mentioned, for this study, 10 hypotheses were proposed. In order to test these hypotheses, we applied Pearson product-moment correlation analysis (for H1, H1.1, H1.2, H1.3 H2, H2.1, H2.2, H2.3 and H3), multiple regression analysis (for H1 and H2) and the computer software MedGraph –Iprogram Jose (for H4).

4.6.1 Research Hypothesis 1 (H1, H1.1, H1.2, H1.3)

Three hypotheses (from H1.1, H1.2 and H1.3) were proposed because there are three variables considered for export intermediaries networking. In order to examine the relationship between each of these variables and IOR, these three hypotheses were aimed. To execute that, we examined the correlation between each of the variables and IOR by Pearson correlation.

4.6.2 Pearson Product-Moment Correlation Analysis

The relationship between the three variable of export intermediary networking on IOR was analyzed by applying Pearson product-moment correlation analysis. Initial analyses pointed out for having no violation of the normality assumption, linearity, and homoscedasticity. The relation between IOR and export intermediary networking is discussed in this section. It was proposed that:

H1: Export intermediary networking by SMEs is positively correlated to international opportunity recognition in SMEs.

- H1.1: Marketing capabilities exchanges between Export intermediary and SMEs is positively correlated to IOR in SMEs.
- H1.2: experience assets exchanges between Export intermediary and SMEs is positively correlated to IOR in SMEs.
- H1.3: Relation assets exchanges between Export intermediary and SMEs is positively correlated to IOR in SMEs.

Tables 4.24 present the Pearson correlation matrix acquired for the three interval-scaled variables. The result shows that export intermediary networking by SMEs is positively correlated to international opportunity recognition in SMEs ($r=.818$, $p<.01$).

As it obvious from Table 4.24, the marketing capabilities were significant statistically and positively related to IOR (r=.664, p<.01). It is proved that marketing capabilities exchanges between export intermediaries and SMEs mostly help SMEs to recognize international opportunities

Experience and knowledge assets which considered as the second variable was proven to have positive significant correlation with IOR at p<0.01 level (r=.663) (Table 4.24).It reflects the fact that experience assets exchanges between Export intermediary and SMEs is positively correlated to international opportunity recognition in SMEs.

Relation assets as the third variable, has been proven that have a positive significant correlation with IOR at p<0.01 level (r=.553) (Table 4.24).This result shows that the third variable exchanges between Export intermediary and SMEs is correlated positively to international opportunity recognition in SMEs.

Table 4.24 : Pearson correlation between variables

Pearson correlation between Networking and IOR (H1)			
		Networking	IOR
Networking	Pearson Correlation	1	.818[**]
	Sig. (2-tailed)		.000
	N	265	265
IOR	Pearson Correlation	.818[**]	1
	Sig. (2-tailed)	.000	
	N	265	265
Pearson correlation between Marketing and IOR (H1.1)			
		Marketing capabilities	IOR
Marketing capabilities	Pearson Correlation	1	.664[**]
	Sig. (2-tailed)		.000
	N	265	265
IOR	Pearson Correlation	.664[**]	1
	Sig. (2-tailed)	.000	
	N	265	265
Pearson correlation between Experience and IOR (H1.2)			

		Experience Assets	IOR
Ex	Pearson Correlation	1	.663**
	Sig. (2-tailed)		.000
	N	265	265
IOR	Pearson Correlation	.663**	1
	Sig. (2-tailed)	.000	
	N	265	265

Pearson correlation between Relation Assets and IOR (H1.3)

		Relation Assets	IOR
Relation Assets	Pearson Correlation	1	.539**
	Sig. (2-tailed)		.000
	N	265	265
IOR	Pearson Correlation	.539**	1
	Sig. (2-tailed)	.000	
	N	265	265

**. Correlations are significant at the 0.01 level (2-tailed).

In conclusion, of the outcome from Pearson correlation analyses of this study, there is favorable resources exchanges between SMEs and export intermediaries for international opportunities recognition (IOR) and it can firmly imply that export intermediaries' resources like, relation assets, marketing capabilities and experience assets are quite closely related to IOR.

To state the matter differently, we can say that the hypothesized relationship (positive) between each networking variable and IOR was confirmed by the data. Hence, it is impossible to reject H1, H1.1, H1.2 and H1.3, which are supported accordingly.

However, between three variables, marketing capability has the strongest correlation with IOR, following with experience and IOR. Relation assets have the less correlation with IOR between other two variables.

4.6.2.2 Multiple Regression Analysis

Test H1 has been tested by executing multiple regression analysis and analyses the relationship of international opportunity recognition with export intermediary networking. Initial results reflect the fact that all the assumptions of multiple regressions were proven. The regression model for this research is as follows:

$$\text{Export Intermediaries Networking} = a + b_1 MC + b_2 EA + b_3 RA + \varepsilon$$

- MC=Marketing Capabilities
- EA= Experience Assets
- RA= Relation Assets
- a=Constant
- b=Coefficients
- ε =Standard error of the estimate

In this study, first hypothesis is correlated to export intermediary networking of the three resources (marketing capabilities, experience assets, relation assets and) and IOR. The accomplishment of the first specific aim of this research study has been proven by testing this hypothesis means it has proven the relationship of export intermediaries networking and IOR.

Multiple regression analysis was applied as a testing method. The results are presented in Table 4.25.Marketing capabilities, experience assets, and relation assets are three independent variables that were entered into the regression model and account for 67 per cent of the variance (R squared) in IOR. As it is shown by the F-value of 183.793 in Model Summary table, it is highly significant. Therefore, first hypothesis substantiated.

Table 4.25 : Relationship between export intermediaries networking and IOR(Model Summary)

R	R^2	Adjusted R^2	Std. Error of the Estimate	F	Sig.
.824[a]	.679	.675	.602	183.793	.000[a]

a Predictors: (Constant), Marketing capabilities, Experience assets, Relation assets

b Dependent Variable: IOR

Table 4.26 : Influence of export intermediaries networking on IOR(Coefficients)

	Unstandardized Coefficients		Standardized Coefficients		
	B	Std. Error	Beta	t	Sig.
(Constant)	.770	.104		7.432	.000
Marketing capabilities	.321	.029	.431	10.966	.000
Experience assets	.270	.031	.359	8.683	.000
Relation assets	.203	.027	.287	7.483	.000

a Dependent Variable: IOR

The variable with the largest beta value in absolute, in analyzing the scale of the coefficients, has remarkable effect on the dependent variable (Sekaran, 2003).The strength and extent of effect of each one of the export intermediaries networking variables would have on IOR was concentrated in Table 4.26.

As can see from the Table 4.26, marketing capabilities has the highest number in Beta is (.431), which is significant statistically. Beta of .359 belongs to experience assets, which are the next strongest and influential variable.

.287 was the standardized Beta value of the variable of relation assets, which is significant statistically. However, relation assets have the lowest influence on IOR among three other variables.

This result indicates that more of the respondents recognized international opportunities by marketing and experience assets exchange of export intermediary.

In the conclusion of the outcomes of the multiple regression analysis, it is deducible that the largest beta coefficient is marketing capabilities β =.431 which reflects strongest unique contribution to explain international opportunity recognition while relation assets β = .287 made less contribution (Table 4.26). This results demonstarte that SMEs are not strong in experience assets and marketing and to compensate these resources, they rely on their networking with export intermediaries.

4.6.3   Research Hypothesis 2 (H2)

Three hypotheses (from H2.1, H2.2 and H2.3) were proposed because there are three variables considered for export intermediaries networking. In order to examine the relationship between each of these variables and export satisfaction, these three hypotheses were aimed. To execute that, we were examined the correlation between each of the variables and export satisfaction by Pearson correlation.

4.6.4 Pearson Product-Moment Correlation Analysis

The relationship between the three variable of export intermediary networking on export satisfaction was analyzed by applying Pearson product-moment correlation analysis. Initial analyses pointed out for having no violation of the normality assumption, linearity, and homoscedasticity. The relation between export satisfaction and export intermediary networking is discussed in this section. It was proposed that:

H2: Export intermediary networking by SMEs is positively correlated to export performance in SMEs.

- H2.1: Marketing capabilities exchanges between Export intermediary and SMEs is positively correlated to export satisfaction in SMEs.
- H2.2: Experience assets exchanges between Export intermediary and SMEs is positively correlated to export satisfaction in SMEs.
- H2.3: Relation assets between Export intermediary and SMEs is positively correlated to export satisfaction in SMEs.

Tables 4.27 present the Pearson correlation matrix acquired for the three interval-scaled variables. The result shows that export intermediary networking by SMEs is positively correlated to export satisfaction in SMEs ($r=.758$, $p<.01$).

Table 4.27 : Pearson correlation between Networking and ES (H2)

		Networking	ES
Networking	Pearson Correlation	1	.758**
	Sig. (2-tailed)		.000
	N	265	265
ES	Pearson Correlation	.758**	1
	Sig. (2-tailed)	.000	
	N	265	265

Pearson correlation between marketing and ES (H2.1)

		Marketing capabilities	ES
Marketing capabilities	Pearson Correlation	1	.603**
	Sig. (2-tailed)		.000
	N	265	265
ES	Pearson Correlation	.603**	1
	Sig. (2-tailed)	.000	
	N	265	265

Pearson correlation between experience and ES (H2.2)

		Experience assets	ES
Experience Assets	Pearson Correlation	1	.614**
	Sig. (2-tailed)		.000
	N	265	265
ES	Pearson Correlation	.614**	1
	Sig. (2-tailed)	.000	
	N	265	265

Pearson correlation between relation assets and ES (H2.3)

		Relation Assets	ES
Relation Assets	Pearson Correlation	1	.511**
	Sig. (2-tailed)		.000
	N	265	265
ES	Pearson Correlation	.511**	1
	Sig. (2-tailed)	.000	
	N	265	265

**. Correlations are significant at the 0.01 level (2-tailed).

As it obvious from Table 4.27, the experience assets as the second variable were significant statistically and positively related to export satisfaction (r=.614, p<.01). It is proved that experience assets exchanges between export intermediaries and SMEs mostly help SMEs to have satisfaction with their exporting.

Marketing capability which considered as the first variable was proven to have positive significant correlation with IOR at p<0.01 level (r=.603) (Table 4.27).It reflects the fact that marketing capability exchanges between Export intermediary and SMEs is positively correlated to export satisfaction in SMEs.

Relation assets as the third variable, has been proven that have a positive significant correlation with IOR at p<0.01 level (r=.511) (Table 4.27).This result shows that the third variable exchanges between Export intermediary and SMEs is correlated positively to export satisfaction in SMEs.

In conclusion, of the outcome from Pearson correlation analyses of this study, there is favorable resources exchanges between SMEs and export intermediaries for export satisfaction and it can firmly imply that export intermediaries' resources like, relation assets, marketing capabilities and experience assets are quite closely related to export satisfaction.

To state the matter differently, we can say that the hypothesized relationship (positive) between each networking variable and export satisfaction was confirmed by the data. Hence, it is impossible to reject H2, H2.1, H2.2 and H2.3, which are supported accordingly.

However, between three variables, experience assets have the strongest correlation with export satisfaction, following with marketing capability and relation assets. Relation assets have the less correlation with export satisfaction between other two variables.

4.6.4.2 Multiple Regression Analysis

Test H2 has been tested by executing multiple regression analysis and analyses the relationship of export satisfaction with export intermediary networking. Initial results reflect the fact that all the assumptions of multiple regressions were proven.

In this study, first hypothesis is correlated to export intermediary networking of the three resources (marketing capabilities, experience assets, and relation assets) and export satisfaction. The accomplishment of the first specific aim of this research study has been proven by testing this hypothesis means it has proven the relationship of export intermediaries networking and export satisfaction.

Multiple regression analysis was applied as a testing method. The results are presented in Table 4.28.Marketing capabilities, experience assets, and relation assets are three independent variables that were entered into the regression model and account for 57 per cent of the variance (R squared) in export satisfaction. As it is shown by the F-value of 119.873 in Model Summary table, it is highly significant. Therefore, first hypothesis substantiated.

Table 4.28 : Relationship between export intermediaries networking and ES (Model Summary)

R	R^2	Adjusted R^2	Std. Error of the Estimate	F	Sig.
.761[a]	.579	.575	.674	119.873	.000[a]

a Predictors: (Constant), Marketing capabilities, Experience assets , Relation assets

b Dependent Variable: ES

The variable with the largest beta value in absolute, in analyzing the scale of the coefficients, has remarkable effect on the dependent variable (Sekaran, 2003).The strength and extent of effect of each one of the export intermediaries networking variables would have on export satisfaction was concentrated in Table 4.29.

Table 4.29 : Influence of export intermediaries networking on ES(Coefficients)

	Unstandardized Coefficients		Standardized Coefficients		
	B	Std. Error	Beta	t	Sig.
(Constant)	.996	.116		8.592	.000
Marketing capabilities	.278	.033	.383	8.515	.000
Experience assets	.246	.035	.334	7.064	.000
Relation assets	.194	.030	.281	6.397	.000

a Dependent Variable: ES

As can see from the Table 4.29, marketing capabilities has the highest number in Beta is (.383), which is significant statistically. Beta of .334 belongs to experience assets, which are the next strongest and influential variable.

.281 was the standardized Beta value of the variable of relation assets, which is significant statistically. However, relation assets have the lowest influence on export satisfaction among three other variables.

This result indicates that most of the respondents were satisfied by marketing and experience assets exchange between export intermediary and SMEs.

In the conclusion of the outcomes of the multiple regression analysis, it is deducible that the largest beta coefficient is marketing capabilities β =.383 which reflects strongest unique contribution to explain export satisfaction while relation assets β = .281 made less contribution (Table 4.29). This results demonstarte that

SMEs are not strong in experiencing assets and marketing to compensate these resources they rely on their networking with export intermediaries. The outputs of SPSS of the results of correlation and regression analysis are presented in Appendix.

4.6.5   Research Hypothesis 3 (H3)

In order to examine the relationship between IOR and export satisfaction, one hypothesis were aimed. To execute that, we examined the correlation between IOR and export satisfaction by Pearson correlation.

The relationship between IOR on export satisfaction was analyzed by applying Pearson product-moment correlation analysis. Initial analyses pointed out for having no violation of the normality assumption, linearity, and homoscedasticity. The relation between export satisfaction and IOR is discussed in this section. It was proposed that:

H3: International opportunity recognition in SMEs is positively correlated to SME's export satisfaction.

Tables 4.30 present the Pearson correlation matrix acquired for this interval-scaled variables. The result shows that IOR is positively correlated to export satisfaction in SMEs (r=.815, p<.01).

Table 4.30 : Pearson correlation between IOR and ES (H3)

		IOR	ES
IOR	Pearson Correlation	1	.815**
	Sig. (2-tailed)		.000
	N	265	265
ES	Pearson Correlation	.815**	1
	Sig. (2-tailed)	.000	
	N	265	265

**. Correlation is significant at the 0.01 level (2-tailed).

As it obvious from Table 4.30, the IOR variable were significant statistically and positively related to export satisfaction (r=.815, p<.01). It is proved that SMEs are able to have more satisfaction of their exporting by the international opportunities which recognized by export intermediaries networking.

In conclusion, of the outcome from Pearson correlation analyses of this study, we can say that the hypothesized relationship (positive) between IOR and export satisfaction was confirmed by the data. Hence, it is impossible to reject H3, which are supported accordingly.

4.6.6   Research Hypothesis 4 (H4, H4.1, H4.2, H4.3)

Three hypotheses (H4.1, H4.2, and H4.3) were proposed to analyze the mediating effect of IOR on the relationship between export intermediary networking and export satisfaction because basically there are three variables considered for export intermediaries networking.

A third variable or mediator (IOR), within a meditational framework (Holmbeck, 1997; Baron & Kenny, 1986) can account for the relationship between an independent variable and a dependent variable in a various ways. In order to test the mediation hypotheses three-step procedure was suggested by (Baron and Kenny, 1986).Based on the research of Baron and Kenny (1986), in order to support a mediating relationship maintain that the following conditions must be accomplished.

- First, there should be a significant association between the independent variable and the mediator.
- Secondly, there should be also a significant association between the independent variable and dependent variable.
- Lastly the relationship between the independent and dependent variables should significantly reduce (partial mediation), disappear (full mediation), or not change the relationship between an independent and dependent variable (no mediation) after the mediator is entered.

In this study in order to test mediation, followed online MedGraph -Iprogram software (Jose, 2008) which was suggested by Jose (2008) and Howell (2010). Mediation among three variables graphically is presented by MedGraph program.

Several research projects applied MedGraph-I for describing mediation among three variables (e.g. Weir and Jose, 2008; Kuvaas, 2009; Cabrera*et al.*, 2009; Godos-Dı'ez *et. al*, 2011). There are various advantageous to apply this particular software. These advantageous could be the ability for obtaining rapid feedback about whether a proposed mediation process has happened or not (Jose, 2008), ability to key in statistical information about covariance relationships among three variables quickly and easily, and clarify the mediation role by Baron and Kenny (1986). In addition, it clarifies the mediation role by (Baron and Kenny, 1986) and (Jose, 2003) at the same time and in one process.

Howell (2010) indicated that MedGraph created by Paul Joes is very useful and very-well written description of meditation. The steps of MedGraph–Iprogram's process are mentioned in proceeding:

First step: Under consideration, input the names of the three variables (independent, dependent and mediator Variables) in order to create the figure.

- Between the pairs of variables, input the raw correlations (Pearson)
- Input the sample size.
- Hit "submit".

Second step: Mediating variable should regressed on independent variable (In this step independent variable consider as the independent variable and mediating variable is the dependent variable).

- Should input B (unstandardized regression coefficient) and input standard error.

Third step: Outcome variable regressed on independent variable and mediating variable (In second step, outcome variable consider being the dependent variable, and that mediating variable and independent variable are considered as independent variables)

- Should input B (unstandardized regression coefficient), standard error and beta (standardized regression coefficient) of mediating variable.

Last Step: Finally input the standardized regression coefficient of independent variable or Beta and press "submit".

As the result of submitting the data, many computed outputs and figures present. Initially, display informs the user whether no, partial, or full mediation was acquired which is quit important. Afterward along with an associated p-value the Sobel's z-score is given. Following by reporting of two beta weights, which reflects the size of the direct and indirect influences of the IV on the DV. Lastly, the figure will be drawn and it should present beta weights, variable names in the proper places and asterisks indicating significance levels. The beta weights computed after the mediator has been included in the regression equation is reported by the two beta weights in parentheses (Shackman, 2005).

For testing the mediating role of IOR between three variables (marketing capabilities, experience assets and relation assets) with export satisfaction, the results of MedGraph Iprogram is analyzed, which is presented in following figures. Furthermore, the results related to the total mediating effect of the three variables on the export gratification are discussed.

4.6.6.1 The mediating effect of IOR between the relationship of marketing capability and export satisfaction (H4.1)

Measurement of mediation was executed by two regressions following the recommendations of Baron and Kenny (1986) using Medgraph (Jose, 2003).In order to test mediation, first it is required that all three variables should be significantly correlated with each other (Baron and Kenny, 1986).

In this study Marketing capabilities is significantly correlated with IOR, r=.664, p<.001; and export satisfaction, r=.603), p<.001. Besides that, IOR is correlated with export satisfaction, r= .815, p<.001. Therefore, the initial requirements (Baron and Kenny, 1986) are satisfied by this result.

Two different regressions were conducted in case that this precondition was satisfied. First of all the potential mediating variable (IOR) was returned to the independent variable (marketing capabilities). Second, the dependent variable (export satisfaction) was returned to IOR and the marketing capabilities variable.

The Sobel's z statistic was computed for each potential meditational model to recognize whether or not mediation had occurred and in case that it had happened, whether it was full or partial mediation.

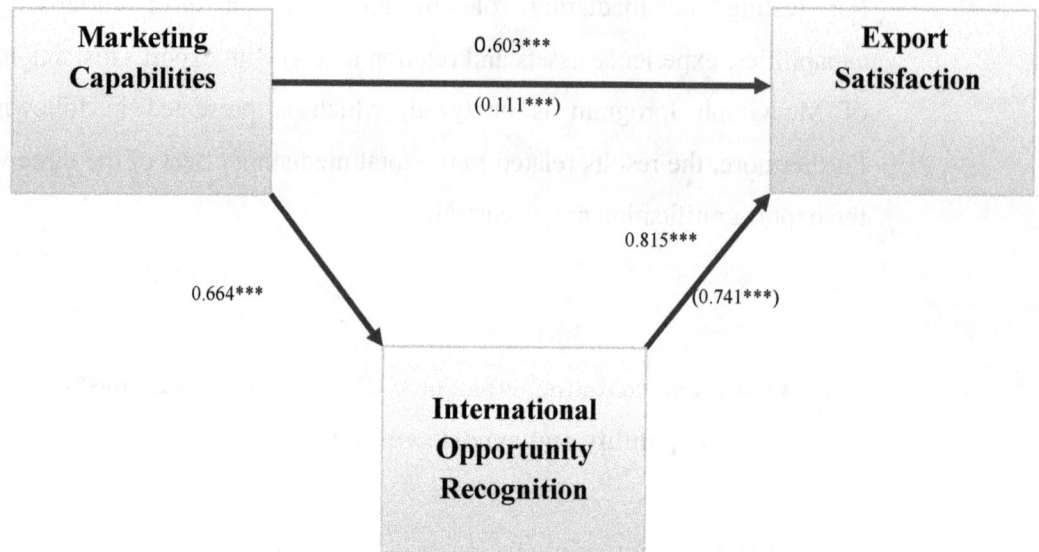

International opportunity recognition is mediated by the relationship between marketing capabilities and export satisfaction
Type of mediation:
Jose (2003): Full
Baron and Kenny (1986): Significant
Direct: .111
Indirect: .492

Figure 4.4   The mediating effect of IOR between the relationship of marketing capability and export satisfaction (H4.1)

The direct path from marketing capabilities to export satisfaction, which is presented in Figure 4.4, remained significant after IOR was included in the analysis. Although the basic relationship was significantly reduced from β=0.603 to β=0.111 (Sobel z-value = 10.66;   p<.001).Therefore, IOR significantly mediated the relationship between marketing capabilities and export satisfaction.

Furthermore the direct path (mediating path) (.111) is not stronger than, the indirect path (.492) from marketing capabilities to export satisfaction. The two beta weights in parentheses that indicate in Figure 4.4 show the beta weights after the mediator was added to the model.

4.6.6.2 The mediating effect of IOR between the relationship of experience assets and export satisfaction (H4.2)

In order to test mediation, first it is required that all three variables should be significantly correlated with each other (Baron & Kenny, 1986). Experience assets is significantly correlated with IOR r=.663, p<.001; and export satisfaction, r=.614, p<.001. Besides that, IOR is correlated with export satisfaction, r= .815, p<.001.Therefore, the initial requirements (Baron and Kenny, 1986) are satisfied by this result.

Two different regressions were conducted in case that this precondition was satisfied. First of all the potential mediating variable (IOR) was returned to the independent variable (Experience assets). Second, the dependent variable (export satisfaction) was returned to IOR and the experience assets variable.

The Sobel's z statistic was computed for each potential meditational model to recognize whether or not mediation had occurred and in case that it had happened, whether it was full or partial mediation.

The direct path from marketing capabilities to export satisfaction that is presented in Figure 4.5, remained significant after IOR was included in the analysis. Although the basic relationship was significantly reduced from β=0.614 to β=0.132 (Sobel z-value= 10.47; p<.001). Therefore, IOR partially mediated the relationship between experience assets and export satisfaction.

Furthermore the direct path (mediating path) (.132) is not stronger than, the indirect path (.482) from experience assets to export satisfaction. The two beta weights in parentheses that indicate in Figure 4.5 show the beta weights after the mediator was added to the model.

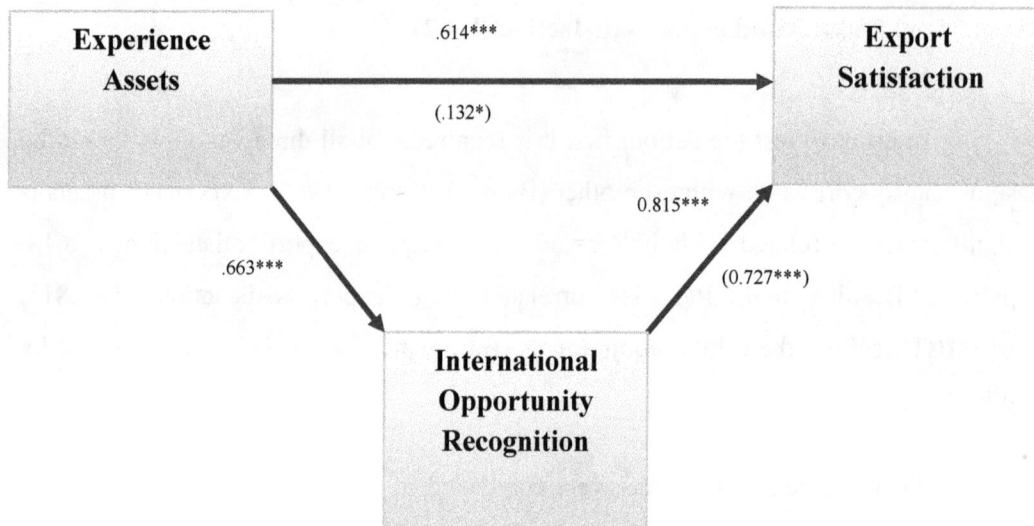

International opportunity recognition is mediated by the relationship between
experience assets and export satisfaction
Type of mediation:
Jose (2003): Partial
Baron and Kenny (1986): Significant
Direct:0.132
Indirect: 0.482

Figure 4.5   The mediating effect of IOR between the relationship of experience
assets and export satisfaction (H4.2)

4.6.6.3 The mediating effect of IOR between the relationship of relation assets and export satisfaction (H4.3)

In order to test mediation, first it is required that all three variables should be significantly correlated with each other (Baron & Kenny, 1986). Relation assets is significantly correlated with IOR, r=.539, p<.001; and export satisfaction, r=.511, p<.001.Besides that, IOR is correlated with export satisfaction, r= .815, p<.001.

Therefore, the initial requirements (Baron and Kenny, 1986) are satisfied by this result.

Two different regressions were conducted in case that this precondition was satisfied. First of all the potential mediating variable (IOR) was returned to the independent variable (Relation assets). Second, the dependent variable (export satisfaction) was returned to IOR and the relation assets variable.

The Sobel's z statistic was computed for each potential meditational model to recognize whether or not mediation had occurred and in case that it had happened, whether it was full or partial mediation.

The direct path from relation assets to export satisfaction, which is presented in Figure 4.6, remained significant after IOR was included in the analysis. Although the basic relationship was significantly reduced from β=.511 to β=.101 (Sobel z-value=11.20; p<.001).Therefore, IOR significantly mediated the relationship between relation assets and export satisfaction.

Furthermore the direct path (mediating path) (.101) is not stronger than, the indirect path (.41) from relation assets to export satisfaction. The two beta weights in parentheses that indicate in Figure 4.6 show the beta weights after the mediator was added to the model.

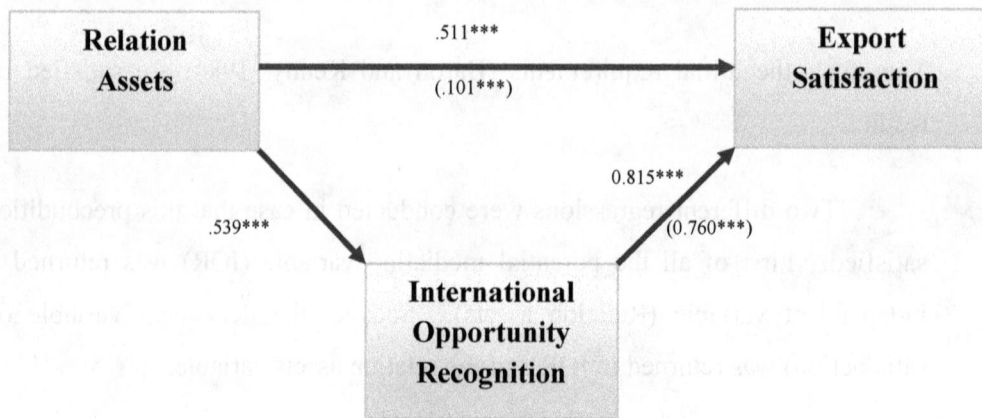

International opportunity recognition is mediated by the relationship between
relation assets and export satisfaction
Type of mediation:
Jose (2003): Full
Baron and Kenny (1986): Significant
Direct: 0. 101
Indirect: 0. 41

Figure 4.6   The mediating effect of IOR between the relationship of relation
assets and export satisfaction (H4.3)

4.6.6.4 The mediating effect of IOR between the relationship of export
intermediaries networking and export satisfaction (H4)

Hypothesis (H4) was applied to test the total mediating effect of the three
variables (marketing capabilities, experience assets and relation assets) on the export
satisfaction. A third variable or mediator (IOR), within a meditational framework
(Holmbeck, 1997; Baron and Kenny, 1986) can account for the relationship between
an independent variable and a dependent variable in a various ways.

In order to test mediation, first it is required that all three variables should be
significantly correlated with each other (Baron and Kenny, 1986). Export
intermediary networking is significantly correlated IOR, $r=.818$, $p<.001$; and export
satisfaction, $r=.758$, $p<.001$.Besides that, IOR is correlated with export satisfaction,

r= .815, p<.001.Therefore, the initial requirements (Baron and Kenny, 1986) are satisfied by this result.

Two different regressions were conducted in case that this precondition was satisfied. First of all the potential mediating variable (IOR) was returned to the independent variable (Export intermediary networking). Second, the dependent variable (export satisfaction) was returned to IOR and the export intermediary networkingvariable.

The Sobel's z statistic was computed for each potential meditational model to recognize whether or not mediation had occurred and in case that it had happened, whether it was full or partial mediation.

The direct path from export intermediary networking to export satisfaction which is presented in Figure 4.7, remained significant after IOR was included in the analysis. Although the basic relationship was significantly reduced from β=.758 to β=.277 (Sobel z-value = 8.99; p<.001).Therefore, IOR partially mediated the relationship between networking and export satisfaction.

Furthermore the direct path (mediating path) (.277) is not stronger than, the indirect path (.481) from export intermediary networking to export satisfaction. The two beta weights in parentheses that indicate in Figure 4.7 show the beta weights after the mediator was added to the model.

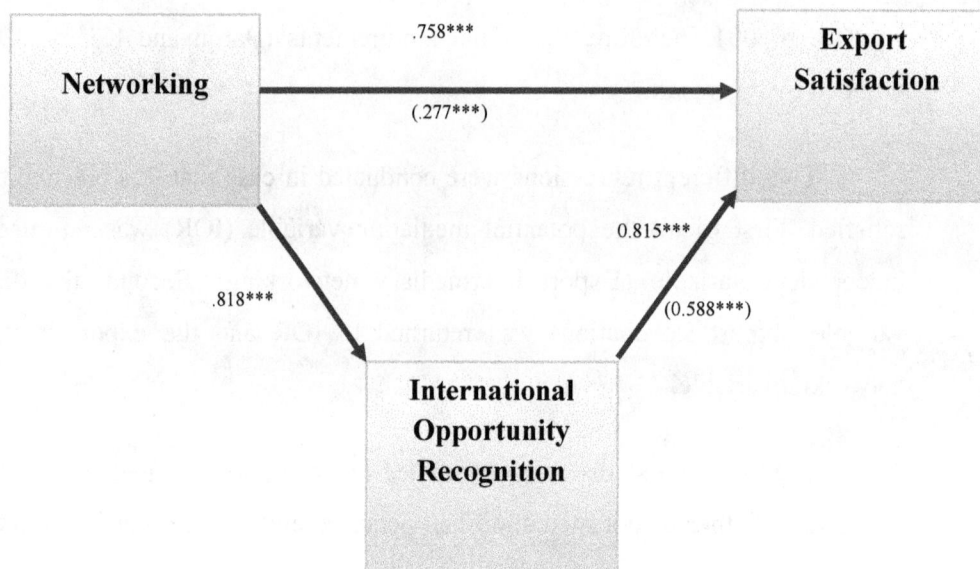

International opportunity recognition is mediated by the relationship between networking and export satisfaction
Type of mediation:
Jose (2003): Partial
Baron & Kenny (1986): Significant
Direct: .277
Indirect: .481

Figure 4.7   The mediating effect of IOR between the relationship of export intermediaries networking and export satisfaction (H4)

4.7   Conclusion

The aim of this chapter was to explore the 10 research questions among the manufacturer SMEs in Malaysia. The first objective examined whether there is any correlation between export intermediary networking and international opportunities recognition and the second objective examined whether there is any correlation between export intermediary networking and export satisfaction. To address these two objectives, Pearson coefficient correlation and multiple regression analysis were performed.   In addition, the third objective was tested by Pearson coefficient correlation to determine whether there is any correlation among international opportunity recognition and export satisfaction.

Furthermore, the forth objective investigated the mediating effect of international opportunity recognition on the relationship between networking and export satisfaction. To answer this objective, path analysis for mediation by Med-Graph online software was conducted. Preliminary analyses carried out confirmed that the assumptions underlying each test employed in this study were not violated.

The findings showed that marketing capabilities, experience assets, relation assets and finally export intermediaries networking have positive correlation with international opportunity recognition and export satisfaction. In addition, international opportunity recognition was found to have a high positive significant correlation with export satisfaction.

The results also, showed that international opportunity recognition was mediating significantly the relationship of marketing capability and relation assets with export satisfaction.   In addition, international opportunity recognition was mediating partially the relationship of experience assets and networking with export satisfaction.

Results of the study pointed out that, 67 percent of the variance in IOR has been significantly explained by the networking. Furthermore, 57 percent of the variance in export satisfaction has been significantly explained by the networking.

Table 4.31 summarizes the results of propositions and hypothesis testing that has been conducted in Chapter four. As can see from the table, all of the propositions tested were supported.

Table 4.31 : Results of tasting all of the researches' hypothesis

Hypotheses	Description	Results
H1	Export intermediary networking by SMEs has relationship with international opportunity recognition in SMEs.	Supported
H1.1	Marketing capabilities exchanges between Export intermediary and SMEs is positively correlated to international opportunity recognition in SMEs.	Supported
H1.2	Experience assets exchanges between Export intermediary and SMEs is positively correlated to international opportunity recognition in SMEs.	Supported
H1.3	Relation assets exchanges between Export intermediary and SMEs is positively correlated to international opportunity recognition in SMEs.	Supported
H2	Export intermediary networking by SMEs has relationship with export satisfaction in SMEs.	Supported
H2.1	Marketing capabilities exchanges between Export intermediary and SMEs is positively correlated to export satisfaction in SMEs.	Supported
H2.2	Experience assets exchanges between Export intermediary and SMEs is positively correlated to export satisfaction in SMEs.	Supported

H2.3	Relation assets exchanges between Export intermediary and SMEs is positively correlated to export satisfaction in SMEs.	Supported
H3	International opportunity recognition in SMEs is positively correlated to SME's export satisfaction	Supported
H4	There is a mediating effect of international opportunity recognition on the relationship between export intermediary networking and export satisfaction.	Supported
H4.1	There is a mediating effect of international opportunity recognition on the relationship between marketing capabilities and export satisfaction.	Supported
H4.2	There is a mediating effect of international opportunity recognition on the relationship between experience assets and export satisfaction.	Supported
H4.3	There is a mediating effect of international opportunity recognition on the relationship between relation assets and export satisfaction.	Supported

CHAPTER 5

DISCUSSION AND CONCLUSION

5.1   Introduction

This study adopts the network-based view derived from International Entrepreneurship (IE) literature and examines its applicability to international opportunity recognition. Findings are obtained from manufacturers, which had export in the context of Malaysian SMEs and support the importance of network-based view in explaining international opportunity recognition. The outcomes substantiate the empirical link between export intermediaries' resources exchanges (marketing capabilities, experience assets, and relation assets) between export intermediary and SMEs on international opportunity recognition and export satisfaction. Thus, the findings of this research expand the IE literatures, respond to calls for more research on international opportunity recognition as well as provide useful managerial application to export managers of Malaysian manufacturers SMEs and their intermediaries having business network to exchange the resources for international markets. Moreover, study contributes to export literatures by investigating the network-based theory.

The organization of this chapter is as follows: 5.2) Major findings and discussion, 5.3) Theoretical contributions, 5.4) Managerial implication, 5.5) Limitations of the present study, 5.6) Implications for future research and 5.7) Conclusion.

5.2   Major Findings and Discussion

The findings suggest that the relationship among SMEs and export intermediaries cause to compensate the resources scarcities in SMEs. Marketing capability, experience assets and relation assets resources in export intermediaries play a significant role in IOR and export satisfaction in SMEs. Marketing capability has found as the most significant resources in export intermediaries, which lead SMEs to find more opportunities in international markets. Findings from the revised model were discussed in detail in the following sections.

5.2.1   Respondent and Firm's Background finding

The findings from descriptive analysis provide the general characteristics of manufacturer exporting SMEs in Malaysia. The result of respondent's background showed that Majority of managers were male and Chinese. The results also indicate that their ages were between 31 to 40 years old with holding bachelor and master degree with 1 to 10 years experience. The descriptive analysis of the respondent's background provides the general characteristics of exporting SMEs owners and managers in Malaysia. The results showed that most of managers in Malaysian exporting SMEs, which, were using export intermediary for their exporting are male, Chinese, young, less experienced and holding bachelor and Diploma degree. That means young owner and managers with less experience need some special support like an incubator system to get in track of the international markets.

The results of the firm's background provided the age, size, level of export experience, the percentage of export sales and sales agreements with foreign customers, product category of product export venture, countries most exported to, market entry distribution most used, type of the product category exported and the number of countries exported to, which gives a general idea on demographic characteristics of exporting manufacturer SMEs.

The results showed that majority of firms were new established between 6 to 10 years old and were small firms, which had 5 to 50 employees with 6 to 10 years exporting experience. Regarding the percentage of firm's total export sales and firm's total sales agreement with foreign customers the results showed that most of SMEs achieved 21% to 40 % their total export sales and total sales agreement through export intermediary.

Results also showed that majority of SMEs were pharmaceutical and medical equipment producer that were most exported to Southeast Asia. Government agency as most export intermediary introduced by Malaysian SMEs.

The results showed that most of product type of SMEs was business products that are exporting to 6 to 10 countries.

Therefore, the above findings indicate that most of Malaysian manufacturers SMEs which are using export intermediary for their exporting are young, small, less exporting experience, which introduced government agency as their export intermediary to find international opportunity.

These results surprisingly revealed that low individuals (such as their age, experience) and firms characteristics (such as age, size, and experience) in SMEs force them to rely on export intermediaries. Figure 5.1 is a matrix, which, is developed based on the relationship between individual and firms characteristics on using export intermediaries. This matrix shows that SMEs, which were younger in their age smaller in their company, size and had less experience in international market, prefer to rely on export intermediaries for IOR. By acquiring more experience, knowledge and developing global networks, they would be able to attend directly in international markets and their dependence on export intermediary will be lower. On the other words, young SMEs need some special support like an incubator system to get in track of the international markets.

Figure 5.1   Matrix of relationship between individual and
firms characteristics and using export intermediary

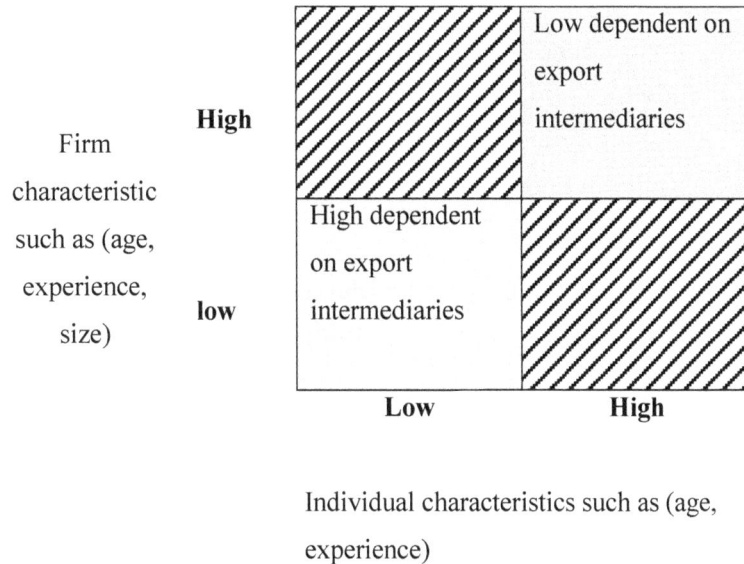

In addition, Malaysian SMEs are using four types of export intermediaries for IOR in order to compensate their resources scarcities and limitations. This four types export intermediaries comprises of 1. Government agency; 2. Foreign intermediary based in foreign market; 3. Malaysian private intermediary based in Malaysia; and finally 4. Foreign private intermediary based in Malaysia. The results indicated that government agencies were the most important intermediary for their IOR. Followed by foreign intermediary in foreign countries and Malaysian private intermediary has been known as the second and third important intermediary to IOR respectively. Figure 5.2 shows the types of export intermediaries used in Malaysian SMEs according to their priority from the most to least.

Figure 5.2   Types of export intermediaries used in
Malaysian SMEs according to their priority from the
most to least.

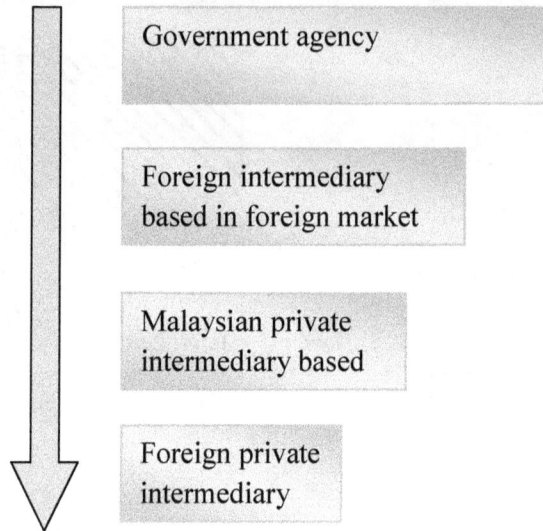

These results show that the Malaysian government programs for SMEs assistance had been effective. These programs motivate SMEs' and young managers to move toward international markets through intermediaries. However, still there is a significant difference between SMEs' share in national exports and GDP. Moreover, they need more incentive and promoting programs in order to increase their export and improve their situation in the global market.

5.2.2 The relation between export intermediary networking and international opportunity recognition (Q1& H1)

A significant contribution of present study is the advancement of the Network-Based View (NBV) within International Entrepreneurship (IE) literature and International Opportunity Recognition (IOR). It was found that there is a significant relationship between export intermediary networking and international opportunity recognition in SMEs. Export intermediaries' resources including marketing capability, experience assets, and relation assets help SMEs to recognize more opportunities in international markets.

Many researches about IE have argued that involvement in business and social networks by entrepreneurs will affect the opportunity recognition and that is the reason how some people realize and exploit opportunities in international markets (e.g. Arenius and DeClercq, 2005; Ellis, 2011; Loane and Bell, 2006; Oviatt and McDougall, 2005; Rutashabya and Jaensson, 2004). Ellis, 2010 and Welch *et al.,* (1971), support stressing the importance of networks in international opportunity recognition and exporting.

In addition, the results illustrated that SMEs with their networking are able to acquire resources for internationalization which is conducted by a number of studies which have initiated that firms are able to achieve resources through their relationships and networking (e.g Zain and Ng, 2006; Chetty *et al.,*2003; Johanson and Vahlne, 1990; Hadjikhani, 1997). In addition, this finding is supported by Johanson and Mattsson, 1988; Kontinen and Ojala, 2010, which indicated that establishing new network or developing the position in the existing network help SMEs to compensate resource scarcities. This finding also is supported by other studies such as (Rutashobya and Jaensson, 2004) which stated, small firms might have to rely on networks to overcome their isolation in the current international market. In addition, this study is supported by Ellis (2003) that indicated SMEs are able to compensate their weakness and recognize the international opportunities by suitable network and potential exchange partner.

The results also reflected the fact that SMEs with their relation with export intermediary are able to acquire resources that they lack such as marketing capability, experience assets, and relation assets. This finding is supported by Theingi (2008), which showed that these three resources of export intermediaries are the intangible resources that SMEs need them for going to international markets and they rely on export intermediaries to acquire them. The relation between SMEs and export intermediary for exchanging resources is supported by other studies such as (Day, 1994; Theingi, 2008; Sharma and Blomstermo, 2003).

In addition, this study found that export intermediaries networking by SMEs lead them to recognize more international opportunity, which is conducted by the study of Gulati et al., (2000) that initiated these relationships, can provide opportunities for the firm.

Moreover, this study found that export intermediaries networking is the important factor for international opportunity recognition between Malaysian SMEs, which is conducted by the study of Senik et al., 2010 that showed networking, or a relationship in Malaysian SMEs is the most important factor for their internationalization process. Also, Hashim and Hassan (2008) agree that networking is crucial for Malaysian SMEs to expand to foreign markets (Senik et al., 2010).

However previous studies have found the relationship between networking and international opportunity recognition, networking and acquire resources, networking and compensate resources for internationalization which were mostly focused on social and business networks. Nevertheless, this study present new kind of networking that is important for SMEs, which wish to move to international markets. This kind of networking introduced with the name of "export intermediary networking" in the present study.

The previous studies about the relationship between SMEs and export intermediaries have focused on different theories such as "Resources dependency theory", "Transaction cost theory", Agency theory", "Institutional theory", "Hole theory", while these days internationalization is fundamentally affected by networking and relationship. Thus, this study examined the networking theory for explaining the relationship between SMEs and export intermediary. Furthermore, current study has found aforementioned relationship as the important factor for international opportunity recognition base on network theory.

5.2.2.1 The relation between marketing capabilities and international opportunity recognition (H1.1)

The findings indicate that marketing capabilities in export intermediary such as effective promotional activities, advertising expenditure, high quality of customer service, strong distribution networks, high quality sales person, effective market research, serving different market segments and ability to introduce the new products quickly, have a positive correlation on IOR in SMEs.

Without marketing capabilities and necessary understanding of export markets, it will be very difficult for firms to identify international opportunities and engage in exporting directly. Since majority of SMEs are young and they are suffering from internal resources such as marketing capabilities, they are able to survive themselves in foreign markets by the marketing capabilities of export intermediary. This result is consistent with prior studies which were conducted many firms pick export intermediaries for their exporting activities and making indirect link between themselves and foreign customers (Ellis, 2010;Ellis, 2001; Balabanis, 2000; Bello et al., 1991; Bello and Williamson, 1985). In addition, Thaingi (2008) in the study of Thailand SMEs showed that marketing is one of the significant resources in export intermediaries.

Therefore, SMEs are able to compensate their marketing capabilities' scarcities by their relation with export intermediaries. Result of this study unveiled the marketing capabilities in compare with experience assets and relation assets, is relatively most important export intermediaries' resource for recognizing international opportunities in SMES.

5.2.2.2 The relation between experience assets and international opportunity recognition (H1.2)

The results found that experience and knowledge assets in export intermediary such as knowledgeable about the requirements of potential customers, overall good experience with respect to the market, adequate experience to sell the products, and supply of market information have a significant positive correlation on IOR in SMEs.

Without experience, knowledge and information making decisions is not easy for entrepreneurs and firm will fail in the market (Baron, 1998; Zahra et al, 2005). Also without experience assets, it will be very difficult for firms to compete in competitive environments. This result is conducted with previous studies (e.g. Zahra et al., 2005; Venkataraman, 1997; Shane and Venkataraman, 2000; Chandra and Styles, 2009; Shepherd and Detienne; 2001) that experience and relevant prior knowledge of entrepreneurs leads them to meet and investigate certain types of information rapidly and recognize opportunities. Ardichivili et al., (2003); Shane, (2000); Park, (2005) indicated that knowledge and experience of the firm are widely recognized in the literature as common and important factors of the opportunity identification process.

In addition, the result, which is obtained from Malaysian SMEs, is consistent with the study of Abdullah (1999) that showed owners who are more experienced achieve higher performance in terms of profit, capital and employment the study of 51 entrepreneurs in SMEs in Kuala Lumpur.

Furthermore, this finding is inconsistent with Shankar (2010) that indicated there is no significant relationship between international knowledge and experience with internationalization in Malaysian SMEs. Moreover, finding of Eriksson et al., (1997) showed that there is no direct effect of the lack of international knowledge on internationalization.

Also Theingi (2008) has found that export intermediaries have important role in introducing experience assets such as knowledge about the requirements of potential customers, overall good experience with respect to the market, adequate experience to sell the products, and supply of market information.

Therefore, this result of study confirmed that SMEs are able to compensate their knowledge and experience scarcities by their relation with export intermediaries. It seems that experience assets compared to the other two firm resources in this study (marketing capabilities, and relation assets), is relatively less important resource for recognizing international opportunities in SMEs.

5.2.2.3 The relation between relation assets and international opportunity recognition (H1.3)

The results also indicated that relation assets capabilities in export intermediaries such as trust and fairness, keeps the promise, helpfulness, positive attitude, long-term relationship, good communication and good reputation, with customers have a positive and significant relationship with IOR in SMEs.

As Etemad (2008) indicated that these days, the interaction between the buyer and the product is deemed to change to the importance of relationship between buyer and seller. Today's, internationalization is a function of multi-polar networks involving special relationship between buyers and sellers (Etemad, 2008). Huge literature suggested that relationship leads SMEs to IOR. This result is consistent with the study of Rutashobya and Jaensson (2004), which have found that the relationship with customers, facilitate IOR.

The significant role of the relationship between supplier and customers on internationalization have examined by previous studies such as (Bradley *et al.,* 2006; Leavy, 1990; Fawcett and Birou, 1992; Holland *et al.,* 1992; Monczka and Carter, 1988; Kalwani and Narayandas, 1995; Paliwoda and Bonaccorsi, 1994; Schonberger, 1986; O'Neal and Bertrand, 1991; Kalwani and Narayandas, 1995; Johanson and Mattsson, 1988; Chetty and Holm, 2000; Majkgard and Sharma, 1998).

Because most of SMEs are young in the markets and they do not know customers in foreign markets and have not networking or relationship with them, therefore they might pay more attention to export intermediaries' relation assets in knowing customer and utilizing IOR. Therefore, this result of study confirmed that SMEs are able to compensate their relation assets scarcities by their relation with export intermediaries. It seems that relation assets compared to the other two firm resources in this study (marketing capabilities, and relation assets), is relatively less important resource for recognizing international opportunities in SMEs.

In conclusion, this study found the positive correlation between all three resources including; marketing capabilities, experience assets, and relation assets with IOR. Marketing capability compared to experience assets, and relation assets consistently contribute more to IOR. This finding implies that exporting SMEs should invest in developing their networking with intermediaries to access resources specially marketing capabilities rather than solely relying on their capabilities. If they just rely on their own resources, they would not tolerate the uncertainties and risks of overseas markets and they would fail in international market (Acs and Preston, 1997).

SMEs with developing their networking with export intermediaries will understand foreign market conditions and implement export marketing activities effectively and efficiently and identify more opportunities in international markets. Hence, the empirical finding on the relative importance of export intermediary networking to access marketing capability, experience assets, and relation assets for IOR is an important contribution of the study.

5.2.3 The relation between export intermediaries networking and export satisfaction (Q2& H2)

This study makes a significant contribution regarding the effects of export intermediary networking on export satisfaction in SMEs. The findings showed that export intermediary networking appears to have a significant and positive relationship with export satisfaction. This finding supports previous study conducted by (Aldrich *et al.,* 1987; Blundel, 2002; Cell and Baines, 2000; Hillebrand and Biemans, 2003; Ambler *et al.,* 1999; Ling-yee and Ogunmokun, 2001) which, support the empirical link between effective networks and firm export performance and conducted by (Birley, 1985; Larson, 1992) which, indicated the beneficial effects of networking activity.

Developing networking with export intermediaries by SMEs, help them to acquire resources (marketing capabilities, experience assets and relation assets) for export activities. Many studies about exporting have revealed that resources have the essential role in export performance and internationalization (e.g. Zou and Stan, 1998; Leonidou *et al.,* 2002) and between firm resources and export performance there is a straight relationship (Bloodgood *et al.,* 1996; Morgan *et al.,* 2004; Wilkinson and Brouthers, 2006; Yang *et al.,* 1992). However, the resource limitations of SMEs force them to rely on their networking with other individuals or firms to compensate their resource scarcities. This study, found that export intermediaries networking as a kind of networking help SMEs to improve their export performance.

In addition, this result is consistent by the study of (Rabino, 1980; Zacharakis, 1997; Wilkinson and Brouthers, 2006) which, the relationship between SMEs and export intermediaries lead to higher export performance, profitability, productivity and firm satisfaction (Terjesen *et al.,* 2006; Rabino, 1980; Zacharakis, 1997; Wilkinson and Brouthers, 2006).

Applying of intermediaries has been argued in order to achieve a higher international performance in the entrepreneurial context (Rabino, 1980; Shepherd and Zacharakis, 1997) and network cooperation between exporters and export intermediaries is considered very important (Ling-yee and Ogunmokun, 2001) due to the resources exchange. SMEs through intermediaries can improve their profitability and productivity. Wilkinson and Brouthers (2006) stated that using services of export intermediaries is positively associated with export performance (Wilkinson and Brouthers, 2006).

Hence, in order to achieve full potential, exporters must pay special attention to the unique competencies of intermediaries (Ling-yee and Ogunmokun, 2001) and SMEs should develop their networking with export intermediaries to acquire necessary resources to success in exporting due to their lackness. The clear implication here is that managers must support a relationship management strategy, since it is a critical determinant of export success.

5.2.3.1 The relation between marketing capabilities and export satisfaction (H2.1)

The findings indicate that marketing capabilities in export intermediary such as high quality of customer service, strong distribution networks, effective promotional activities, advertising expenditure, high quality sales person, effective market research, serving different market segments and ability to introduce the new products quickly, have a positive correlation on export satisfaction in SMEs.

The result is consistent with previous empirical studies (Katsikeas *et al.*, 1996; Pope and Ralph, 2002; Wang and Olsen, 2002) which were conducted that marketing capability has a positive influence on strategic export performance. Without marketing capabilities and necessary understanding of export markets, it will be very difficult for firms to survive in today's uncertain and intense competitive environments (Theingi, 2008). In addition, the result is consistent with previous empirical studies, which were conducted that marketing capability was found to be directly responsible for export profitability (Pope and Ralph, 2002; Wang, 2002) and successful export business operation (Constantine*et al.*, 1996). Moreover, previous studies support that; marketing knowledge, promotional efforts and assessment of export market developments have a positive correlation with export performance (Constantine*et al.*, 1996; Katsikeas *et al.*, 1996).

Moreover, the literature of export activities suggests in the marketing of many manufacturers, export intermediaries play an important role (Munro and Beamish, 1987; Rosson and Ford, 1982; Theingi, 2008). Therefore, SMEs are able to acquire marketing capabilities by developing their networking with export intermediaries due to the lack of marketing capabilities. It seems that marketing capabilities compared to the other two export intermediaries resources in this study (experience assets, and relation assets), is relatively most important export intermediaries' resource for export satisfaction.

5.2.3.2 The relation between experience assets and export satisfaction (H2.2)

The results found that export experience and knowledge as a firm's intangible resources such as knowledgeable about the requirements of potential customers, overall good experience with respect to the market, adequate experience to sell the products, and supply of market information have a significant positive correlation on export satisfaction.

This finding is consistent with the study of Ling-yee and Ogunmokun, (2001) which was conducted that firms with short experience in exporting lead to export success and study of Madsen (1989) that indicated that there is positive relationship between experience in exporting and export performance.

SMEs may hire export intermediaries because they lack necessary knowledge and experience in operation in international markets. Therefore, SMEs are able to better export in foreign markets by the export intermediaries' knowledge and corporation to develop their experience assets.

5.2.3.3 The relation between relation assets and export satisfaction (H2.3)

The results found that relation assets such as, strong trust and fairness, long-term relationship, good communication, helpfulness in emergency case, positive attitude toward any complaints, good reputation, and also keeping their promise have a positive and significant relationship with export satisfaction in SMEs (r=.511).

This study found that SMEs are able to achieve export satisfaction with their relation to export intermediaries to compensate their relation assets scarcities. Export intermediaries with possessing their long-term relation with customers are able to help SMEs to move to international markets and also help customers to find manufacturer.

This finding is conducted with the study of Leonidou and Kaleka, (1998), which indicated that the relationship between buyer and seller in global markets associated to some degree with the export involvement and study of Styles and Ambler, (1994). This fact indicated that this relationship in global markets is vital to successful export activities and study of Ford (2002) that stated that business relationships are important resources for firm's development.

Therefore, export managers might pay more attention to export intermediaries' relationships assets in utilizing export satisfaction in SMEs due to the lack of relation assets in their internal firm resources.

In conclusion, all three variables including; marketing capabilities, experience assets, and relation assets, have positive correlation with export satisfaction. Marketing capabilities compared to experience assets and relation assets contribute more to export satisfaction. Therefore, the findings indicate that all export intermediaries' resources are interdependent and crucial to achieve export success that is consistent with the study of Theingi (2008).

This finding implies that exporting SMEs should invest in developing their networking with intermediaries to access resources specially marketing capabilities rather than solely relying on their capabilities. If they just rely on their own resources, they would not tolerate the uncertainties and risks of overseas markets and they would fail in international market (Acs and Preston, 1997). SMEs with developing their networking with export intermediaries will achieve resources and implement export activities effectively and efficiently. Hence, the empirical finding on the relative importance of export intermediary networking to access resources on export satisfaction is an important contribution of the study. The results showed that marketing capabilities, experience assets and relation assets are highly correlated to export satisfaction.

5.2.4 The relationship between international opportunity recognition (IOR) on export satisfaction (H3)

The findings showed that IOR appear have a high and positive correlation with export satisfaction. This finding supports previous studies such as OECD (2008) that indicated the importance of IOR in export activities and study of (Chandler and Jansen, 1992, Baum *et al.*, 2001) that indicated IOR and export performance are interlaced. This result is consistent with the study of Chandler and Jansen (1992), which indicated opportunity recognition skills are optimistically interrelated to venture performance and study of Baum *et al.*, (2001), that indicated there is relationship between opportunity recognition skills and firm's growth. In addition, Sambasivan *et al.*, (2009) stated that ability to possess opportunities recognition is highly correlated with profitability and a firm's growth.

In addition, studies in different countries emphasize on this relationship between internationalization and firm performance. For example in Singapore, has been found a positive correlation between them (Pangarkar, 2008). In India, they recognized that there is a U-shaped relation between firm internationalization and performance (Contractor, 2007). In addition, it was implied that those firms that go earlier to international markets benefit more in terms of performance (Contractor, 2007).

Furthermore, international opportunity recognition has been recognized as the main factor to be successful in IE studies by several researchers (e.g. Zahra *et al.*, 2005; Leonidou*et al.*, 2002; Shaw and Darroch, 2004; Dimitratos and Jones, 2005; Julien and Ramangalahy, 2003). The relation between IOR and export performance in the literature is well established and SMEs with recognizing more international opportunities could increase their performance. IOR and firm performance are related; however, previous studies did not investigate the relationship between international opportunities which recognized by export intermediaries and export satisfaction. Therefore, this study found this relation as the positive relationship and this is the important contribution of this study in strategic management and IE fields.

5.2.5 International opportunity recognition mediate the relationship between export intermediaries networking and export satisfaction (H4)

This study makes a significant contribution regarding the IOR as the mediate factor between export intermediary networking and export satisfaction in SMEs. It is not surprising, as the sample, firms are manufacturing exporters and IOR has highly correlation with networking and export satisfaction.

However, opportunity recognition in entrepreneurship research with influence of mediating has been considered in only very few studies. Some of this few researches include, the study of Sambasivan *et al.*, (2009) which shows that the mediating affect of opportunity recognition skills as the mediator between the qualities skills and venture performance. Also in another study, Kickul and Walters (2002) pointed to the role of opportunity recognition skills as a mediator between strategic orientation of the entrepreneurial firm and e-commerce innovations in Internet companies. Butler *et al.* (2003) have examined that opportunity recognition has mediated the relationship between social and business network, and performance.

Therefore, this study found a significant contribution of the mediating role of IOR between the relationship of networking and export. This base relationship between export intermediary networking and export satisfaction is affected by the degree of international opportunity recognition.

Furthermore, the findings indicate that IOR mediate the relation between marketing capabilities and export satisfaction in SMEs. The results also indicate that IOR mediate the experience assets in export intermediary and export satisfaction. Moreover, IOR mediate the relation assets and export satisfaction.

5.3   Theoretical Contributions

5.3.1   Application of network-based view (RBV)

Based on the background of export intermediary networking and research on international opportunity recognition, current study contributes to the network theory. Of course wideness of this topic requires more research on international opportunity recognition (Oviatt and McDougall, 2005; Zahra *et al.,* 2005; Ellis, 2011; Dimitratos and Jones, 2005). Also significance of the correlation between networking and opportunities recognition for internationalization requires further studies (Singh, 2000; Ellis, 2011, 2000). This study is an effort to extend the network theory of internationalization by indicating that expert intermediary networking has a vital role in the international opportunity recognition of SMEs in order to compensate resources scarcities.

Current study contributes to the IE literatures and examines network theory and its applicability to international opportunity recognition. This study also respond to calls for more research on international opportunity recognition (Dimitratos and Jones, 2005; Ellis, 2011; Oviatt and McDougall, 2005; Zahra *et al.,* 2005, Kontinen and Ojala, 2010).

As discussed in Chapter II, International Opportunity Recognition (IOR) is the first and most significant step in SMEs internationalization while it is one of the important barriers for moving to international market (OECD, 2008).   Many researchers have argued upon IE and its contribution in business and social networks by entrepreneurs will affect the opportunity recognition (Aldrich and Zimmer, 1986; Arenius and DeClercq, 2005; Johanson and Mattson, 1988; Coviello and Munro, 1997; Loane and Bell, 2006; Meyer and Shak, 2002; Ellis, 2011; Oviatt and McDougall, 2005; Rutashabya and Jaensson, 2004; Singh, 2000). Previous studies have focused on the role of individuals and firms characteristics and they ignored the role of external factors (Arenius and DeClercq, 2005; Hessels and Terjesen, 2010; Terjesen and Hessels, 2007), but recent evidences show that firms' internationalization is facilitated and influenced by its relationships with others in its network. Therefore, the focus of studies on individuals and firms characteristics has changed to the focus on relationships and networks (Etemad and Wright, 2008) because opportunity identification is fundamentally affected by network structure (Ellis, 2011). SMEs suffer from the individual's cognitive limitation and weakness in the firm's resources for IOR and move to international market (Vandekerckhove and Dentchev, 2005).

Hence, this study contributes on important step toward verifying the vital effect of networking between firms and export intermediaries to compensate the resources scarcities for IOR. This study has revealed that intermediaries can perform an important function by linking SMEs and customers in the host country and gain advantages over direct exchange in a number of ways by their marketing, experience assets and relation assets that otherwise would not have been connected. Previous studies about the relationship between SMEs and export intermediary have focused on transactional cost theory (e.g. Karunaratna and Johnson, 1997; Peng and Ilinitch, 1998; Lau, 2008), institutional theory (e.g. DiMaggio and Powell, 1983), agency theory (for example, Karunaratna and Johnson, 1997) and resource dependency theory. While internationalization is fundamentally affected by relationship and networks, so this study applied network theory for explaining the relationship between SMEs and export intermediaries for exchanging resources to recognize international opportunities and export satisfaction.

These empirical findings on firm and export intermediary resources substantiate a unique contribution to IE literature. The practical application of NBV in IE literature has been highlighted by revealing the direct relationship between export intermediary networking with IOR and export satisfaction. In addition, the empirical findings of this research also further the understanding of NBV to exchange the resources for internationalization. The results help in the development of a networking theory, which considered as a new approach in IE literature.

The study also confirms that export managers prefer to use export intermediary for IOR because they are new and not familiar with foreign market and they lack required resources to internationalization.

5.3.2 Contribution to SME research in Southeast Asia

Since most of the research on SMEs within the area of International Entrepreneurship (IE) is in west and very little attention has done to the Southeast Asia such as Malaysia, therefore the findings from this research provide a unique contribution to SME research in developing economies like Malaysia. Based on the fact that majority number of respondents of this study were Chinese, the networking and relational orientation were found high correlation to IOR and export satisfaction. This result is conducted by the study of Ling-yee and Ogunmkun (2001) that stated China compared with US has the higher level of relational orientation. In addition, Senik *et al.* (2010) showed that networking is the most important factor for Malaysian SMEs internationalization.

The findings from descriptive analysis provide the general characteristics of manufacturer exporting SMEs in Malaysia. These results surprisingly revealed that low individuals and firms characteristics in SMEs force them to rely on export intermediaries. For example, SMEs that were younger in their age, smaller in their company size, and had less experience in international market, prefer to rely on export intermediaries for IOR. By acquiring more experience, knowledge and developing global networks, they would be able to attend directly in international markets.

In addition, Malaysian SMEs are using four types of export intermediaries for IOR in order to compensate their resources scarcities and limitations. These four types export intermediaries comprises of 1.Government agency; 2.Foreign intermediary based in foreign market; 3.Malaysian private intermediary based in Malaysia; and finally 4.Foreign private intermediary based in Malaysia. The results indicated that government agencies were the most important intermediary for their IOR. Followed by foreign intermediary in foreign countries and Malaysian private intermediary has been known as the second and third important intermediary to IOR respectively.

The empirical findings offer a comprehensive image of the importance of export intermediary networking in recognizing international opportunities in

Malaysian SMEs. The study emphasizes that Malaysian manufacturer SMEs should pay special attention to employing intermediaries, which enrich in marketing capabilities, experience assets as well as relation assets and broadening their products. These findings are particularly important for resource-constrained SMEs, as they need to focus on developing resources and capabilities, which influence their IOR and export satisfaction. Thus, this research provides a significant contribution to the sparse body of international entrepreneurship literature on Malaysian SMEs by enhancing the understanding of the characteristics of successful manufacturer SMEs to recognize more opportunities in foreign markets.

5.4 Managerial Implication

5.4.1 Implications for SMEs export managers

From a managerial point of view, SMEs managers with limited resources should concentrate on actively looking for networking with export intermediary that will provide them with novel resources on international opportunities and export satisfaction. The clear implication for managers is that they must support a relationship management strategy. Managers should pay special attention to the role of export intermediary to compensate their resources scarcities, since resources are the most important factors for internationalization.

This study indicates that export intermediary networking is an effective relationship between SMEs and export intermediary, which found as a critical and significant key factor for achieving IOR and export success. The results suggest that marketing capabilities followed by relation assets and experience assets of export intermediary play as the important factors to achieve IOR and export satisfaction.

The findings help to further understand and stress the importance of export intermediary networking to compensate SMEs resources including; marketing capabilities, experience assets, and relation assets. Managers should select export intermediaries that have adequate resources for internationalization specially marketing capabilities, since it was found as the most important resources in export intermediary to IOR and export satisfaction. Thus, it would be unwise for export managers to consider establishing their own integrated channels and rely on their own resources and eliminating export intermediaries if they have no potential substitute for export intermediary resources.

This study also has implication for export intermediary managers. This study suggests that export intermediary should try to improve their marking capability, market knowledge and experience, and their relation with customers because manufacturers are likely to continue using services from export intermediaries for compensating resources scarcities and going to international markets. SMEs manufacturers mostly look for some intermediary that are strong in these intangible resources. Intermediary with these resources can make big differences in international opportunity recognition and export satisfaction. These intangible resources are difficult to replace. Consequently, intermediaries stand to gain high bargaining power against exporters.

5.4.2   Implication for Policy Makers and Malaysian Government

The results of this study provide some directions for Malaysian government on how to help Malaysian SMEs in order to recognize more opportunities in international markets. There are at least 18 local ministries and 60government agencies, which are helping Malaysian SMEs development. International trade plays a large role in Malaysian economy. Syed Zamberi (2010) showed that in Malaysian SMEs, sales managers were alert of the government support in Malaysia and they achieve this assistance for their export activities. Despite of government supporting programs in Malaysian SMEs, still there is a significant difference between SMEs' share in national exports and GDP. These differences might be the focus of government support programs on financial supports (OECD, 2008). While intangible resources such as experience, specific knowledge, relation assets and marketing skills are, less easy to recognize but they are necessary resources for internationalization and usually have more effect on higher export performance while SMEs are suffering from their scarcities.

Malaysian GDP was reported around 750 billion Malaysian Dollar in 2010 and national export reported around 64 Billion Malaysian Dollar (The European Central Bank). Figure 5.3 shows the GDP and Malaysian national export.

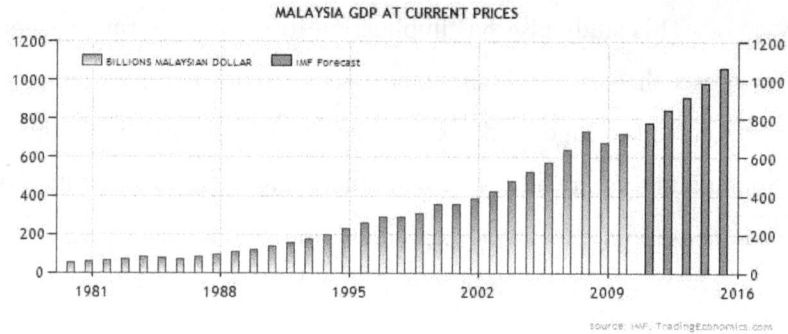

Figure 5.3   GDP reported by the Negara Bank in 2010

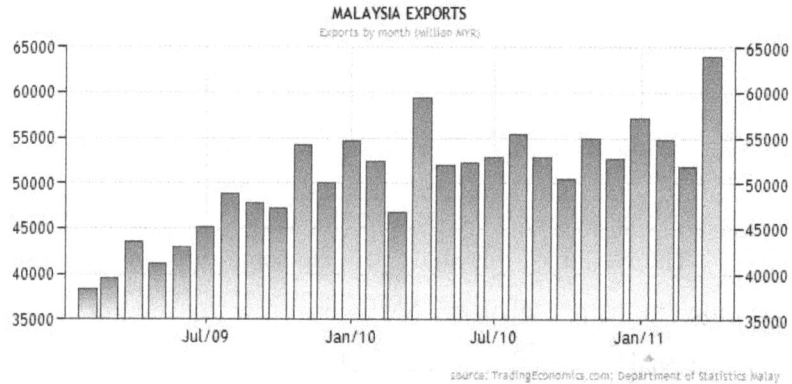

Figure 5.4   National export reported by the Negara Bank in 2010

Thus, SMEs contribution to export revenue is far less than their contribution to GDP. Therefore SMEs manufacturer in Malaysia have big potential for increasing their exports share. Moreover, they need more incentive and promoting programs in order to increase their export and improve their situation in the global market. Seyed zamberi (2010) indicated that government should do more effort for promoting and encouraging SMEs to operate the programs.

5.5   Limitations of the Study

However, the results of this study are strong and interesting but faced some limitation. Those limitations of this study are as follows:

First, the findings might be country-specific because the results were derived from a sample of Malaysian SMEs and findings of this study cannot be generalized beyond Malaysia. SMEs in different countries have different definition surrounding with different cultures and environment, which could affect the results of the study. This study recommends studies from diverse countries and different cultures to test the robustness of this study.

Second, due to time and cost constraints, a quantitative study was conducted for this research. Since international entrepreneurship, opportunity recognition and network theory is still a relatively new research area; qualitative study such as interviews with the export intermediaries and entrepreneurs might be able to increase further the understanding of this research area and can better explicate the relationships among the diverse constructs.

Third, this study exploited a cross-sectional technique where data were collected at a single point of time, (In this study, data were collected in 2010). Therefore, it provided only a snapshot view of the Malaysian SMEs. Cross-sectional data lack an ability to detect changing variables and, as a consequence, it is not possible to draw strong conclusions about the causal relationships between constructs in the model (Malhotra, 1999).Longitudinal data would be suitable in the future for a similar study. Nevertheless, longitudinal methods also have their own boundaries such as high cost and potentially high bias through attrition of the sample population (Weiss and Heide, 1993).

Forth, this study faced the difficulty of collecting data from Malaysian SMEs. Because some companies listed in FMM directory were not updated, regularly their information and some of emails failed or their telephone numbers were not answered. This was might be due to closing down of companies, changed their email addresses or their phone number when contacted. In addition, there was difficult to convince the respondents on the phone to cooperate and fill out the questionnaire due to foreign accent. Moreover, there was difficulty in the collecting because they were afraid of disclosing the data to their competitors or even to their export intermediaries since they are concerned that this disclosure of information might have negative consequences on their relation with export intermediaries.

Fifth, this study focused almost exclusively on independent SMEs manufacturing exporters. They would have been more perfectly measured by including the service sectors SMEs.

Sixth, this study was found on the perception of managers in SMEs and did not include export intermediaries viewpoint. They would have been more accurately measured by including the export intermediary's perspective. Future study could be enhanced by including both exporters and export intermediaries to provide information, which would be stronger than the data collected solely from the perceptions of exporters.

Seventh, the measurement scales for all constructs in this study were based from prior studies mostly investigated in the US and west. Therefore, developing and improving measurement scales is required for future research.

Eighth, the sample did not include SMEs that had failed in their exporting and just focused on the exporting SEMs. Future studies on SMEs, which they failed on exporting, would be better explaining the result of study.

In addition, since owners or managers supply the information related to export activity SMEs, this study might meet a problem of self-reported Prejudice. The above-mentioned limitations of this study could be supposed as a literature gap that could provide the foundation for future work in IE research. The next section highlights some suggestions for further research.

Furthermore, future research into three-way relationships among manufacturers, export intermediaries and overseas customers would be more beneficial in obtaining accurate information (Peng and Ilinitch, 1998). Future studies can also see more variables, other than marketing, experience assets, and relation assets, which are able to be integrated in the framework. Moreover, more export research should be conducted from a network-based view. It would be beneficial to know other types of networking for SMEs to enhance their resources capabilities and recognize more opportunities in international markets.

5.6   Conclusion and discussion

This study attempts to investigate the applicability of the network-based view in explaining the relationship between export intermediary and SMEs to compensate SMEs resources scarcities and recognize opportunities in international markets and enhance export satisfaction.

Export intermediary resources such as marketing capabilities, experience assets, and relation assets, are key success factors in international opportunity recognition and export satisfaction that SMEs can achieve these resources through their networking with export intermediary.

Export managers should not rely on their own resources for internationalization, since they do not have potential intangible resources for internationalization. They should develop their resources before starting internationalization through their networking with other parties in the environment such as export intermediary. They should also be careful when they select appropriate export intermediaries, as intermediary resources influence IOR and strategic export performance and they can facilitate internationalization due to their unique intangible resources.

A more thorough understanding of network theory in achieving resource and recognize international opportunity would have been achieved by examining how the interaction between SMEs and export intermediary would have an effect on IOR and export satisfaction and by investigating dyadic data from both parties.

This study suggests that government can enhance the seminars and training especially on how SMEs access to international markets and how recognize international opportunities. These programs may help SMEs to recognize more opportunities in international markets and increase their export satisfaction, especially in an early stage of internationalization. It could also help Malaysian economy to increase their national export and decrease the differences between GDP and national export in the future.

Moreover, this study suggests that Malaysian SMEs should be encouraged to compensate their resources scarcities with their relation and networking with other parties in the environment for their international operations. Training could at least show how they can compensate their resources scarcities and make SMEs confidence to active internationally and success in international markets. The programs could also be advised to teach SMEs on how to make networks with other parties specially with those export intermediaries that are strong in intangible resources such as marketing, relation, experience and knowledge.

Lastly, should be special attention to the foreign export intermediaries in Malaysia since it is one kind of the export intermediaries for helping SMEs to move international markets and it has huge potential due to their familiarity with different language, culture and even geographical location in destination markets and they can act as a bridge to connect two different markets. Therefore Malaysian government can do more support in foreign export intermediaries in Malaysia specially immigrant entrepreneurs as a foreign business owners which can introduce more international opportunities.

In summary, this study highlights the importance of export intermediary networking to compensate resource scarcities such as marketing capability, experience assets, and relation assets for IOR and export satisfaction of Malaysian manufacturer SMEs. This study has confirmed the importance of networking to IOR and export performance and, thus, provided a significant contribution to IE and export marketing literature and practical guidelines to Malaysian government policy makers, export intermediaries, and exporting SMEs in Malaysia. In addition, Figure 5.5 indicates all the results of this study in one figure, which addresses research question, and all hypothesis and the results of all hypothesis in this study.

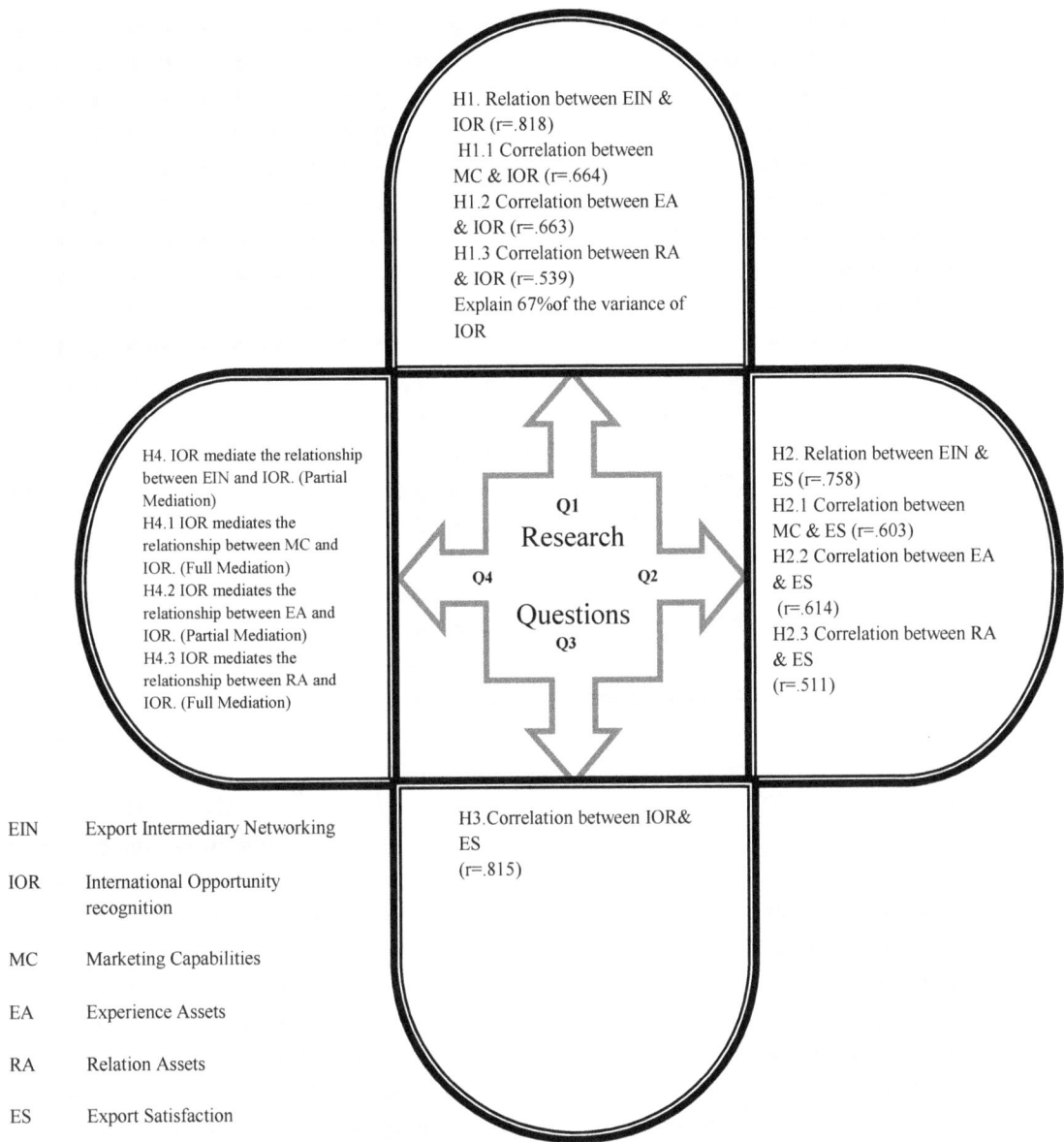

H1. Relation between EIN &
IOR (r=.818)
 H1.1 Correlation between
MC & IOR (r=.664)
H1.2 Correlation between EA
& IOR (r=.663)
H1.3 Correlation between RA
& IOR (r=.539)
Explain 67%of the variance of
IOR

H4. IOR mediate the relationship
between EIN and IOR. (Partial
Mediation)
H4.1 IOR mediates the
relationship between MC and
IOR. (Full Mediation)
H4.2 IOR mediates the
relationship between EA and
IOR. (Partial Mediation)
H4.3 IOR mediates the
relationship between RA and
IOR. (Full Mediation)

Q1
Research

Q4   Q2

Questions
Q3

H2. Relation between EIN &
ES (r=.758)
H2.1 Correlation between
MC & ES (r=.603)
H2.2 Correlation between EA
& ES
 (r=.614)
H2.3 Correlation between RA
& ES
(r=.511)

H3.Correlation between IOR&
ES
(r=.815)

EIN   Export Intermediary Networking

IOR   International Opportunity
        recognition

MC   Marketing Capabilities

EA   Experience Assets

RA   Relation Assets

ES   Export Satisfaction

Figure 5.5   Results of this study in one picture

REFERENCES

Aaker, D. A. (1989). Managing Assets and Skills: The Key to a Sustainable Competitive Advantage. *alifornia management review*, 32(2), 91-107.

Abdullah, M. Perception and attitude of small and medium industries' entrepreneurs towards training in Malaysia: A case of Penang. *In The Proceedings of Second Asian Academy of Management Conference: Towards management excellence in the 21st Century Asia.* Langkawi, Malaysia; University of Science Malaysia. 1997.

Abdullah, M.A. Myths and Realities of Small and Medium Enterprises in Malaysia. *In International Conference on Small and Medium Enterprises at New Crossroads: Challenges and Prospects.* Penang, Malaysia; University of Science Malaysia. 1999.

Achrol, S.R. and Kotler, P. (1999). Marketing in the Network Economy. *Journal of Marketing*, 63(Special Issue), 146–63.

Acs, Z. J. and Preston, L. (1997). Small and Medium-Sized Enterprises, Technology , and Globalization: Introduction to a Special Issue on Small and Medium-Sized Enterprises in the Global Economy. *Small Business Economics*, 9,1-6.

Acs, Z. J, Dana, L. and Jones, M. V. (2003). Toward New Horizons: The Internationalisation of Entrepreneurship. *Journal of International Entrepreneurship*, 1, 5-12.

Acs, Z. J. , Morck, R., Shaver, J. M. and Yeung, B. (1997). The Internationalization of Small and Medium Enterprises: A Policy Perspective. *Small Business Economics*, 9(1), 7-20.

Agndal, H. and Chetty, S. (2007). The impact of relationships on changes in internationalisation strategies of SMEs. *European Journal of Marketing*, 41(11/12), 1449-1474.

Agndal, H., Chetty, S. and Wilson, H. (2008). Social capital dynamics and foreign market entry. *International Business Review*, 17(6), 663-675.

Aldrich, H. and Waldinger., R. Trends in Ethnic Businesses in the United States. In R.Waldinger, H. Aldrich, and R.Ward ed. *Ethnic Entrepreneurs: Immigrant Businesses in Industrial Societies*. Newbury, CA: Sage. 1990.

Aldrich, H. and Zimmer, C. Entrepreneurship through social networks: In D. L. Sexton and R. W. Smilor ed. *The Art and Science of Entrepreneurship*. Ballinge, MA: Cambridger, pp. 3- 23. 1986.

Aldrich, H.E, Jones, T.P. and McEvoy, D. Ethnic advantage and minority business development. In R. Ward & R. Jenkins ed. *Ethnic Communities in Business: Strategies for Economic Survival*. Cambridge: Cambridge University Press, pp. 189–210. 1984.

Alerck, P.L. and Settle, R.B., *The Survey Research Handbook*, Boston, MA: Homewood, Ill. (1985).

Alvarez, R. (2004). Sources of export success in small- and medium-sized enterprises: the impact of public programs. *International Business Review*, 13(3), 383-400.

Ambler, T., Styles, C. and Xiucun, W. (1999). The effect of channel relationships and guanxi on the performance of inter-province export ventures in the People's Republic of China. *International Journal of Research in*

Marketing, 16(1), 75-87.

Andersen, O. and Kheam, L.S. (1998). Resource-based theory and international growth strategies: an exploratory study. *International Business Review*, 7, 163-184.

Anderson, J. C. and Narus, J.A. (1990). A model of distributor firm and manufacturer firm working partnerships. *Journal of Marketing*, 54(1), 42-58.

Ardichivili, A., Cardonzo, R. and Sourav, R. (2003). A theory of entrepreneurial opportunity identification and development. *Journal of Business Venturing*, 18(1), 105–123.

Arenius, P. and DeClercq, D. (2005). A Network-based Approach on Opportunity Recognition. *Small Business Economics*, 24(3), 249-265.

Atuahene-Gima, K., (1993 a). Determinants of Inward Technology Licensing Intentions: An Empirical Analysis of Australian Engineering Firms. *Journal of Product Innovation Management*, 10(3), 230-240.

Atuahene-Gima, K. (1993 b). Relative Importance of Firm and Managerial Influences on International Technology Licensing Behaviour. *International Marketing Review*, 10(2).

Atuahene-Gima, K. (1995). The influence of new product factors on export propensity and performance: an empirical analysis. *Journal of International Marketing*, 3(2), 11–28.

Axelsson, B. and Johanson, J. (1992). Foreign market entry:the Textbook vs. the Network View. In B. Axelsson & G. Easton, eds. Industrial Networks: A New View of Reality. London: Routledge, 218-234.

Bagozzi, R.P. (1975). Marketing as exchange. *Journal of Marketing*, 39(4), 32-9.

Balabanis, G.I. (2000). Factors Affecting Export Intermediaries' Service Offerings:

The British Example. International Business, 31(1), 83-99.

Balabanis, G.I. and Katsikea, E.S. (2003). Being an entrepreneurial exporter: does it pay? *International Business Review*, 12(2), 233-252.

Baldauf, A., Cravens, D. W. and Wagner, U. (2000). Examining Determinants of Export Performance in Small Open Economies. *Journal of World Business*, 35(1), 61-79.

Baldwin, J. R. and Gu, W. (2004). Trade Liberalization: Export-market Participation, Productivity Growth, and Innovation. Oxford Review of Economic Policy, 20(3), 372-392.

Baldwin, John R. and Gu, W. (2003). Export-Market Participation and Productivity Performance in Canadian Manufacturing. Canadian Journal of Economics/Revue Canadienne d`Economique, 36(3), 634-657.

Barney, J., Wright, M. and Ketchen, D.J. (2001). The resource-based view of the firm: Ten years after 1991. *Journal of Management*, 27(special issue editors), 625-641.

Barney, J.B. (2001). Is the Resource-Based " View " A Useful Perspective for Strategic Management Research? Yes. The Academy of Management Review, 26(1), 41-56.

Barney, J.B. (1986). Strategic Factor Markets: Expectations, Luck, and Business Strategy. *Management Science*, 32(10), 1231-1241.

Baron, R. and Tang, J. (2009). Entrepreneurs' Social Skills and New Venture Performance: Mediating Mechanisms and Cultural Generality. *Journal of Management*, 35(2), 282-306.

Baron, R.A. (1998). Cognitive mechanisms in entrepreneurship,why and when entrepreneurs think differently than other people. *Journal of Business*

Venturing, 13, 275-294.

Baron, R.A., (2007). Opportunity Recognition as Pattern Recognition: How Entrepreneurs "Connect the Dots" to Identify New Business Opportunities. *Academy of Management Perspective*, 104-120.

Baron, R.M. and Kenny, D.A., (1986). The Moderator-Mediator Variable Distinction in Social Psychological Research: Conceptual, Strategic, and Statistical Considerations. *Journal of Personality and Social Psychology*, 51(6), 1173–1182.

Barrett, C.B. (1997). Food Marketing Liberalization and Trader Entry: Evidence from Madagascar. World Development, 25(5), 763–777.

Baum, J.R., Locke, E.A. and Smith, K.G. (2001). A Multidimensional Model of venture Growth. *Academy of Management Journal,* 44(2), 292-303.

Bausch, A. and Krist, M. (2007). The Effect of Context-Related Moderators on the Internationalization-Performance Relationship: Evidence from Meta-Analysis. *Management International Review*, 47(3), pp.319 - 347.

Beamish, P. W and Killing, P.J. *Cooperative strategies: European perspectives*, San Francisco, CA: New Lexington Press. 1997.

Beamish, P. W. The internationalisation process for smaller Ontario firms: A research agenda. In A. Rusman. ed. *Research in global strategic management*. Greenwich, Conn: JAI Press. 1990.

Bearden, W.O. and Netemeyer, R.G. *Handbook of Marketing Scales: Multi-Item Measures for Marketing and Consumer Research* 2nd ed. Thousand Oaks, CA: Sage Publications. 1998.

Begley, T.M. and Boyd, D.P. (1987). Psychological characteristics associated with performance in entrepreneurial firms and smaller businesses. *Journal of*

Business Venturing, 2(1), 79-93.

Bell, J.D. (1995). The internationalisation of small computer software firms a further challenge to "stage" theories. *European Journal of Marketing*, 29(8), 60-75.

Bello, D. C. and Williamson, N.C. (1985). The American Export Trading Company: Designing a new international marketing institution. *Journal of Marketing*, 49(4), 60–69.

Bello, D., Urban, D. and Verhage, B.J. (1991). Evaluating Export Middlemen in Alternative Channel Structures. *International Marketing Review*, 8(5), 49–64.

Bello, Daniel C and Lohtia., R. (1995). Export Channel Design: The Use of Foreign Distributors and Agents. *Journal of the Academy of Marketing Science*, 23(2), 83-93.

Bijmolt, T.H.A. and Zwart, P.S. (1994). The Impact of Internal Factors on the Export Success of Dutch Small and Medium-Sized Firms. *Journal of Small Business Management*, 32(2), 69–83.

Birley, S., Cromie, S. and Myers, A. (1991). Entrepreneurial networks: their emergence in Ireland and overseas. *International Small Business Journal*, 9(4), 56-74.

Birley, Sue. (1985). The role of networks in the entrepreneurial process. *Journal of Business Venturing*, 1(1), 107–117.

Blankenburg, D. (1995). A network approach to foreign market entry. In K. Moller, ed. Business Marketing: An Interaction and Network Perspective. 375-405.

Blaschke, J. and Ersoz, A. (1986). The Turkish economy in West Berlin. *International Small Business Journal*, 48(3), 38–45.

Blomstermo, A., Eriksson, K. ,Lindstrand, A., Sharma, D. D. (2004). The perceived usefulness of network experiential knowledge in the internationalizing firm. *Journal of International Management*, 10(3), 355.

Blomstermo, A., Sharma, D. D. and Sallis, J. (2006a) Choice of foreign market entry mode in service firms. *International Marketing Review*, 23(2), 211–229.

Blomstermo, A., Sharma, D. D and Sallis, J. (2006 b). Choice of foreign market entry mode in service firms. *Journal of International Marketing*, 23(2), 211-229.

Bloodgood, J., Sapienza, H. J. and Almeida, J.G. (1996). The internationalization of new high-potential U.S. ventures: Antecedents and outcomes. Entrepreneurship Theory and Practice, 20, 61-76.

Blundel, R. (2002). Network Evolution and the Growth of Artisanal Firms: A Tale of Two Regional Cheese Makers. Entrepreneurship and Regional Development, 14, 1-30.

Boissevain, J. and Grotenbreg, H. Ethnic enterprise in the Netherlands: the Surinamese of Amsterdam. In R. Goffee and R. Scase ed. *Entrepreneurship in Europe*. Beckenham, Kent: Croom Helm, 105–130. 1987.

Bonaccorsi, A. (1992). On the Relationship between Firm Size and Export Intensity. *Journal of International Business Studies*, 23(4), 605-635.

Bonacich, E. and Light., I., (1988). Immigrant Entrepreneurs, Berkley, CA: University of California Press.

Bowyer, D., *Going Global, Part II-A Three-Part Series Covering Tips, Advice, and Resources to Help You Turn Your Company into a Global Presence on the*

Internet. 2002.

Boyce, J., *Market Research in Practice*, McGraw Hill Australia. 2002.

Bradley, F., Meyer, R. and Gao, Y. (2006). Use of supplier-customer relationships by SMEs to enter foreign markets. *Industrial Marketing Management*, 35(6), 652-665.

Brenner, G. and Toulouse, J.-M. (1990). Business Creation among the Chinese Immigrants in Montreal. *Journal of Small Business and Entrepreneurship*, 7(4), 38-44.

Brockhaus, R.H. and Horowitz, P.S., The Psychology of the Entrepreneur: The Art and Science of Entrepreneurship. In F. K. Norris ed. *Entrepreneurship: critical perspectives on business and management*. London: Routledge, pp. 25-48. 2002.

Brouthers, L. E. and Xu, K. (2002). Product Stereotypes, Strategy and Performance Satisfaction: The Case of Chinese Exporters. *Journal of International Business Studies*, 33(4), 657-77.

Brown, T.E., Davidsson, P. and Wiklund, J. (2001). An operationalization of Stevenson's conceptualization of entrepreneurship as opportunity-based firm behavior. *Strategic Management Journal*, 22(10), 953-968.

Burt, R.S. (1992). Structural Holes.

Burt, R.S., The network structure of social capital. In R. I. Sutton and B. M. Staw ed. Research in Organizational Behavior. Greenwich, CT: JAI Press, pp. 345-423. 2000.

Butler, J.E and Chamornmarn, W. (1995). Entrepreneurial Characteristics: Reflections of a Changing Economy. *Chulalongkorn Journal of Economics*, 7, 89–110.

Butler, J. E, Brown, B. and Chamornmarn, W. (2003). Informational Networks,

Entrepreneurial Action and Performance. *Asia Pacific Journal of Management*, 20(2), 151-174.

Bygrave, W.D. and Hofer, C.W. (1991). Theorizing about entrepreneurship. *Entrepreneurship Theory and Practice*, 16(2), 13–22.

Cabreraa, P., Auslander, W. and Polgar, M. (2009). Future Orientation of Adolescents in Foster Care: Relationship to Trauma, Mental Health , and HIV Risk Behaviors. *Journal of Child & Adolescent Trauma*, 26(11), 271-286.

Carson, D. and Grant, K. SME marketing competencies: a definition and some empirical evidence. In G.E. Hills, R. W. L. Forge, and D. F. Muzyaka ed. *Research at the Marketing/ Entrepreneurship Interface*. University of Illinois at Chicago. 1993.

Cavusgil, S.T. and Zou, S. (1994). Marketing Strategy-Performance Relationship: An Investigation of the Empirical Link in Export Market Ventures. *Journal of Marketing,* 58(January), 1-21.

Ceglie, G. and Dini, M. SME cluster and network development in developing countries: The experience of UNIDO. In R. de Janeiro ed. *International Conferance on Bulding a Modern and Effective Development service Industry for Small Enterprises.* Vienna: United Nations Industrial Development Organization. 1999.

Chalmin, P. *Traders and Merchants. In Panorama of International Commodity Trading.* Harwood Academic Publishers. 1987.

Chan, T.S. (1992). Emerging Trends in Export Channel Strategy: An Investigation of Hong Kong and Singaporean Firms. *European Journal of Marketing*, 26(3), 18-26.

Chandler, G.N. and Jansen, E. (1992). The founder's self-assessed competence and venture performance. *Journal of Business Venturing*, 7(3), 223-236.

Chandra, Y., Styles, C. and Wilkinson, I. (2009). The recognition of first time international entrepreneurial opportunities: Evidence from firms in knowledge-based industries. *International Marketing Review*, 26(1), 30-61.

Chatterjee, S. and Wernerfelt, B. Related or unrelated diversification: A resource based approach, Institute for Research in the Behavioral, Economic, and Management Sciences, Krannert Graduate School of Management, Purdue University. West Lafayette, Ind. 1986.

Chatterjee, S. and Wernerfelt, B. (1991). The link between resources and type of diversification: Theory and evidence. *Strategic Management Journal*, 12(1), 33-48.

Chell, E. and Baines, S. (2000). Networking, Entrepreneurship and Microbusiness Behaviour. *Entrepreneurship and Regional Development*, 12, 195–215.

Chell, E. and Baines, S. (2000). Networking, Entrepreneurship and Microbusiness Behaviour. *Entrepreneurship and Regional Development*, 12(3), 195–215.

Chen, H. and Chen, T. J. (1998). Network Linkages and Location Choice in Foreign Direct Investment. *Journal of International Business Studies*, 29(3), 445-467.

Chen, M.K. and Wang, S. (2010 a). Expert Systems with Applications. *Expert Systems with Applications*, 37, 694-704.

Chen, M.K. and Wang, S. (2010 b). The critical factors of success for information service industry in developing international market: Using analytic hierarchy process (AHP) approach. *Expert Systems with Applications*, 37, 694-704.

Chetty, S. and Campbell-Hunt, C. (2003). Explosive international growth and problems of success amongst small to medium-sized firms. *International*

Small Business Journal, 21(1), 5-27.

Chetty, S. and Holm, D.B. (2000). Internationalisation of small to medium-sized manufacturing firms: a network approach. *International Business Review*, 9(1), 77-93.

Christensen, P.S. and Peterson, R. Opportunity identification: Mapping the sources of new venture ideas. *In Frontiers of Entrepreneurship Research.* Wellesley, MA: Babson College, pp. 567–581. 1990.

Chryssochoidis, G. and Theoharakis, V. (2004). Attainment of competitive advantage by the exporter–importer dyad: The role of export offering and import objectives. *Journal of Business Research*, 57, 329 - 337.

Churchill, G. A., Marketing Research: Methodological Foundations sixth edn., The Dryden Press. 1995.

Churchill, G. A, (1979). A Paradigm for Developing Better Measures of Marketing Constructs. *Journal of Marketing Research*, 16, 64–73.

Claver, E., Rienda, L. and Quer, D. 2008. Family firms' risk perception: Empirical evidence on the internationalization process. *Journal of Small Business and Enterprise Development*, 15(3), 457–471.

Coase, R.H. (1937). The Nature of the Firm. Economica, New Series, 4(16), pp.386-405.

Cobanoglu, C. and Cobanoglu, N. (2003). The effect of incentives in web-based surveys: application and ethical considerations. *International Journal of Market Research*, 45(4), 475-489.

Collarelli-O'Connor, G.C. and Rice, M. (2001). Opportunity recognition and breakthrough in large established firms. *California Management Review*, 43(2), 95– 116.

Contractor, F.J. (2007). Is International Business Good for Companies? The
    Evolutionary or Multi- Stage Theory of Internationalization vs. the
    Transaction Cost Perspective. *Journal of Management Review*, 47(3), 453 -
    475.

Cooper, C.J., Cooper, S.P, Junco, D., Eva M. S. (2006). Web-based data collection:
    detailed methods of a questionnaire and data gathering tool. *Epidemiol
    Perspect Innov*, 3(1).

Cooper, D.J., Hinings, B., Greenwood, R., Brown, J. L. (1996). Sedimentation and
    Transformation in Organizational Change: The Case of Canadian Law
    Firms. *Organization Studies*, 17(4), 623-647.

Cooper, R.G., Edgett, S.J. and Kleinschmidt, E.J., Portfolio Management for New
    Products: Picking The Winners. *In Reading Mass*. Addison-Wesley. 1998.

Cooper, Z.G. (1999). Product Innovation Best Practices Series From Experience:
    The Invisible Success Factors In Product Innovation From Experience: The
    Invisible Success Factors in Product Innovation. *Journal of Product
    Innovation Management*, 16(2), 115-133.

Corbett, A.C. (2007). Learning asymmetries and the discovery of entrepreneurial
    opportunities. *Journal of Business Venturing*, 22, 97 - 118.

Coviello, N.E and Munro, H. J. (1995). Growing the entrepreneurial firm:
    Networking for international market development. *European journal of
    Marketing*, 29(7), 49-61.

Coviello, N. and Munro, H., (1997). Network Relationships and the
    Internationalisation Process of Small Software Firms. *International
    Business Review*, 6(4), 361-386.

Coviello, N. E. and McAuley, A. (1999). Internationalization and the smaller firms:
    a Review of Contemporary Emprical research. *Management International*

Review, 39(3), 223-256.

Coviello, N. E and McAuley, A. (1999). Internationalization and the smaller firms: a Review of Contemporary Emprical research. *Management International Review*, 39(3), 223-256.

Coviello, N. E. and Cox, M.P. (2006). The resource dynamics of international new venture networks. *Journal of International Entrepreneurship*, 4(2–3), 113–132.

Crant, J.M., (1996). The proactive personality scale as a predictor of entrepreneurial intentions. *Journal of Small Business Management*, 34, 42–49.

Creswell, J.W. *Research Design: Qualitative and Quantitative Approaches*, Sage Publications. 1994.

Crick, D. and Spence, M. (2005). The internationalization of "high performing" U.K. high-tech SMEs: a study of planned and unplanned strategies. *International Business Review,* 14(2), 167-185.

Crick, D., Chaudhry, S. and Batstone, S. (2001). An Investigation into the Overseas Expansion of Small Asian-Owned U.K. Firms. *Small Business Economics*, 16, 75–94.

Crosa, B., Aldrich, H. E. and Keister, L., *Is There a Wealth Affect? Financial and Human Capital as Determinants of Business Startups Wellesley*. In Frontiers of Entrepreneurship Research. MA: Babson College. 2002.

Curtin, P.D. *Cross- cultural Trade in World History*, Cambridge: University Press. 1984.

D.Hunt, S. and Morgan, R. M. (1995). The comparative Advantage Theory of Competition. *Journal of Marketing*, 59, 1-15.

Dana, L.P. (1995). Entrepreneurship in a remote sub-arctic community: Nome,

Alaska. *Entrepreneurship: Theory and Practice*, 20(1), 55–72.

Dana, L.P. (1996). Self-employment in the Canadian sub-arctic: an exploratory study. *Canadian Journal of Administrative Sciences*, 13(1), 65–77.

Dana, L.P. (2001). Introduction Networks, Internationalization & Policy. *Small Business Economics*, 16, 57-62.

Dana, L. Paul. (1995). Small business in a non-entrepreneurial society: the case of the Lao people's democratic republic (Laos). *Journal of Small Business Management*, 33(3), pp.95–102.

Dana, L. P, Etemad, H. and Wright, R. (2008). Networking as a Means to value creation. *International Journal of Entrepreneurship and Small Business*, 5(2), 109-126.

Dana, L. P, Etemad, H. and Wright, R.W. (2008). Toward a paradigm of symbiotic entrepreneurship. *Journal of Entrepreneurship and Small Business*, 5(2), 109-126.

Dana, L.P. , Etemad, H. and Richard W. W. *The Theoretical Foundations of International Entrepreneurship International Entrepreneurship: Globalization of Emerging Businesses.* In R. W. Wrigh ed. Stamford: JAI Press, pp. 3–22. 1999.

Dana, L.P.(1999). Entrepreneurship in Pacific Asia: Past, Present & Future, Singapore: World Scientific.

Dana, L.P and Etemad, H. (1995). SMEs – Adapting Strategy for NAFTA: A Model for Small and Medium- Sized Enterprises. *Journal of Small Business & Entrepreneurship*, 12(3), 4–17.

Dana, L.P and Hamid, E. (1994). A Strategic Response Model for the Internationalization of Small or Medium-Sized Australian Enterprises.

Bond Management Review, 4(1), 31-42.

Dana, Leo-Paul, Etemad, H. & Wright, R.W. (1999). The Impact of Globalization on SMEs. *Global Focus*, 11(4), 93–105.

Davidsson, P., Delmar, F. and Wiklund, Johan, *Entrepreneurship and the Growth of Firms, Massachusetts*: Edvard Elgar. 2006.

Davis, R.N. and Nolen-Hoeksema, S. (2000). Cognitive Inflexibility Among Ruminators and Nonruminators. *Cognitive Therapy & Research*, 24(6), 699–711.

Day, George S. (1994). The Capabilities of Market-Driven Organizations. *The Journal of Marketing,* 58(4), 37-52.

Day, G. S. and Wensley, R. (1988). Assessing Advantage: A Framework for Diagnosing Competitive Superiority. *Journal of Marketing*, 52(April), 1-29.

DeClercq, D.D., Hessels, J. and Stel, A. (2008). Knowledge spillovers and new ventures' export orientation. *Small Business Economics*, 31(3), pp.283-303.

DeTienne, D.R and Cardon, M.S., (2007). Entrepreneurial exit strategies: The case for intention.

DeTienne, Dawn R and Cardon, Melissa S. The impact of new venture design on entrepreneurship. In Babson College. *Entrepreneurship Research Conference (BCERC).* 2008.

DeTienne, D. R. (2010). Entrepreneurial exit as a critical component of the entrepreneurial process: Theoretical development. *Journal of Business Venturing*, 25(2), 203-215.

DeTienne, D. R. and Chandler, G.N., (2007). The Role of Gender in Opportunity

Identification. *Entrepreneurship Theory and Practice*, 31(3), 365 - 386.

Delamar, F. The psychology of the entrepreneur. In S. Carter and D. Jones-Evans, ed. *Enterprise and Small Business: Principles, Practice and Policy*. Prentice Hall. London: Prentice Hall, 132–154. 2000.

Deligonul, S., Kim, D., Roath, A. S, Cavusgil, E. (2006). The Achilles' heel of an enduring relationship: Appropriation of rents between a manufacturer and its foreign distributor. *Journal of Business Research*, 59, 802 - 810.

Delmar, F., Davidsson, P. and Gartner, W. B. (2003). Arriving at the High Growth Firm. *Journal of Business Venturing*, 18(2), 189-216.

Denzin, N.K. and Lincoln, Y.S., *Handbook of Qualitative Research* 2nd ed., Sage Publications, Thousand Oaks. 1994.

Dess, G. G. and Robinson, R.B., (1984). Measuring organizational performance in the absence of objectives measures: the case of the privately-held firm and conglomerate business unit. *Strategic Management Journal*, 5(3), 265-273.

DiMaggio, P. and Powell, W. (1983). The iron cage revisited: Institutional isomorphism and collective rationality in organizational fields. *American Sociological Review*, 48(2), 147–160

.

Diamantopoulos, A. and Winklhofer, H.M. (2001). Index Construction with Formative Indicators: An Alternative to Scale Development. *Journal of Marketing Research*, 38(2), 269–277.

Dimitratos, P and Jones, M. (2005). Future directions for international entrepreneurship research. *International Business Review*, 14(2), 119-128.

F M M. Federation of Malaysian Manufacturer (FMM) 40th ed. 2009.

Easton, G. and Hakansson, H. (1996). Markets as Networks: Editorial introduction. *International Journal of Research in Marketing*, 13, 407-413.

Eckhardt, J.T. and Shane, S.A. (2003). Opportunities and Entrepreneurship. *Journal of Management*, 29(3), 333-349.

Eisenhardt, K.M. (1989). Building theories from case study research. *Academy of Management Review*, 14(4), 532–550.

Elfring, T. and Hulsink, W. (2003). Networks in Entrepreneurship: The Case of High-technology Firms. *Small Business Economics,* 21(4), 409–422.

Ellis, P. (2003). Are International Trade Intermediaries in Economic Catalysts Development? A New Research Agenda. *Journal of International Marketing*, 11(1), 73-96.

Ellis, P. and Pecotich, A. (2001). Social factors Influencing Export Initiation in Small and Medium-Sized Enterprises. *Journal of Marketing research*, (Februry), 119-130.

Ellis, P.D. (2003). An International Trade Intermediariers catalysts in Economic Development? A New research agenda. *Journal of International Marketing*, 11(1), 73-96.

Ellis, P.D. (2010). International trade intermediaries and the transfer of marketing knowledge in transition economies. *International Business Review*, 19(1), 16-33.

Ellis, P.D. (2003). Social Structure and Intermediation: Market-making Strategies in International Exchange. *Journal of Management Studies*, 40(7), 1683-1708.

Ellis, P.D. (2011). Social ties and international entrepreneurship: Opportunities and constraints affecting firm internationalization. *Journal of International Business Studies*, 42(1), 99-127.

Eriksson, K., Johanson, J., Majkgard, A., Sharma, D. D. (1997). Experiential Knowledge and Cost in the Internationalization Process. *Journal of*

International Business Studies, 28(2), 337-360.

Etemad, H. (2004). International Entrepreneurship as a Dynamic Adaptive System: Towards a Grounded Theory. *Journal of International Entrepreneurship*, 2(1/2), 5-59.

Etemad, H. and Ala-Mutka, J. (2006). From seed to born global: Towards a theorical framework. In ASAC. Banff, Alberta, 155-173.

Etemad, H. and Lee, Y. (2003). The Knowledge Network of International Entrepreneurship: Theory and Evidence. *Small Business Economics*, 20, 5-23.

Etemad, H. and Wright, R.W. (2003). Internationalization of SMEs: Toward a New Paradigm. *Small Business Economics*, 20, 1-4.

Fafchamps, M. and Minten, B. (1999). Relationships and traders in Madagascar. *Journal of Development Studies*, 35(6), 1–35.

Fahy, J. ,Hooley, G., Cox, T., Beracs, J., Fonfara, K., Snoj, B (2000). The Development and Impact of Marketing Capabilities in Central Europe. *Journal of International Business Studies*, 31(1), 63-81.

Farh, J., Tsui, A. S., Xin, K., Cheng, B., Anne, J., Katherine, S. T., and Cheng, X. Bor. (1998). The Influence of Relational Demography and Guanxi: The Chinese Case. *Organization*, 9(4), 471-488.

Fawcett, S.E. and Birou, L.M. (1992). Exploring the logistics interface between global and JIT sourcing. *International Journal of Physical Distribution and Logistics Management*, 22(1), 3–14.

Feenstra, R.C. and Hanson, G.HGlobal. Production Sharing and Rising Inequality: A Survey of Trade and Wages. *Handbook of International Economics*, (October). 2001.

Ford, D. (2002). Distribution, Internationalization and Networks: Solving Old problems, Learning new thing and forgetting most of them. *Internationalization Marketing review*, 19(3), 225-35.

Ford, I.D and Rosson, P.J. The relationships between export manufacturers and their overseas distributors. In M. R. Czinkota and G. Tesar ed. *Export Management: An International Context.* New York: Praeger Publishers, pp. 257-75. 1982.

Francis, J. and Collins-Dodd, C. (2004). Impact of Export Promotion Programs on Firm Competencies, Strategies and Performance: The Case of Canadian High-technology SMEs. *International Marketing Review*, 21(4/5).74-495.

Fujita, M. (1995). Small and Medium-Sized Transnational Corporations: Salient Features. *Small Business Economics*, 7, 251–271.

Gadde, L.-E. and Hakansson, H., Analyzing Change and Stability in Distribution Channels—A Network Approach. In I. B.Axelsson and G. Easton ed. *Industrial Networks:ANewViewof Reality.* London: Routledge. 1992.

Gaglio, C.M. and Katz, J.A. (2001). The Psychological Basis of Opportunity Identification: Entrepreneurial Alertness. *Small Business Economics*, 16, 95-111.

Ganesan, S. (1994). Determinants of long-term orientation in buyer–seller relationships. *Journal of Marketing*, 58(2), 1–19.

Garnsey, E. A New Theory of the Growth of the Firm. *In 41st ICSB World conference.* Stockholm. 1996.

Gartner, W. B. (1985). A conceptual framework for describing the phenomenon of new venture creation. *Academy of Management Review*, 10(4), 696–706.

Gartner, W. B. (1988). Who is the Entrepreneur?Is the Wrong Question. *American*

Journal of Small Business, 12(4), 11–31.

Gençtürk, E.F. and Kotabe, M. (2001). The Effect of Export Assistance Program Usage on Export Performance: A Contingency Explanation. *Journal of International Marketing*, 9(2), 51-72.

George, G., Wiklund, J. and Zahra, S. (2005). Ownership and internationalization of small firms. *Journal of Management*, 31(2), 210-233.

Gerbing, D.W. and Anderson, J. C. (1988). An Undated Paradigm for Scale Development Incorporating Unidimensionality and its Assessment. *Journal of Marketing Research*, 25(2), 186–192.

Geringer, J.M. and Hebert, L. (1991). Measuring Performance of International Joint Ventures. *Journal of International Business Studies*, 22(2), 249–263.

Ghauri, P., Lutz, C. and Testom, G. (2003). Using networks to solve export-marketing problems of small- and medium-sized firms from developing countries. *European Journal of Marketing*, 37(5–6), 728–752.

Gilliland, D. and Bello, D.C. (2002). Two Sides to Attitudinal Commitment: The Effect of Calculative and Loyalty Commitment on Enforcement Mechanisms in Distribution Channels. *Journal of the Academy of Marketing Science*, 30(1), 24-43.

Godos-Díez, J. L., Fernández-Gago, R. and Martínez-Campillo, A. (2011). How Important Are CEOs to CSR Practices? An Analysis of the Mediating Effect of the Perceived Role of Ethics and Social Responsibility. *Journal of Business Ethics*, 98, 531-548.

Granovetter, M. (1985). Economic actions and social structure: The problem of embeddedness. *American Journal of Sociology*, 91(3), 481-510.

Grant, R.M. (1991). The Resource-Based Theory of Competitive Advantage: Implications for Strategy Formulation. *California Management Review*

Spring, 33(2), 114–135.

Gregorio, D.D., Musteen, M., and Thomas, D. (2008). International new ventures: The cross-border nexus of individuals and opportunities. *Journal of World Business*, 43(2), 186-196.

Gregorio, D.D., Musteen, M., and Thomas, D.E. (2008). International new ventures: The cross-border nexus of individuals and opportunities. *Journal of World Business*, 43, 186-196.

Greif, A., (1993). Contract Enforceability and Economic Institutions in Early Trade: The Maghribi Traders' Coalition. *American Economic Review*, 83(3), 525-548.

Gulati, R. (1995). Social structure and alliance formation patterns: A longitudinal analysis. Administrative Science Quarterly, 40(4), 619-652.

Gulati, R., Nohria, N. & Zaheer, A. (2000). Strategic networks. *Strategic Management Journal,* 21(3), 203–215.

Haar, J and Ortiz-Buonafina. (1995). The Internationalization Process and Marketing Activities: The case of Brazilian Export Firms. *Journal of Business Research*, 32, 175-181.

Hadjikhani, A. (1997). A note on the criticisms against the internationalization process model. *Management International Review*, 37(2), 43-66.

Hadjikhani, A., Ghauri, P. and Johanson, J. Introduction: Opportunity development in business networks. In P. Ghauri, A. Hadjikhani, and J. Johanson ed. *Managing opportunity development in business networks.* New York: Palgrave, 1–24. 2005.

Hair, J., Anderson, R.,Tatham, R. and Black. W. *Multivariate Data Analysis*. Fifth ed. New Jersey: Prentice-Hall International. 1998.

Hall, R. (1993). A framework linking intangible resources and capabiliites to sustainable competitive advantage. *Strategic Management Journal*, 14(8), 607-618.

Hallén, L., Johanson, Jan & Seyed-Mohamed, N. (1991). Interfirm Adaptation in Business Relationships. *The Journal of Market*ing, 55(2), 29-37.

Harris, R. and Li, Q.C. Review of the Literature: The Role of International Trade and Investment in Business Growth and Development, *Report to UK Trade and Investment,* UK. 2005.

Harris, S. and Wheeler, C. (2005). Entrepreneurs' relationships for internationalization: functions, origins and strategies. *International Business Review*, 14(2), 187-207.

Harrison, B., *Lean and Mean*, New York: Gilford. 1997.

Hashim, M. (2000). SMEs in Malaysia: Past, present and future. *Malaysian Management Review*, 35(1), 22-30.

Hashim, M. K. and Hassan, R. (2008). Internationalization of SMEs: options, incentives, problems and business strategy. *Malaysian Management Review*, 43(1), 63-76.

Hayton, J.C., George, G. and Zahra, S.A. (2002). National Culture and Entrepreneurship: A Review of Behavioral Research. *Entrepreneurship: Theory and Practice*, 26.

Ha°kansson, H. and Johanson, J, Model of Industrial Networks. In A. B and G. Easton ed. *Industrial networks: a new view of reality*. London: Routledge, pp. 32-46. 1992.

Ha°kansson, H. and Snehota, I., *Developing relationships in business networks.* In H. Håkansson and Ivan Snehota ed. London and New York: Routledge. (1995).

Heide, J. B. and John, G. (1988). The role of dependence balancing in safeguarding transaction- specific assets in conventional channels. *Journal of Marketing*, 52(1), 20–35.

Heide, J.B. (1994). Interorganizational Governance in Marketing Channels. *Journal of Marketing*, 58(1), 71–85.

Heide, Jan B. and Miner, A.S. (1992). The Shadow of the Future: Effects of Anticipated Interaction and Frequency of Contact on Buyer-Seller Cooperation. *Academy of Management Journal*, 35(2), 265-291.

Herkenhoff, L.M. National Remuneration (Pay) Preferences: *Cultural Analysis within the Hofstede Model: Using Cultural Values to Untangle the Web of Global Pay, Organization and Labor Studies*. University of Western Australia. (2002).

Herron, L. and Sapienza, H. J. (1992). The entrepreneur and the initiation of new venture launch activities. Entrepreneurship. *Entrepreneurship: Theory and Practice*, 17(1), 49–55.

Hessels, J., and Terjesen, S. (2008). Resource dependency and institutional theory perspectives on direct and indirect export choices. *Journal of Small Business Economics*, 34(2), 203-220.

Hessels, J., and Terjesen, S. *SME Choice of Direct and Indirect Export Modes: Resource Dependency and Institutional*. Theory Perspectives, Netherlands. 2007.

Hillebrand, B. and Biemansb, W.G. (2003). The relationship between internal and external cooperation literature review and propositions. *Journal of Business Research,* 56(9), pp.735-743.

Hills, G. E. and Schrader, R., *Successful Entrepreneur's insights into Opportunity*

Recognition. In Frontiers of Entrepreneurship Research. MA: Babson College: Wellesley. 1998.

Hills, G.E and La Forge, R.W., Marketing and entrepreneurship: the state of the art. In D. L. Sexton and J. D. Kasada ed. The State of the Art of Entrepreneurship. Boston: PWS-Kent Publishing, pp. 164–90. 1992.

Hisrich, R.D. and Peters, M.P., *Entrepreneurship.* 4th ed., Boston: Irwin/McGraw-Hill. 1998.

Hitt, M.E. and Ireland, R.D. (1985). Corporate distinctive competence, strategy, industry and performance. *Strategic Management Journal,* 6(3), 273–293.

Hocutt, M.A. (1998). Relationship Dissolution model: Antecedents of Relationship Commitment and the Likelihood of Dissolving a Relationship. *International Journal of Service Industry Managemen,* 9(2), 189-200.

Holland, C., Lockett, G. and Blackman, L. (1992). Planning for electronic data interchange. *Strategic Management Journal,* 13(7), 539–550.

Hollenstein, H. (2005). Determinants of International Activities: Are SMEs Different? *Small Business Economics,* 24(5), pp.431-450.

Holzmüller, H.H. and Stottinger, B. (1996). Structural Modeling of Success Factors in Exporting: Cross-Validation and Further Development of an Export Performance Model. *Journal of International Marketing,* 4(2), 29- 55.

Houston, F.S., and Gassenheimer, J.B. (1987). Marketing and exchange. *Journal of Marketing,* 51(4), 3-18.

Howell, D. *Statistical Methods for psychology.* In J. Potter et al., eds., Wadsworth. 2010.

Hsieh, C., How can we identify technological opportunities ahead of time? Management Science. 2004.

Hsieh, Y.J. Personal relationship and its influence on export behavior: an empirical study. In American Marketing Association Summer Conference Proceedings. pp. 368–373. 1994.

Hsing, Y.T. (1999). Trading companies in Taiwan's fashion shoe networks. *Journal of International Economics*, 48(1), 101–20.

Hsiu-Mei, H. (2002). Student perceptions in an online mediated environment. *International Journal of Instructional Media*, 29(4), 405-423.

Hughes, A., *Centre For Business Research Conference*, PowerPoint Presentation. 2004.

Hunt, S.D. (1999). The Strategic Imperative and Sustainable Competitive Advantage: Public Policy Implications of Resource-Advantage Theory. *Journal of the Academy of Marketing Science*, 72(2), 144–159.

Hunt, S.D., and Morgan, R.M. (1995). The Comparative Advantage Theory of Competition. *Journal of Marketing*, 59, 1–15.

IFERA, (2003). Family businesses dominate. *Family Business Review*, 16(4), 235–240.

Ilinitch, A.Y. and Peng, M.W. *A Resource-based model of Export performance.* Paper presented at the Academy of Management, Boston, August. 1994

Ilinitch, A., Peng, M.W., Eastin, I., Paum, D., (1993). Developing intangible Resources: The new battleground for export success for small and mid-sized firms.

Inkpen, A.C., and Beamish, P.W. (1997). Knowledge, Bargaining Power, and the. Instability of International Joint Ventures. *The Academy of Management Review*, 22(1), 177-202.

Jap, S. D and Ganesan, S. (2000). Control mechanisms and the relationship life cycle: implications for safeguarding specific investments and developing commitment. *Journal of Marketing Research*, 37(2), 227–245.

Jap, S.D and Anderson, E. Challenges and Advances in Marketing Strategy Field Research. In C. Moorman and D. R. Lehmann ed. *In Assessing Marketing Strategy Performance*. Cambridge, MA: Marketing Science Institute, pp. 269-292. 2004.

Jensen, M.C. and Meckling, W.H. (1976). Theory of the firm: managerial behavior, agency costs and ownership structure. *Journal of Financial Economics*, 3, 305-60.

Johanson, J and Vahlne, J.-E. (1990). The mechanism of internationalisation. *International Marketing Review*, 7(4), 111-124.

Johanson, J and Vahlne, J.E., (1992). Management of foreign market entry. *Scandinavian International Business Review*, 1(3), pp.9-27.

Johanson, J. and Mattsson, L. Internationalization in industrial systems — A network approach. In Hood and J. E. Vahne ed. *Strategies in global competition*. London: Croom Helm, pp. 303–321. 1987.

Johanson, J. and Mattsson, L.-G. Interorganizational relations in industrial systems: A network approach compared with the transaction cost approach P. J. Buckley and P. N. Ghauri ed. *International Studies of Management and Organization*, 17(1), pp.34–48. 1987.

Johanson, J. and Vahlne, J.-E. (2003). Business relationship learning and commitment in the internationalization process. *Journal of International Entrepreneurship*, 1, 83–101.

Johanson, J. and Wiedersheim-Paul, F. (1975). The internationalisation of the firm:

four Swedish cases. *Journal of International Management Studies*, 12(3), 305–322.

Johanson, J. and Hallen, E. Introduction: Business Relationships and Industrial Networksl. In L. Hallen and Jan Johanson ed. In Advances in International Marketing: *A Research Annual*. Greenwich,: JAI Press Ing, p. xiii-xxiii. 1989.

Johanson, J. and Mattson, L.G. Internationalization in industrial systems - a network approach. In N. Hood and J.E. Vahlne ed. *Strategies in Global Competition*. London: Croom Heln, pp. 287-314. 1988.

Johanson, J. and Vahlne, J.E. (2006). Commitment and Opportunity Development in the Internationalization Process: A Note on the Uppsala Internationalization Process Model. *Business Economics*, 46(2), 165 - 178.

Johanson, J. and Vahlne, J.E. (1992). Management of Foreign Market Entry. *Scandinavian International Business Review*, 1(3), 9-27.

Johanson, J. and Vahlne, J.E. (1977). The Internationalization Process of The Firms: A Model of Knowledge Development and Increasing Foreign Market Commitments. *Journal of International Business Studies*, 8(1), 23-32.

Johnston, R. and Lawrence, P.R. (1988). Beyond Vertical Integration—The Rise of theValue Adding Partnership. *Harvest Business Review*, 66(4), 95-101.

Jones, C.I., 1999. Growth: With or without Scale Effects? American Economic Review, 89(2), 139-144.

Jones, M.V and Coviello, N.E. (2005). Internationalisation: Conceptualising an Entrepreneurial Process of Behaviour in Time. *Journal of International Business Studies*, 36(3), 284-303.

Jose, P.E. (2003). MedGraph-I: A Programme to Graphically Depict Mediation Among Three Vari- ables: The Internet Version, Version 2.0',. Victoria

University of Wellington, Wellington, New Zealand.

Jose, P.E. and Brown, I. (2008). When does the gender difference in rumination begin? Gender and age differences in the use of rumination by adolescents. *Journal of Youth and Adolescence.*, 37(2),180-192.

Judd, C.M. and Kenny, D.A. (1981). Process analysis: Estimating mediation in treatment evaluations. *Evaluation Review*, 5(5), 602–619.

Julien, P.-andré and Ramangalahy, C. (2003). Competitive Strategy and Performance of Exporting SMEs:An Empirical Investigation of the Impact of Their Export Information Search and Competencies. *Entrepreneurship Theory and Practice*, 27(3),227-245.

Kalwani, M.U. and Narayandas, N. (1995). Long-term manufacturer-supplier relationships: Do they pay off for supplier firm*? Journal of Marketing*, 59(1), 1–16.

Karunaratna, A.R. and Johnson, L.W., Classification Of Opportunistic Behaviour By Foreign Agents and Distributors. *In Marketing in the third Millenium*. New York. 1999.

Karunaratna, A.R. and Johnson, L.W. (1997). Initiating and Maintaining Export Channel Intermediary Relationships. *Journal of International Marketing*, 5(2), 11-32.

Katsikeas, C. and Piercy, N.F., (1993). Adapting Export Business Relationships: The Greek Experience in the UK. *Marketing Intelligence & Planning*, 11(2), 22-7.

Katsikeas, C. S. and Morgan, R.E. (1994). Differences in Perceptions of Exporting Problems Based on Firm Size and Export Market Experience. *European Journal of Marketing*, 28(5), 17–35.

Katsikeas, C. S., Deng, S.L. and Wortzel, L.H., (1997). Perceived Export Success

Factors of Small and Medium-Sized Canadian Firms. *Journal of International Marketing*, 5(4), pp.53-72.

Katsikeas, C. S., Leonidou, L. C. and Morgan, N. a. (2000). Firm-Level Export Performance Assessment: Review, Evaluation, and Development. *Journal of the Academy of Marketing Science*, 28(4), 493-511.

Katsikeas, C.S and Piercy, N. F. (1993). Long-Term Export Stimuli and Firm Characteristics in a European LDC. *Journal of International Marketing*, 1(3), 23-47.

Katsikeas, C.S., Piercy, N.F. and Ioannidis, C. (1996). Determinants of export performance in a European context. *European Journal of Marketing*, 30(6), 6-35.

Kenny, D.A., Kashy, D.A. and Bolger, N. Data analysis in social psychology. In D. T. Gilbert, S. T. Fiske, and G. Lindzey ed. *The handbook of social psychology*. New York: McGraw- Hill, pp. 233–265. 1998.

Kickul, J. and Walters, J. (2002). Recognizing new opportunities and innovations: The role of strategic orientation and proactivity in Internet firms. *International Journal of Entrepreneurial Behaviour & Research*, 8(6), 292-308.

Kieley, J.M. CGI scripts: Gatewaysto World-Wide Webpower. Behavior Research Methods. *In Instruments and Computers.* pp. 165-169. 1996.

Kim, L. and Nugent, J.B. (1997). Transaction costs and export channels of small and medium-sized firms. *Contemporary Economic Policy*, 15(1), 104-120.

Kirpalani, V. and MacIntosh, N. (1980). International marketing effectiveness of technology-oriented small firms. *Journal of International Business Studies*, 11(3), 81–90.

Kirzner, I.M, *Competition and Entrepreneurship*, Chicago: University of Chicago Press. 1973.

Kirzner, I.M. (1999). Creativity and/or Alertness: A Reconsideration of the Schumpeterian Entrepreneur. *Review of Austrian Economics*, 11, 5–17.

Kirzner, I.M. (1997). Entrepreneurial discovery and the competitive market process: an Austrian approach. *Journal of Economic Literature*, 35(1), 60–85.

Kirzner, I.M. (1985). Discovery and the Capitalist Process, Chicago: University of Chicago Press.

Kirzner, Israel M. Entrepreneurship:Austrian school of economics. *In Perception, opportunity, and profit: Studies in the theory of entrepreneurship*. Chicago: University of Chicago Press. 1979.

Kirzner, Israel.M. *Competition and Entrepreneurship*, Chicago: Published in the University of Chicago. 1978.

Knight, G. (2000). Entrepreneurship and Marketing Strategy: The SME Under Globalization. *Journal of International Marketing*, 8(2), 12-32.

Knight, G. (1997). Firm Orientation and Strategy under Regional Market Integration: A Study of Canadian Firms. *International Executive*, 39(3), 351-74.

Koen, P. and Kohli, P. (1998). Idea generation:who has the most profitable ideas? *Engineering Management Journal*, 10(4), 35-40.

Koen, P.A. and Kohli, P. *Idea generation: who comes up with the most profitable products?*. Wellesley, MA: Babson College. 1998.

Kogut, B. (2000). The network as knowledge: generative rules and the emergence of structure. *Strategic Management Journal*, 21(3), 405-425.

Kogut, B. and Kulatilaka, N. (1994). Operating Flexibility, Global Manufacturing, and the Option Value of a Multinational Network. *Management Science*, 40(1), 123-139.

Kojima, K. and Ozawa, T. *Japan's General Trading Companies: Merchants of Economic Development*. 1984.

Komulainen, H., Mainela, T. and Tahtinen, J. (2006). Social networks in the initiation of a high-tech firm's internationalisation. *International Journal of Entrepreneurship and Innovation Management*, 6(6), 526 - 541.

Komulainen, H., Mainela, T.,Tahtinen, J. (2005). Intermediary Roles in Value Co-Creation. Building Social Capital in NetworksCurtin University of Technology, 11-14.

Kontinen, T. and Ojala, A. (2010). The internationalization of family businessess: A review of extant research. *Journal of Family Business Strategy*, 1(2), 97–107.

Kontinen, Tanja and Ojala, Arto, (2010). Network ties in the international opportunity recognition of family SMEs. *International Business Review*, 1-14.

Kotkin, J. *Tribes: How Race, Religion, and Identity Determine Success in the New Global Economy*, New York: Random House. 1992.

Krueger, N. (1993). The Impact of Prior Entrepreneurial Exposure on Perceptions of New Venture Feasibility and Desirability. *Entrepreneurship Theory and Practice*, 18(1), 5-21.

Krueger, N. and Brazeal, D. (1994). Entrepreneurial Potential & Potential Entrepreneurs. *Entrepreneurship Theory and Practice*, 18(3), 91-104.

Kumar, V., Aaker, D. A. and Day, G. S., Essentials of Marketing Research, John Wiley and Sons, Inc. 1999.

Kuvaas, B. (2009). A test of hypotheses derived from self-determination theory among public sector employees. *Employee Relations*, 31(1), 39-56.

Ladbury, S. Choice, chance or no alternative? Turkish Cypriots in business in London. In R. Ward and R. Jenkins ed. *Ethnic Communities in Business: Strategies for Economic Survival*. Cambridge: Cambridge University Press, pp. 89–124. 1984.

Lane, P.R. and Milesi-Ferretti, G.M. *International Investment Patterns*. 2004.

Larson, A., 1992. Network dyads in entrepreneurial settings: a study of the governance of exchange relationship. *Administrative science quarterly*, 37(1), pp.76-104.

Lau, H.-fuk. (2008). Export channel structure in a newly industrialized economy. *Asia Pacific Journal of Management*, 25, 317-333.

Leavy, B. The supplier relationship and competitive strategy. In H. E. Glass ed. Handbook of business strategy. Boston' Warren: Gorham and Lamont, pp. 16:1–16:5. 1990.

Lee, H. and Danusutedjo, D. *Export Electronic Intermediaries*, Washington D.C. (2000).

Lee, J. (2006). Family Firm Performance: Further Evidence. *Family Business Review*, 19(2), 103-114.

Leonidou, L. and Katsikeas, Constantine S. (1996). The Export Development Process: An Integrative Review of Empirical Models. *Journal of International Business Studies,* 27(3), 517-551.

Leonidou, L., Katsikeas, Constantine S. and Samiee, S. (2002). Marketing strategy determinants of export performance: a meta-analysis. *Journal of Business Research,* 55(1), 51-67.

Leonidou, Leonidas C. (2004). An analysis of the barriers hindering small business export development. *Journal of Small Business Management*, 42(3), 279–302.

Leonidou, Leonidas C. and Kaleka, A. a, (1998). Behavioural aspects of international buyer-seller relationships: their association with export involvement. *International Marketing Review*, 15(5), 373-397.

Levy, S. (1977). Symbols for sale. Harvard Business Review, 37, 117-124.

Li, LEE. (2001). Networks, Transactions, and Resources: Hong Kong Trading Companies' Strategic Position in the China Market. *Asia Pacific Journal of Management*, 18(2001), 279-293.

Li, L. *Export Practices and Performance: A Study of Exporting Companies in the People's Republic of China.* University of Western Australia. 1998.

Light, I. *Ethnic Enterprise in America*, Berkley, CA: University of California Press. 1972.

Lilien, G.L. (1979). Modeling the Marketing Mix Decision for Industrial Products. *Management Science*, 25(2), 191-204.

Ling-yee, L. and Ogunmokun, G.O. (2001). The influence of interfirm relational capabilities on export advantage and performance: an empirical analysis. *International Business Review*, 10(4), 399-420.

Loane, S and Bell, J. (2006). Rapid internationalisation among entrepreneurial firms in Australia, Canada, Ireland and New Zealand: An extension to the network approach. *International Marketing Review*, 23(5), 467-485.

Loane, Sharon. (2006). The role of the internet in the internationalisation of small and medium sized companies. *Journal of International Entrepreneurship*,

3(4), 263-277.

Loewen, J. *The Mississippi Chinese: Between Black and White*, Cambridge: Harvard University Press. 1971.

Lumpkin, G. T. and Dess., G. G. (200)1. Linking two dimensions of entrepreneurial orientation to firm performance: The moderating role of environment and industry life cycle. *Journal of Business Venturing*, 16, 429–451.

Lumpkin, G.T and Dess, G.G. (1996). Clarifying the entrepreneurial orientation construct and linking it to performance. *Academy of Management Review,* 21(1), 135-72.

Lumpkin, G.T. and Lichtenstein, B.B. (2005). The Role of Organizational Learning in the Opportunity Recognition Process. *Entrepreneurship Theory and Practice*, 29(4), 451–472.

Luo, Xueming, G., David, A., Liu, S. S and Shi, L.Z (2004). The Effect of Customer Relationships and social Capital on Firm Performance: A Chinese Business Illustration . *Journal of International Marketing*, 12(4), 25-45.

Luo, Y., Shenkar, O. and Nyaw, M. (2001). A dual parent perspective on control and performance in international joint ventures: Lessons from a developing economy. *Journal of International Business Studies*, 32(1), 41–58.

MacKinnon, D.P. et al. (2002). A Comparison of Methods to Test Mediation and Other Intervening Variable Effects. *Psychological Methods*, 7(1), 83–104.

Madsen, T.K. (1986). Empirical export performance studies: a review of conceptualizations and findings. In S. T. Cavusgil and C. Axinn ed. *Advances in International Marketing*. Greenwich: JAI Press, pp. 177-98.

Madsen, T.K. (1989). Successful Export Marketing Management: Some Empirical

Evidence. *International Marketing Review*, 6(4), 41-57.

Mahajar, A.J. and Hashim, M.K. (2001). Perceptions of International Business Incentives: A Study of Malay Firms in Malaysia. *Songklanakarin Joournal of Social Sciences & Humanities,* 7(3), 363-371.

Majkgard and Sharma. (1998). Client-following and market-seeking strategies in the internationalization of service firms. *Journal of Business-to- Business Marketing,* 4(3), pp.1–41.

Malhotra, N.K. *Marketing research: An applied orientation.* Upper Saddle River. NY: Prentice Hall.1999.

Markman, G.D., Balkin, D.B. and Baron, R.A. (2002). Inventors and New Venture Formation: the Effects of General Self-Efficacy and Regretful Thinking. *Entrepreneurship Theory and Practice*, 27(2), 149–165.

Mathews, J. and Zander, I. (2007). The international entrepreneurial dynamics of accelerated internationalisation. *Journal of International Business Studies*, 38(3), 387-403.

Maxim, P.S. (1999). Quantitative Research Methods in Social Sciences, Oxford University Press.

McClelland, D.C. (1965). N achievement and Entrepreneurship: A Longitudinal Study. *Journal of Personality and Social Psychology,* 1(4), 389-392.

Mcdougall, P.P and Oviatt, B.M. (2003). Some Fundamental Issues in International Entrepreneurship. *Entrepreneurship Theory & Practice*, (7), 1-27.

Meyer, K. and Shak, A. (2002). Networks, Serendipity and SME entry into eastern Europe. *European Management Journal*, 20(2), 179-188.

Michael, S. and Brant, L. (1997). Virtual subjects: Using the Internet as an alternative source of subjects and research environment. *Behavior Research Methods, Instruments. and Computers,* 29(4), pp.496-505.

Michalisin, M.D., Smith, R.D. and Kline, D.M. (1997). In Search of Strategic Assets.

The International Journal of Organizational Analysis, 5(4), 360-387.

Miesenbock, K.J. (1988). Small businesses and exporting: A literature review. *International Small Business Journal*, 6(1), 42-61.

Miller, D. and Dröge, C. (1986). Psychological and Traditional Determinants of Structure. *Administrative Science Quarterly*, 31(4), 539-560.

Miller, D. , DeVries, M. F. R. K. and Toulouse, J.M. (1982). Top Executive Locus of Control and Its Relationship to Strategy-Making, Structure, and Environment. *Academy of Management Journal*, 25(2), 237-253.

Miller, D. and Shamsie, J. (1996). The Resource-Based View of the Firm in Two Environments: The Hollywood Film Studios from 1936 to 1965. *Academy of management journal,* 39(3), 519-543.

Miller, D., Droge, C. and Toulouse, J.-M., (1988). Strategic Process and Content as Mediators between Organizational Context and Structure. *The Academy of Management Journal,* 31(3), 544-569.

Min, P.G.M. and Jaret, C. (1985). Ethnic business success: The case of Korean small business in Atlanta. *Sociology and Social Research*, 69(3), 412–435.

Miner, J.B. (2000). Testing a Psychological Typology of Entrepreneurship Using Business Founders. *Journal of Applied Behavioral Science*, 36(1), 43–69.

Misra, S. and Kumar, E.S. (2000). Resourcefulness:A Proximal Conceptualization of Entrepreneurial Behavior. *Journal of Entrepreneurship*, 9(2), 135–154.

Monczka, R.M. and Carter, J.R. (1988). Implementing electronic data interchange.

Journal of Purchasing and Materials Management, 24(2), 2-9.

Morgan, N., Kaleka, A. and Katsikeas, C.S. (2004). Antecedents of Export Venture Performance: A Theoretical Model and Empirical Assessment. *Journal of Marketing*, 68(1), 90-108.

Morgan, R.M. and Hunt, S. (1999). Relationship-Based Competitive Advantage: The Role of Relationship Marketing in Marketing Strategy. *Journal of Business Research*, 46, 281–290.

Morrel-Samuels, P. (2003). Web-based survey's hidden hazards. *Harvard Business Review*, 81(7), 16-18.

Mort, G.S. and Weerawardena, J. (2006). Networking capability and international entrepreneurship: How networks function in Australian born global firms. *International Marketing Review*, 23(5), 549-572.

Mortanges, C.P. de and Vossen, J. (1999). Mechanisms to Control the Marketing Activities of Foreign Distributors. *International Business Review*, 8(1), 75-97.

Munro, H.J. and Beamish, P., *Distribution methods and export performance, in market entry and expansion modes* P. Rosson and S. Reid, eds., New York: Praeger Publisher. 1987.

Muzychenko, O. (2008). Cross-cultural entrepreneurial competence in identifying international business opportunities. *European Management Journal*, 26(6), 366-377.

Myers, M.B. and Harvey, M. (2001). The Value of Pricing Control in Export Channels: A Governance Perspective. *Journal of International Marketing*, 9(4), 1-29.

Nahapiet, J. and Ghoshal, S. (1998). Social Capital, Intellectual Capital, and the

Organizational Advantage. *Academy of Management Review*, 23(2), pp.242-266.

Nakaoka, T., Saito, E. and Fujikawa, K. Asia-Pacific Economies and Small Business, Osaka. 1995.

Nakos, G., Brouthers, K.D. and Brouthers, L. E. (1998). The Impact of Firm and Managerial Characteristics on Small and Medium-sized Greek Firms' Export Performance'. *Journal of Global Marketing*, 11(4), 23-47.

Nee, G.Y. and Wahid, N.A. (2010). The Effect of ISO 14001 Environmental Management System Implementation on SMEs Performance: An Empirical Study in Malaysia. *Journal of Sustainable Development*, 3(2), 215-220.

Nitisch, D., Beamish, P. and Makino, S. (1996). Entry mode and performance of Japanese FDI in Western Europe. *Management International Review*, 36(1), 27–43.

Nummela, N., Saarenketo, S. and Puumalainen, K., (2004). A Global Mindset—A Prerequisite for Successful Internationalization? Canadian *Journal of Administrative Science*, 21(1), pp.51-64.

Nunnally, J.C., *Psychometric Theory*, New York: McGraw- Hill. 1978.

OECD. *Globalization and Small and Medium Enterprises* (SMEs). I2nd ed. Paris. 1997.

OECD. Promoting Entrepreneurship and Innovative SMEs in a Global Economy. *In 2nd OECD Conference of Ministers Responsible for Small and Medium-Sized Enterprises (SMEs)*. Istanbul, Turkey: OECD. 2004.

OECD. *Removing Barriers to SME Access to International Markets*, Singapore: OECD Publishing. 2008.

Ohmae, K. (1989). The Global Logic of Strategic Alliances. *Harvard Business Review,* (March-April), 143-154.

Ojala, A. (2009). Internationalization of knowledge-intensive SMEs: The role of network relationships in the entry to a psychically distant market. *International Business Review*, 18(1), 50–59.

Oviatt, B. and Mcdougall, P.P. (2005). Toward a Theory of International New Ventures.*Journal of International Business Studies*, 36(1), 29-41.

Oviatt, B. M. and Mcdougall, p. p. (2005). Defining International Entrepreneurship and Modeling the Speed of Internationalization. *Entrepreneurship, Theory and Practice*, 29(5), 537–553.

Oviatt, B.M and Mcdougall, P. P. (2005). The Internationalization of Entrepreneurship. *Journal of International Business Studies*, 36(1), 2-8.

Oystein, M. (2000). SMEs and international marketing: investigating the differences in export strategy between firms of different size. *Journal of Global Marketing*, 13(4), 22.

Ozgen, E. and Baron, R. (2007). Social sources of information in opportunity recognition: Effects of mentors, industry networks, and professional forums. *Journal of Business Venturing,* 22(2), 174-192.

O'Neal, C. and Bertrand, K. *Developibng a winning J.1.T. marketing strategy—the industrial marketer's guide*, New Jersey, Englewood Cliffs: Prentice Hall. 1991.

Paliwoda, S.J. and Bonaccorsi, A.J. (1994). Trends in procurement strategies within the European aircraft industry. *Industrial Marketing Management*, 23(3), 235-244.

Pallant, J. *SPSS Manual. A step by step guide to data analysis using SPSS for windows*. 15th ed. 2007.

Pangarkar, N. (2008). Internationalization and performance of small- and medium-sized enterprises. *Journal of World Business*, 43(4), 475-485.

Park, J.S. (2005). Opportunity recognition and product innovation in entrepreneurial hi-tech start-ups: a new perspective and supporting case study. *Technovation,* 25(7), 739-752.

Peng, M.W. *behind the Success and Failure of US Export Intermediaries*, Quorum: Westport. 1998.

Peng, M.W. and Delios, A. (2006). What determines the scope of the firm over time and around the world? An Asia Pacific perspective. *Asia Pacific Journal of Management,* 23(4), 385-405.

Peng, M.W. and York, A.S. (2001). Behind Intermediary Performance in Export Trade: Transactions, Agents and Resources. *Journal of International Business Studies*, 32(2), 327-346.

Peng, M.W., Wang, D.Y.L. and Jiang, Y. (2007). An Institutation-Based view of international Business strategy: A focus Emerging Economies. *Journal of International Business Studies*, (8), 1-38.

Peteraf, M.A. (1993). The cornerstones of competitive advantage: a resource-based view. *Strategic Management Journal*, 14, 179-191.

Peteraf, M.A. and Barney, J.B. (2003). Unraveling The Resource-Based Tangle. *Managerial and Decision Economics*, 24(4), 309-323.

Piercy, N. F., Kaleka, A. and Katsikeas, C. S. (1998). Sources of Competitive Advantage in High Performing Companies. *Journal of World Business*, 33(4), 378-393.

Piercy, N. F, Katsikeas, C.S. and Cravens, D.W. (1997). Examining the Role of Buyer-Seller Relationships in Export Performance. *Journal of World*

Business, 32(1), 73-86.

Pope, R. (2002). Why Small Firms Export: Another Look. *Journal of Small Business Management,* 40(1), 17-26.

Porter, M.E. and Fuller, M.B. *Coalitions and Global Strategy. Competition in Global Industries.* Boston. Harvard Business School. (1986).

Porter, M.E and Linde, C.V.D. (1995). Toward a New Conception of the Environment-Competitiveness Relationship. *The Journal of Economic Perspectives,* 9(4), 97-118.

Porter, M.E. (1986). Coalitions and Global Strategy. In Michael E. Porter, ed. Competition in global industries. Boston: Harward Business school press, 314.

Porter, Michael E. (1990). The Competitive Advantage of Nations, New York: Free Press.

Prasad, V.K., Ramamurthy, K. and Naidu, G.M. (2001). The Influence of Internet-Marketing Integration on Marketing Competencies and Export Performance. *Journal of International Marketing,* 9(4), 82-110.

Rabino, S. (1980). An examination of barriers to exporting encountered by smaller manufacturing companies. *Management International Review,* 20(1), 67-73.

Ramaswami, S.N. and Yang, Y. Perceived barriers to exporting and export assistance requirements. In T. Cavusgil and Michael R. Czinkota ed. *International perspectives on trade promotion and assistance.* Westport: Quorum books. 1990.

Rasli, A. *Handbook for Postgraduate Social Scientists,* Johor: UTM Press. 2006.

Rauch, J.E. *Trade and Search:* Social Capital, Sogo Shosha, and Spillovers. 1996.

Ray, D.M., Asley Momijan, W., McMullan, E., Ko, S. *Comparison of Immigrant Armenian Entrepreneurs in Los Angeles and Immigrant Chinese Entrepreneurs in Calgary*, Calgary, Canada. 1988.

Rindfleisch, A. and Heide, J.B. (1997). Transaction Cost Analysis: Past, Present, and Future Applications. *Journal of Marketing,* 61(4), 30-54.

Rindfleisch, A., Malter, A.J, Ganesan, S. and Moorman, C. (2008). Cross-Sectional Versus Longitudinal Survey Research: Concepts, Findings, and Guidelines. *Journal of Marketing Research*, 45(3), 261-279.

Roberts, E. (1991). Entrepreneurs in high technology: Lessons from MIT and beyond, New York: Oxford University Press.

Robertson, C. and Chetty, S.K. (2000). A Contingency-Based Approach to Understanding Export Performance. *International Business Review*, 9(2), 211-235.

Robinson, J., Shaver, P. and Wrightsman, L. Criteria for scale selection and evaluation. In J. Robinson, P. Shaver, and L. Wrightsman, eds. *In Measures of Personality and Social Psychological Attitudes.* San Diego, CA: Academic Press, pp. 1–16. (1991).

Root, F.R. *Entry Strategies for International Markets*, San Fransisco: Lexington Books. 1994.

Rosson, P.J and Ford, I.D. (1982). Manufacturer-Overseas Distributor Relations and Export Performance. *Journal of International Business Studies*, 13(2), 57-72.

Rotter, J.B. (1966). Generalized expectancies for internal versus external control of reinforcement. Psychological Monographs, 80(1), 1-28.

Rullani, E. Enhancing the competitiveness of SMEs in the global economy:

Strategies and policies. *In Conference for Ministers responsible for SMEs and Industry Ministers.* Bologna, Italy. 2000.

Rutashabya, L. and Jaensson, J.E. (2004). Small Firms' Internationalization for development in Tanzania: exploring the Network Phenomenon. *International journal of Social Economic,* 31(1/2), 159-172.

SBA. (2004). Guide to SBA's definitions of small business.

SMIDEC, (2009). SME annual Report, kuala lampur.

Salancik, G.R. and Pfeffer, J. (1978). A social information processing approach to. job attitudes and task design. *Administrative science quarterly,* 23(2), 224-53.

Sambasivan, M., Abdul, M. and Yusop, Y. (2009). Impact of personal qualities and management skills of entrepreneurs on venture performance in Malaysia:Opportunity recognition skills as a mediating factor. *Journal of Technovation,* 29, 798-805.

Sangsuwan, N. *Success Factors in Export Marketing: The Case of Thailand.* 1992.

Sapienza, H. J., DeClercq, D. and Sandberg, W.R., *Antecedence of International and Domestic Learning effort. Learning.* 2004.Sayre, S. *Qualitative Methods for Marketing Research,* Sage Publications, Inc. 2001.

Schmidt, W.C. World-Wide Web survey research: Benefits, potential problerns,and solutions. *In Behavior Research Methods, Instru- ments, & Computers.* pp. 274-279. 1997.

Schonberger, R.J. *World class manufacturing-the lessons of simplicity applied,* New York: The Free Press. 1986.

Schroder, P.J.H., Trabold, H. and Trubswetter, P. *Intermediation in Foreign Trade: When do Exporters Rely on Intermediaries? Traders.* pp.1-20. 2003.

Schumpeter, J. *Capitalism, Socialism, and Democracy.* 3rded. New York: Harper and Row. 1975. (Originally published in 1942 by Harper and Brothers).

Schumpeter, J. *Capitalism, Socialism, and Democracy*. In H. Row ed. New York. 1934.

Sekaran, U. *Research methods for business: a skill building approach*. 4thed. New York: John Wiley and Sons. 2003.

Senik, Z. , Isa, R. , Scott-Ladd, B. and Entrekin, L. (2010). Influential Factors for SME Internationalization: Evidence from Malaysia. *Journal of Economics and Management*, 4(2), 285 - 304.

Seow, C. and Liu, J. (2006). Innovation in Maintenance Strategy through Six Sigma: Insights of a Malaysian SME. (2006) IEEE International Conference on Management of Innovation and Technology, 793-797.

Seringhaus and Rosson. (1998). Management and performance of international trade fair exhibitors: Government stands vs. independent stands. *International Marketing Review,* 15(5), 398–412.

Shackman, A.J. (2005). Research Program.

Shane, S. 2000. Prior Knowledge and the Discovery of Entrepreneurial Opportunities.

Shane, S. and Venkataraman, S. (2000). The Promise of Enterpreneurship as a Field of Research. *The Academy of Management Review,* 25(1), 217-226. *Organization Science*, 11(4), 448-469.

Shankar, C., Pandian, S., Sulaiman, M. and Munusamy, J. (2010). The moderating effect of firm size: Internationalization of small and medium enterprises (SMEs) in the manufacturing sector. *African Journal of Business Management,* 4(14), 3096-3109.

Shankar, C., Sulaiman, M. and Pandian, S. (2010). The Determinants of Internationalization of Small and Medium Enterprises (Smes): A Case in

Malaysia. *World Applied Sciences Journal*, 10(10), 1202-1215.

Shankar, C., Sulaiman, M. and Yusoff, Y.M. (2010). Internationalization and Performance: Small and Medium Enterprises (SMEs) in Malaysia. International *Journal of Business and Management*, 5(6), 27-37.

Sharma, D. D. and Johanson, J. (1987). Technical Consultancy in Internationalization.
International Marketing Review, 4(4), 20-29.

Sharma, D.D and Blomstermo, A. (2003). The internationalization process of Born Globals: A network view. *International Business Review*, 12, 739–753.

Shaw, V. and Darroch, J. (2004). Barriers to Internationalisation: A Study of Entrepreneurial New Ventures in New Zealand. *Journal of International Entrepreneurship,* 2(4), 327-343.

Shepherd, D. A. and Zacharakis, A. Conjoint analysis:A window of opportunity for entrepreneurship research. In J. Katz ed. *Advances in entrepreneurship, firm emergence and growth.* Greenwich: JAI Press, pp. 203-248. 1997.

Shepherd, D.A. and DeTienne, D.R. (2005). Prior Knowledge, Potential Financial Reward and Opportunity Identification. *Journal of Entrepreneurship: Theory and Practice*, 29.

Shepherd, D. A. and DeTienne, D.R. *Discovery of opportunities: anomalies, accumulation and alertness.* 2001.

Sherer, P.D. and Lee, K. (2002). Institutional Change in Large Law Firms: A Resource Dependency and Institutional Perspective. *Academy of Management Journal*, 45(1), 102-119.

Shipley, D., Cook, D. and Barnett, E. (1989). Recruitment, Motivation, Training and Evaluation of Overseas Distributors. *European Journal of Marketing,*

23(2), 79-93.

Shook, C.L., Priem, R.L. and Mcgee, J.E. (2003). Venture Creation and the Enterprising Individual: A Review and Synthesis. *Journal of Management*, 29(3), 379–400.

Singh, R. *Entrepreneurial Opportunity Recognition through Social Networks*. New York: Garland Publishing. 2000.

Singh, R., Hills, G. E., Hybels, R.C. and Lumpkin, G.T. Opportunity recognition through Social Network Characteristics of Entrepreneurs. *In Frontiers of Entrepreneurship Research.* Wellesley: Babson College. 1999.

Singh, R., Hills, G.E. (1999). Frontiers in Entrepreneurship Research. *In Frontiers in Entrepreneurship Research.* Wellesley, MA: Babson College.

Sirmon, D.G. and Hitt, M.A. (2003). Managing Resources: Linking Unique Resources, Management, and Wealth Creation in Family Firms. *Entrepreneurship Theory and Practice,* 27(4), pp.339–358.

Skinner, D., Tagg, C. and Holloway, J. (2000). Managers and Research: The Pros and Cons of Qualitative Approaches. *Management Learning*, 31(2), 163-179.

Snow, C.C., Miles, R.E. and H.J. Coleman, J. (1992). Managing 21st Century Network Organizations. *Organizational Dynamics*, 20, 5–20.

Srivastava, R.K., Fahey, L. and Christensen, H.K. (2001). The resource-based view and marketing: The role of market-based assets in gaining competitive advantage. *Journal of Management*, 27(6), 777-802.

Steenkamp, J.-B.E.M. (2001). The role of national culture in international marketing research. *International Marketing Review,* 18(1), 30-44.

Stempel, G.H. Content analysis. In G. H. Stempel and B. Westley, eds. *Research methods in mass communications*. Englewood Cliffs, NJ: Prentice-Hall, pp. 119-143. 1981.

Stevenson, H.H. and Jarillo, J.C. *A paradigm of entrepreneurship: Entrepreneurial management. In Entrepreneurship: concepts, theory and perspective*. pp. 156-170. 1990.

Stewart, W.H., Watson, W.E., Carland, J.C., Carland, J.W. (1998). A proclivity of entrepreneurship: a comparison of entrepreneurs, small business owners, and corporate managers. *Journal of Business Venturing*, 14, pp.189–214.

Styles, C. and Ambler, T. (1994). Successful Export Practice:The UK Experience. *International Marketing Review*, 11(6), 23-47.

Styles, C. and Seymour, R.G. (2006). Opportunities for marketing researchers in international entrepreneurship. *International Marketing Review*, 23(2), 126-145.

Susman, G.I. *Small and Medium sized enterprise and global economy*. G. I. Susman and E. Elgar (Ed.) Uk: Edward Elgar Publishing Limited. 2007a.

Susman, G.I. *Small and Medium-Sized Entreprise and the Global Economy*. The Pennsy. G. I. Susman and E. Elgar ed. Uk: Edward Elgar Publishing Limited. 2007b.

Syed Zamberi, A. and Siri R.X. (2010). Stress and coping styles of entrepreneurs: a Malaysian survey. *International Journal of Entrepreneurship*, 14.

Terjesen, S. (2005). Senior women managers: leveraging embedded career capital in new ventures. *Career Development International*, 10(3), 246–259.

Terjesen, S., O'Gorman, C. and Acs, Z. J. (2008). Intermediated mode of internationalization: new software ventures in Ireland and India. *Entrepreneurship & Regional development*, 20, 89-109.

Terjesen, S. and Hessels, J., (2007). Indirect Internationalization of Small Ventures:

A Development and Test of Two Theories. *In Frontiers of Entrepreneurship Research.*

Theingi. *The Influence of Marketing Control and a Resource-based view (RBV) on. Export Performance of SMEs in Tailand.* PhD Thesis. The University of Western Australia. 2008.

Theingi, Purchase, S. and Phungphol, Y. (2007). The Role of the Firm's Resources in Relationship Development Stages: Case Studies in Thailand. *Journal of International Entrepreneurship.*

Thurasamy, R., Mohamad, O., Omar, A. and Marimuthu, M. (2009). Technology Adoption among Small and Medium Enterprises (SME's): A Research Agenda. *Engineering and Technology*, 41(May), 943-946.

Timmons, J.A. *New Venture Creation: Entrepreneurship for the 21st Century.* 1999.

Trabold, H. (2002). Export Intermediation: An Empirical Test of Peng and Ilinitch. *Journal of International Business Studies*, 33(2), 327-344.

Tsang, E.W.K. (1998). Can guanxi Be a Source of Sustained Competitive Advantage for Doing Business in China? *The Academy of Management Executive*, 12(2), 64- 73.

Vandekerckhove, W. and Dentchev, N.A. (2005). A Network Perspective on Stakeholder Management: Facilitating Entrepreneurs in the Discovery of Opportunities. Journal *of Business Ethics*, 60(3), 221-232.

Venkataraman, S. Advances in entrepreneurship, firm emergence, and growth. In J. Katz and R. Brockhaus, eds. *The distinctive domain of entrepreneurship research: An editor's perspective.* Greenwich, CT: Elsevier Ltd., pp. 119-138. 1997a.

Venkataraman, S., The Distinctive Domain of Entrepreneurship Research. *In*

Advances in Entrepreneurship, Firm Emergence, and Growth. Greenwich: JAI Press, pp. 119–138. 1997b.

Venkataraman, S., The distinctive domain of entrepreneurship research: An editor's perspective. In J. Katz and R. Brockhaus, eds. *Advances in entrepreneurship, firm emergence, and growth*. Greenwich, CT: JAI Press. 1997c.

Venkatraman, N. and Ramanujam, V. (1986). Measurement of Business Performance in Strategy Research: A Comparison of Approaches. *Academy of Management Review*, 11(4), pp.801-14.

Wang, Olsen, J.E. and Guangping. (2002). Knowledge, Performance and Exporter Satisfaction: An Expolatory Study. *Journal of Global Marketing,* 15(3/4), pp.39-62.

Wang, Y.-lin, (2008). *Organizational Learning, Entrepreneurial Opportunity recognition, and Innovation Performance in High Technology Firms in Taiwan.* PhD Thesis. University of Illinois at Urbana-Champaign.

Weerawardena, J. and Mort, G. (2006). Investigating social entrepreneurship: A multidimensional model. *Journal of World Business*, 41(1), 21-35.

Weerawardena, J.(2003). The role of marketing capability in innovation-based competitive strategy. *Journal of Strategic Marketing*, 11(1), 15-35.

Weerawardena, Jay and O'Cass, A.,(2004). Exploring the characteristics of the market-driven firms and antecedents to sustained competitive advantage. *Industrial Marketing Management,* 33(5), pp.419-428.

Weerawardena, J. , O'Cass, A. and Julian, C. (2006). Does industry matter? Examining the role of industry structure and organizational learning in innovation and brand performance. *Journal of Business Research*, 59(1), 37-45.

Weir, K.F. and Jose, P.E. (2008). A Comparison of the Response Styles Theory and the Hopelessness Theory of Depression in Preadolescents. *The Journal of Early Adolescence*, 28(3), 356-374.

Weiss, A.M. and Heide, J. B. (1993). The nature of organizational search in high technology markets. *Journal of Marketing Research*, 30(2), 220−233.

Welch, D. et al. (1996). Network analysis of a New Export Grouping Scheme: The Role of Economic and Non-economic relation. *International Journal on Research in Marketing*, 13, 463-477.

Welch, D.E. ,Welch, L.S., Young, L.C.,Wilkinson, I.F. (1998). The Importance of Networks in Export Promotion: Policy Issues. *Journal of lnternutionul Marketing*, 6, 66- 82.

Werbner, P. Business in trust: Pakistani entrepreneurship in the Manchester Garment Trade. In R. Ward and R. Jenkins ed. *Ethnic Communities in Business: Strategies for Economic Survival.* Cambridge: Cambridge University Press, pp. 166–188. 1984.

Whitely, W., Doughterty, T.M. and Dreher, G.F. (1991). Relationship of Career Mentoring and Socioeconomic Origin to Managers' and Professionals' Early Career Progress. *Academy of Management Journal*, 34(2), 331–351.

Wilkinson, I., Young, L. and Freytag, P.V.,(2005). Business Mating: Who Chooses Whom and Gets Chosen? Industrial Marketing Management, 34,669 – 680.

Wilkinson, I.F. and Young, L.C.,(2005). Toward a normative theory of normative marketing theory. *Marketing Theory*, 5(4), 363-96.

Wilkinson, Ian F and Nguyen, V., (2003). A Contingency Model of Export Entry Mode Performance: The Role of Production and Transactions Costs. *Australasian Marketing Journal*, 11(3), 44-60.

Wilkinson, T. and Brouthers, L. E, (2006). Trade promotion and SME export performance. *International Business Review*, 15, 233-252.

Williamson, O. E. *The Economic Institutions of Capitalism: Firms, Markets, Relational Contracting.* 1985.

Williamson, O. E. *Markets and Hierarchies: Analysis and Antitrust Implications.* 1975.

Williamson, O. E. *The Mechanisms of Governance.* 1996.

Williamson, O.E. (1996). Economic Organization: The Case for Candor. *Academy of Management Review,* 21(1), 48-57.

Wolff, A.J. and Pett, T.L. (2000). Internationalization of small firms: an examination of export competitive patterns, firm size, and export performance. *Journal of Small Business Management,* 38(2), 34–47.

Wong, B., (1987). The Role of Ethnicity in Enclave Enterprises: A Study of the Chinese Garment Factories in New York City. *Human Organization,* 46(2), pp.120-130.

Woodcock, C.P., Beamish, P. W. and Makino, S., (1994). Ownership-Based Entry Mode Strategies and International Performance. *Journal of International Business Studies,* 25(2), 253–273.

Yang, Y.S., Leone, R.P. and Alden, D.L. (1992). A market expansion ability approach to identify potential exporters. *Journal of Marketing,* 56(1), 84-96.

Yli, H., Autio, E. and Tontti, V. Social capital, knowledge, and the international growth of technology-based new firms. Knowledge Creation Diffusion Utilization. 2000.

Young, M.N., Peng, M.W. , Ahlstrom, D., Bruton, G.D and Jiang, Y. (2008). Corporate Governance in Emerging Economies: A Review of the Principal–Principal Perspective. *Journal of Management Studies,* 45(1),

196-220.

Young, S., Dimitratos, P. and Dana, L.P. (2003). International Entrepreneurship Research: What Scope for International Business Theories? *Journal of International Entrepreneurship*, 1(1), 31-42.

Zacharakis, A.L. (1997). Entrepreneurial entry into foreign markets: A transaction cost perspective. *Entrepreneurship Theory and Practice*, 21, 23-39.

Zacharakis, A. L. and Meyer, G.D. (1998). A Lack of Insight: Do Venture Capitalists Really Understand Their Own Decision Process? Business Venturing, 13, 57-76.

Zahra, S, Korri, J. and Yu, J. (2005). Cognition and international entrepreneurship: implications for research on international opportunity recognition and exploitation. *International Business Review,* 14(2), 129-146.

Zahra, S. A. and Gravis, D.M. (2000). International Corporate Entrepreneurship and Firm Performance: The Moderating Effect of International Environmental Hostility. *Journal of Business Venturing*, 15, 469-492.

Zahra, S. and Dess, G. G. (2001). Entrepreneurship as a Field of Research: Encouraging Dialogue and Debate. *The Academy of Management Review*, 26(1), 8-10.

Zahra, S. (2005). A Theory of International New Ventures: A Decade of Research. *Journal of International Business Studies*, 36(1), 20–28.

Zain, M. and NG, S.I. (2006). The Impacts of Network Relationships on SMEs' Internationalization Process. *Thunderbird International Business Review*, 48(2), 183-205.

Zietsma, C., (1999). Opportunity knocks or does it hide, Frontiers of

Entrepreneurship Research. *Frontiers of Entrepreneurship Research.*

Zikmund, W.G. *Business Research Methods seventh.* South-Western: Thomson. 2003.

Zikmund, W.G. *Essentials of Marketing Research.* the Dryden Press. 1999.

Zikmund, W.G. *Exploring Marketing Research.* the Dryden Press. 1997.

Zou, Shaoming and Stan, S. (1998). The determinants of export performance: a review of the empirical literature between 1987 and 1997. *International Marketing Review,* 15(5), 333-356.

APPENNDIX A

Questionnaire

@UTM

Dear Sir/Madam

SURVEY ON INTERNATIONAL OPPORTUNITY RECOGNITION AND
EXPORT SATISFACTION IN SMEs

This is a study on the role of export intermediary on international opportunity recognition and export performance of small and medium sized firms to fulfill the requirements for the degree of PhD at Universiti Teknologi Malaysia.

Your participation in filling out this questionnaire will be vital for the completion of this study. Therefore, kindly complete this questionnaire. I realize that your time is valuable but the questionnaire would take only approximately 30 minutes to complete.

I would like to stress that your data will not be disclosed to any third party. All information will be analyzed in general and no references will be made to specific individuals or firms. At the end of this research study, companies participating in this study, researcher will send a summary of the findings upon request.

In case of any ambiguity and inquiry, please do not hesitate to contact me at *+60-0177288247* or email me at sahar.swan2@gmail.com. Your cooperation is essential and would be greatly appreciated.

Sincerely yours
Sahar Ahmadian
Ph.D Student

1. RESEARCH'S CRITERIA

Note: For the following questions please provide information about your firm by choosing "Yes" or "No".

1) Is your firm a manufacturing exporter?

Yes ☐   No ☐

2) Are the employees of your firm less than 150 employees?

Yes ☐   No ☐

3) Is your firm an independent business base in Malaysia?

Yes ☐   No ☐

4) Is your firm using export intermediary to export the products?

Yes ☐   No ☐

Note1: If the answers of all above questions are "Yes", your firm is qualified to attend to this survey, otherwise no need to fill the rest.

Note2: The questionnaire should fill by the owner-manager, general-manager, sales and marketing manager, export manager, or production manager. If you are not mentioned persons, please pass it to the related managers.

Note3: For filling the rest of questions, please think of one of your companies' products that were exported via export intermediary and use this product export venture as a source of reference when answering the questions.

UTM

2. RESPONDENT'S BACKGROUND

Note: For the following questions please provide information about yourself.

5 Gender?

        1) Male ☐   2) Female ☐

6 Ethnic group?

        1) Malay ☐   3) Indian ☐

        2) Chinese ☐   4) Others ☐

7 Age?

        1) 20 - 30 ☐   4) 51 - 60 ☐

        2) 31 - 40 ☐   5) More than 60 ☐

        3) 41 - 50 ☐

8 Educational status?

        1) Primary school ☐   4) Bachelor ☐

        2) Secondary school ☐   5) Master ☐

        3) Diploma ☐   6) Higher than master ☐

9 How long you have experience in exporting business?

        1) 1 - 5 years ☐   4) 16-20 years ☐

        2) 6 - 10 years ☐   5) Over 20 years ☐

        3) 11 - 15 years ☐

3. FIRM'S BACKGROUND

Note: Please provide the following information about the firm you are working with.

10. Age of your firm?

1) 1-5 years ☐	4) 16-20 years ☐
2) 6-10 years ☐	5) More than 20 years ☐
3) 11-15 years ☐	

11. Number of employees in your firm?

1) 1 - 4 employees ☐	4) 101-150 employees ☐
2) 5 - 50 employees ☐	
3) 51 - 100 employees ☐	

12. How long has your firm engaged in exporting?

1) 1-5 years ☐	4) 16 - 20 years ☐
2) 6 - 10 years ☐	5) More than 20 years ☐
3) 11 - 15 years ☐	

13. What is the percentage of your firm's total export sales come from agent or distributor?

1) 1% - 20% ☐	4) 61% - 80% ☐
2) 21% - 40% ☐	5) More than 81% ☐
3) 41% - 60% ☐	

14. What is the percentage of your firm's sales agreements with foreign customers come from agent or distributor?

1) 1% - 20% ☐	4) 61% - 80% ☐
2) 21% - 40% ☐	5) More than 81% ☐
3) 41% - 60% ☐	

UTM

15. Which of the following is the product category of your firm's product export venture?

1)Agricultural products & machinery	☐	13)Industrial & engineering products & services	☐
2)Automotive parts & components	☐	14)Iron & steel products	☐
3)Building material, machinery & related products	☐	15)Laboratory equipment, fittings & services	☐
4)Cement & concrete products	☐	16)Paper, packaging, labeling & printing	☐
5) Ceramic & tiles	☐	17)Pharmaceutical, medical equipment, cosmetics & toiletries	☐
6) Chemical & adhesive products	☐	18)Plastic products & resins	☐
7)Electrical & electronics products	☐	19)Playground equipment	☐
8)Environmental & waste management	☐	20)Rubber products	☐
9)Food & beverage	☐	21)Financial institutions	☐
10)Furniture & wood related products	☐	22)Inspection, certification & consultancy services	☐
11)Gifts, stationery & office supplies	☐	23)Manufacturing solutions	☐
12)Household products & appliances	☐	24)Logistic	☐

16. In which of the following regions/countries is this product export venture most exported to by using export intermediary? (Please select only one).

1) North America ☐   7) Northern Europe ☐
2) South America ☐   8)Oceania ☐
3) Central America ☐   9) Eastern Asia ☐
4)Eastern Europe ☐   10) Southeast Asia ☐
5)Western Europe ☐   11) Africa ☐
6)Southern Europe ☐   12) Mid East ☐

17. Which of the following export intermediaries have you mostly used for identify international opportunities?

1) Foreign intermediary based in Malaysia ☐
2) Malaysian private intermediary (based in Malaysia) ☐
3) Foreign intermediary based in foreign market ☐
4) Government agency (based in Malaysia) ☐

18. How would you describe the product that you are currently exporting?

1) Business goods ☐   2) Consumer goods ☐

19. The number of countries exported to?

1) 1 - 5 countries ☐   4)16-20 countries ☐
2) 6 - 10 countries ☐   5)More than 20 countries ☐
3)11 - 15 countries ☐

UTM

4. EXPORT INTERMEDIARIES NETWORKING
4.1 MARKETING CAPABILITIES

Instruction: The following statements describe your opinion about exporting processes in your organization. Please indicate your agreement to each statement by circling a number from 1 to 5 where 1 = "highly disagree" and 5 = "highly agree"

	Highly disagree	Disagree	Natural	Agree	Highly agree
	1	2	3	4	5

20. Our distributor/agent has high quality of customer service.   1 2 3 4 5

21. Our distributor/agent has effective promotional activities (e.g. advertising and trade show) in gaining market share/sales growth.   1 2 3 4 5

22. Our distributor/agent has high quality sales person.   1 2 3 4 5

23. Our distributor/agent has strong distribution networks.   1 2 3 4 5

24. The advertising expenditure of our firm is significantly reduced through our distributor/agent.

25. Our distributor/agent has not strong and effective market research.   1 2 3 4 5

26. Our distributor/agent is able to introduce our new products very fast.   1 2 3 4 5

27. Our distributor/agent is able to serve different market   1   2   3   4   5
segments.

4.2 EXPERIENCE ASSETS

28. Our distributor/agent is knowledgeable about the   1   2   3   4   5
requirements of potential customers.

29. Our distributor/agent has overall good experience with   1   2   3   4   5
respect to the market.

30. Our distributor/agent has not adequate experience to sell   1   2   3   4   5
the products.

31. Our distributor/agent has overall good market   1   2   3   4   5
information.

4.3 RELATION ASSETS

32. There is strong trust and fairness between our   1   2   3   4   5
distributor/agent and our customers.

33. Our distributor/agent keeps their promise with the   1   2   3   4   5
customers.

34. Our distributor/agent is not helpful in the any emergency   1   2   3   4   5
case of customers.

35. Our distributor/agent has positive attitude toward any   1   2   3   4   5
complaints of customers.

UTM

36. There is long-term relationship between our   1   2   3   4   5
distributor/agent and the customers.

37. There is good communication between our   1   2   3   4   5
distributor/agent and the customers.

38. Our distributor/agent has good reputation in the foreign   1   2   3   4   5
market.

5. OPPORTUNITY RECOGNITION

39. Through our distributor/agent we have found foreign   1   2   3   4   5
opportunities in the more different countries.

40. Through our distributor/agent we have found foreign   1   2   3   4   5
opportunities in more markets with the different cultures.

41. Through our distributor/agent we have not found foreign   1   2   3   4   5
opportunities in more markets with the different
languages.

42. We achieve greater foreign sales volumes through our   1   2   3   4   5
distributor/agent sale.

43. We achieve greater foreign market share through our   1   2   3   4   5
distributor/agent sale.

44. We achieve greater sales agreements volumes with   1   2   3   4   5
foreign customers through our distributor/agent sale.

6. EXPORT SATISFACTION

45. We are satisfied with the foreign sales growth in our firm   1   2   3   4   5
by using agent/distributor.

46. We are satisfied with the firm's export market share by   1   2   3   4   5
using agent/distributor.

47. We are not satisfied with the number of countries which   1   2   3   4   5
our firm is exporting via agent/distributor.

48. We are satisfied with the overall export performance by   1   2   3   4   5
using agent/distributor.

Please indicate below if you would like to receive a summary of the finding of this research study.

☐ Yes, I would like to be sent a copy of the finding (please indicate your email address below).
Your email address: ……………………..

☐ No, I do not wish to receive a copy of the findings.

www.ingramcontent.com/pod-product-compliance
Lightning Source LLC
Chambersburg PA
CBHW080538090426
42733CB00016B/2618